The Moot Court Advisor's Handbook

The Moot Court Advisor's Handbook

SECOND EDITION

The Legal Writing Institute

James Dimitri

Melissa E. Love Koenig

Susie Salmon

CAROLINA ACADEMIC PRESS

Durham, North Carolina

Library of Congress Cataloging-in-Publication Data

Names: Dimitri, James, author. | Love Koenig, Melissa E., author. | Salmon, Susie, author. | Legal Writing Institute.
Title: The moot court advisor's handbook / The Legal Writing Institute, James Dimitri, Melissa E. Love Koenig, and Susie Salmon.
Description: Second edition. | Durham, North Carolina : Carolina Academic Press, 2023. | Includes bibliographical references and index.
Identifiers: LCCN 2023024092 | ISBN 9781531019495 (paperback) | ISBN 9781531019501 (ebook)
Subjects: LCSH: Moot courts—United States.
Classification: LCC KF281.A2 M66 2023 | DDC 340.071/173—dc23
LC record available at https://lccn.loc.gov/2023024092

Carolina Academic Press
700 Kent Street
Durham, North Carolina 27701
(919) 489-7486
www.cap-press.com
Printed in the United States of America

To Annie, Mom, Lisa, and Mom D.
for their unwavering love, support, and encouragement.
—J.D.

To Jonathan and Olivia, and my parents, George and Edith.
Thank you for always being there for me and
showing me what great advocacy is.
—M.E.L.K.

To my parents, Michael and Nan, and my brother, Jeff.
I will never be part of a better team. And to all the residents of thc
#houseofterriers. Wherever I am, you are my home.
—S.S.

Contents

Acknowledgments for the Second Edition

Many people helped make this second edition better. University of Arizona Law student Marley Grosskopf provided research for Chapters One and Six, and fellow student Erica Litle cite-checked, proofread, and contributed invaluable suggestions to Chapters One, Two, Five, and Six. Professor Lisa Mazzie is a great colleague and mentor at Marquette Law School who is always instrumental in drafting the Marquette bylaws and handbook. Marquette's Donnette Tinsley and Marquette law student Andrew Depkon proofread Chapter Four. Lane McFadden of Indiana's Maurer School of Law, a member of the Legal Writing Institute's Moot Court Committee, shared indispensable feedback on a late draft of Chapter Six. University of Arizona Law's Debbie Martin and Barbara Vandervelde helped with some tricky, last-minute formatting issues.

For the appendices, Heather Baxter of Shepard Broad College of Law at Nova Southeastern University was kind enough to share the syllabus for her moot court course.

None of this would be possible without the support and shared wisdom of our colleagues at University of Arizona Law, Marquette, and IU McKinney. And of course, this entire endeavor continues to be inspired by generations of moot court competitors, who teach us something new every year.

Finally, we owe a great debt of gratitude to everyone at Carolina Academic Press for their patience and grace as we revised this second edition through a global pandemic that changed the world—and the practice and teaching of law—forever.

Acknowledgments

Writing this book has been one of the most rewarding experiences of our careers. We could not have accomplished this without the generosity and support of many people, and we would like to recognize them here.

First, this has truly been a collaborative process. Each of us is grateful to have worked with such capable and tireless colleagues, both on this book and on the Legal Writing Institute's Moot Court Committee. The experience of collaborating on this book together has made us better writers, mentors, and teachers.

None of us springs from the earth fully formed—not even law professors—and much of the wisdom in this book originated outside its authors. Professor Melissa Tatum not only helped draft the sample bylaws and inspired ideas shared in Chapter Five, she has been an invaluable mentor and colleague. Professor Julie Ferdon shared years of institutional memory about moot court and moot court competitions when Professor Salmon first joined Arizona Law. JJ Arevalo made last-minute edits and formatting on the first edition a breeze. Arizona Law Dean Marc Miller has consistently supported legal-skills competitions and Professor Salmon's work on this book. The Marquette Moot Court Executive Board and Professor Jessica Slavin helped draft the bylaws and handbook, and the students, faculty, and administration at Marquette are to be thanked for their unfailing support. Dean Joseph Kearney is a true champion of appellate advocacy, moot court, and legal writing at Marquette Law School. IU McKinney's Moot Court Board also helped draft several documents in the appendices—including bylaws, internal competition rules, and scoring rubrics—for which we are quite thankful. And Professor Dimitri owes a debt of gratitude to IU McKinney's faculty and administration for their steady and robust support of his work on this book and of IU McKinney's Moot Court Society.

Many people also read portions of this book and provided invaluable advice and support. Professor Suzanne Rabe has not only been a longtime mentor and advisor, she also reviewed drafts of Chapters One, Two, and Five, and provided insightful feedback and encouragement. Professor Sarah Ricks encouraged us to write the book in the first place and helped us get started. And Professor Allison Martin provided indispensable input to Professor Dimitri during his work on Chapter Three, giving suggestions on how to simplify that chapter.

None of this would have been possible without the students. Your struggles, triumphs, humor, intelligence, and persistence inspired virtually everything in this book. Every year, we have the privilege of meeting a new group of you. The diverse viewpoints and experiences you bring to the law-school endeavor enrich us and shape who we are as teachers, mentors, coaches, and human beings. In particular, we would like to thank Arizona Law's ABA National Appellate Advocacy Competition teams, Arizona Law's Moot Court Boards, the Marquette Law School Moot Court Association and teams, and IU McKinney's Moot Court Society.

Of course, we owe a great debt to the Legal Writing Institute's Board of Directors for their support of the Moot Court Committee's formation in 2008 and for their support of this book. Without the Board's encouragement, the writing of *The Moot Court Advisor's Handbook* simply would not have been possible.

Finally, thanks to Carolina Academic Press, and particularly Linda Lacy, for your indulgence and for being a dream and delight to work with over these past two years.

About the Authors

The Legal Writing Institute (LWI) is a non-profit organization dedicated to improving legal writing by providing a forum for discussion and scholarship about legal writing, analysis, and research. LWI promotes these activities through its publications, workshops, specialty conferences, and the national biennial conferences held in even-numbered years.

The Legal Writing Institute has over 2,800 members and includes representatives from 38 different countries. We are the second largest organization of law professors in the United States. Only the Association of American Law Schools (AALS) involves more members of the legal academic community. LWI sponsors many different working committees and projects, including the Moot Court Committee.

James Dimitri is a Clinical Professor of Law at Indiana University Robert H. McKinney School of Law. Drawing on his experience as an appellate attorney for the Office of the Indiana Attorney General, Professor Dimitri advised IU McKinney's Moot Court Board for two decades, guiding the Board in its running of the school's internal appellate advocacy competition, the Honorable Robert H. Staton Intramural Moot Court Competition. He has also advised several award-winning interscholastic teams, including teams representing IU McKinney in the ABA National Appellate Advocacy Competition. Professor Dimitri co-founded the Legal Writing Institute's Moot Court Committee and is a past co-chair of the Committee.

Melissa E. Love Koenig is a Professor of Legal Writing at Marquette Law School, where she teaches Appellate Writing and Advocacy in addition to other legal writing courses. Professor Love Koenig co-advises the moot court program at Marquette, which includes the Law School's Jenkins Honors Moot Court Competition and the National Moot Court Competition's Region VIII Round. She also coaches the New York City Bar Association's National Moot Court Competition team and the William B. Spong Moot Court Tournament team. Prior to teaching, Professor Love Koenig gained experience in appellate practice as a clerk to the Honorable N. Patrick Crooks of the Wisconsin Supreme Court and later in private practice in Milwaukee as a litigator. She continues to consult on appellate cases and is a past chair of the State Bar of Wisconsin's Appellate Practice Section Board. Professor Love Koenig co-founded the Legal Writing Institute's Moot Court Committee and is a past Committee co-chair.

Susie Salmon is Director of Legal Writing and Clinical Professor of Law at University of Arizona, James E. Rogers College of Law. She teaches first-year Legal Research, Analysis, and Communication and upper-level writing seminars, and she has coached the College's ABA National Appellate Advocacy Competition teams since 2010. For many years, she ran the College's internal Fegtly 2L Moot Court Competition, supervised the Moot Court Board, and chaired the Legal Skills Competition Board. For the 2022–24 biennium, Professor Salmon serves as President of the Board of Directors of the Legal Writing Institute. She also is a past co-chair of the LWI Moot Court Committee. Before joining Arizona Law, Professor Salmon spent nine years as a litigator at large private law firms in California and Arizona. As a law student, she had the honor of participating in the moot court program at University of California Law, San Francisco, as both an advocate and a student coach.

Contributors

Chapter 1: Introduction

Lead Author and Editor: Susie Salmon

Contributor:
Melissa E. Love Koenig

Chapter 2: Administering a Moot Court/ Legal Skills Competition Program

Lead Author and Editor: Susie Salmon

Contributor:
Allison Martin

Chapter 3: Managing an Internal Moot Court Competition

Lead Author and Editor: James Dimitri

Contributors:
Gail Mullins
Connie S. Smothermon

Chapter 4: Advising External Competition Teams

Lead Author and Editor: Melissa E. Love Koenig

Contributors:
Todd Bruno
Christopher G. Evers
Victoria Lowery
Allison Martin
Edward H. Telfeyan

Chapter 5: Developing and Managing (or Hosting) an External Moot Court Competition

Lead Author and Editor: Susie Salmon

Chapter 6: Virtual Moot Court Competitions

Lead Author and Editor: Susie Salmon

Online Materials

Printable versions can be found at
www.caplaw.com/mootcourt

Password: access29

The Moot Court Advisor's Handbook

CHAPTER 1

Introduction

THIS CHAPTER WILL HELP YOU TO:

- **Understand what "moot court" means;**
- **Learn some of the history of moot court and moot court programs;**
- **Understand the benefits of moot court participation;**
- **Understand how moot court activities may satisfy some of the newer ABA Standards for law schools.**

Perhaps you are a law professor who has just been asked to advise a moot court team. Or maybe you teach an appellate advocacy course or run an internal moot court competition. You might be an attorney recruited by a law school to coach a team. Or—lucky you—your school's entire moot court program might just have been dropped in your lap.

Whatever your role, congratulations! Moot court and other legal-skills competitions can be among the most rewarding experiences law school offers, both for the students and for the coach or professor.

No matter what your role or level of experience or whether you're a full-time or adjunct faculty member or practitioner—this book is designed to be a resource of sound advice and best practices for running moot court and other legal-skills competitions. Drawing on the combined expertise of the authors and the Legal Writing Institute's Moot Court Committee, this handbook can be your soup-to-nuts manual for building and administering a moot court program, a handy reference guide for the moot court newcomer, or anything in between.

I. What Is Moot Court?

Strictly defined, "moot court" refers to courses and competitions involving appellate advocacy. Participants usually receive a truncated version of an appellate record and anywhere from one to a handful of questions for review. Participants then research and brief the legal and factual issues and deliver oral arguments on those issues before a mock appellate court.

Moot court falls under the larger umbrella of legal-skills competitions, and many schools use "moot court" as a generic term to refer to the school's advocacy or competition programs. Over the years, the number and variety of moot court and other legal-skills competitions has grown exponentially.[1] Although many of the broader topics in this book—overall administration, advising teams, managing competitions—apply equally to a variety of legal-skills competitions, when it comes to the details, this text will focus primarily on traditional appellate advocacy competitions.

Programs across the country vary widely in how they address moot court in the curriculum. At some schools, moot court is a required, graded course. At others, it is not a course at all, but simply an extracurricular activity that some students choose to pursue. Some schools manage moot court within the legal-writing department. Others have an independent director of advocacy who oversees moot court, trial advocacy, and the student "moot court board" or "board of advocates." Some schools leave moot court entirely to student organizations; others have complex, structured, faculty-run programs.

Depending on your role, you may just need to learn your school's organizational scheme and how to work effectively within that scheme. You may, however, have a voice in how your school's moot court program is organized and run. In that case, Chapter Two of this book offers guidance on administering a moot court or legal-skills-competition program. Chapter Three provides tips on managing an internal moot court

1. LSU Law School, which maintains a list of moot court and alternative dispute resolution—not including trial advocacy, transactional, or other legal-skills competitions—on its website, currently lists sixty-five competitions. LSU L. Ctr. Advoc. Programs, *List of National Moot Court Competitions*, LA. STATE U. L. SCH. (2019), https://www.law.lsu.edu/advocacy/resources/list-of-national-moot-court-competitions/ (last visited Feb. 8, 2023).

competition, and Chapter Four addresses advising interscholastic competition teams. Chapter Five is helpful if your school hosts an external moot court competition, especially if you will be doing so for the very first time. Chapter Six, new to the second edition, provides guidance on organizing and hosting virtual moot court competitions and preparing students to compete in them. Finally, the appendices and online resources provide sample documents you can use to create your own bylaws, judging guidelines, scoring rubrics, competition rules, and other materials.

First, however, this text provides a brief introduction to moot court, its history, and its potential as a pedagogical tool.

II. History of Moot Court

Moot court exercises and competitions are among the oldest traditions in legal education. In Old English, the meanings of "moot" encompassed argument, discussion, and meeting for judicial or legislative purposes.[2] References to "a moot" appear as early as 997, in the laws of Aethelred the Unready, when it referred to something that sounds very similar to today's grand jury.[3] Moot court—or the use of oral argument of fictitious cases as a pedagogical tool—appears to have originated in the English Inns of Court beginning in the sixteenth century.[4] The Inns of Court grew out of the more informal apprenticeship system, by which aspiring lawyers learned the profession through observing and mimicking the activities of experienced lawyers.[5] These institutions formalized

---

2. "moot, n.1," OXFORD ENGLISH DICTIONARY, https://www.oed.com/view/Entry/122011?rskey=tKUXYy&result=1#eid (last visited Feb. 8, 2023).

3. Rufus Fleming, *The Scottish Jury: Landmarks in the History of Jury Trial*, 5 MICH. L. REV. 520, 527 (1906–07).

4. MOHAMED RACHID & CHARLES R. KNERR, BRIEF HISTORY OF MOOT COURT: BRITAIN AND U.S.1 (2000) *available at* https://files.eric.ed.gov/fulltext/ED442343.pdf; *see also* Jeffrey D. Jackson & David R. Cleveland, *Legal Writing: A History from the Colonial Era to the End of the Civil War*, 19 LEGAL WRITING: J. LEGAL WRITING INST. 191, 196 (2014); Anton-Hermann Chroust, *The Beginning, Flourishing, and Decline of the Inns of Court: The Consolidation of the English Legal Profession after 1400*, 10 VAND. L. REV. 79, 81 (1956).

5. John T. Gaubatz, *Of Moots, Legal Process, and Learning to Learn the Law*, 37 U. MIAMI. L. REV. 473, 477 (1983).

a structured system of instruction composed of three basic components intended to build skill in legal argument: attendance in court, participation in readings, and "instructional exercises."[6] The instructional exercises—sometimes called "moots," "bolts," or "putting a case," depending on their complexity—required students to put forth and argue cases of varying legal difficulty.[7] These exercises occurred daily and were considered rigorous and practical educational experiences.[8]

Although moots began to disappear from the Inns of Court in England over the course of the eighteenth century,[9] early legal education in the United States incorporated moot court as an essential pedagogical tool. Litchfield Law School, the nation's first, conducted optional moot courts for its students.[10] Some of the young nation's finest and most prominent legal minds participated in moot court; for example, the law-preparation curriculum at the College of William and Mary, which John Marshall attended, required regular moot courts.[11] George Wythe—who taught or mentored such distinguished lawyers and politicians as Marshall, Thomas Jefferson, and Henry Clay, among others—began using moot court to teach advocacy skills after he became a professor of law at the College in 1780.[12] In fact, moot court was consid-

6. Gaubatz, *supra* note 5, at 478; *see also* Chroust, *supra* note 4, at 94.

7. Gaubatz, *supra* note 5, at 478–79; *see also* Jackson & Cleveland, *supra* note 4, at 196; Chroust, *supra* note 4, at 109–11.

8. Chroust, *supra* note 4, at 109–11.

9. Jackson & Cleveland, *supra* note 4, at 196; Rachid & Knerr, *supra* note 4, at 4; Chroust, *supra* note 4, at 116–18.

10. Jackson & Cleveland, *supra* note 4, at 201; Albert J. Harno, *Legal Education in the United States: A Report Prepared for the Survey of the Legal Profession* 30 (Bancroft-Whitney Co., 1953). Students at Litchfield Law School were generally required to use hypothetical cases as the subject of their moot court exercises. Donald F. Melhorn, Jr., *A Moot Court Exercise: Debating Judicial Review Prior to Marbury v. Madison*, 12 CONST. COMMENT 327, 327 (1995). On August 31, 1797, however, the students argued a timely and pending legal question: whether the judiciary could void laws as unconstitutional. *Id.* In contrast to the moot courts at William and Mary, which were conducted and presided over by George Wythe and other William and Mary faculty, the moot court program at Litchfield was run by students and modeled after the Yale debating societies. *Id.* at 330. Oral arguments were held every Thursday evening. *Id.*

11. JEAN EDWARD SMITH, JOHN MARSHALL: DEFENDER OF A NATION 79 (1996).

12. Davison M. Douglas, *The Jeffersonian View of Legal Education*, 51 J. LEGAL EDUC. 185, 200–01 (2001); *see also* Jackson & Cleveland, *supra* note 4, at 202.

ered one of Wythe's key teaching innovations.[13] Wythe's students participated in oral arguments before faculty judges once a month at the old colonial Williamsburg capitol.[14] George Nicols, a William and Mary law graduate, imported moot court to Transylvania University in Lexington, Kentucky when he was appointed to teach there in 1799.[15]

The use of moot court as pedagogical tool in American law schools continued at Harvard Law School, the first university school of law in the country, which held appellate moot courts with faculty serving as judges as often as twice a week.[16] Moot courts were "a regular part of the curriculum," and "intended to be as nearly like an actual court as possible."[17] Many other law schools boast equally venerated moot court programs: The University of Virginia's moot court program began in the 1840s, Boston University has offered moot court since the 1870s, and the University of Mississippi's program has existed for over 140 years.[18]

The Langdellian[19] revolution in U.S. legal education at the end of the nineteenth century meant the decline of faculty-supervised moot court and the rise of moots run by student clubs. In the decade after Harvard

---

13. Wythe apparently believed in using simulations to teach skills; his second innovation was the use of a mock legislative assembly to teach his students "the practical art of government." *Id.* at 201–02; *see also* Wythe Holt, *George Wythe: Early Modern Judge*, 58 ALA. L. REV. 1009, 1010 (2007); Jackson & Cleveland, *supra* note 4, at 202.

14. Douglas, *supra* note 12, at 201.

15. *Id.* at 208.

16. Jackson & Cleveland, *supra* note 4, at 211, 221.

17. THE HARVARD L. SCH. ASS'N, THE CENTENNIAL HISTORY OF THE HARVARD LAW SCHOOL, 1817–1917, 144 (1918).

18. Darby Dickerson, *In re Moot Court*, 29 STETSON L. REV. 1217, 1223–24 (2000).

19. Christopher Columbus Langdell, Dean of Harvard Law School from 1870 to 1895, is credited with transforming legal education into what it is today: the three-year degree, teaching by the law-school version of the "Socratic method," much of the standard first-year curriculum, essay exams, and a faculty largely "divorced from practice." *See* Richard K. Neumann, Jr., *Osler, Langdell, and the Atelier: Three Tales of Creation in Professional Education*, 10 LEGAL COMM. & RHETORIC 151, 153 (2013). Somewhat ironically, Langdell seems to have appreciated the value of moot court when he was a law student; he was an "avid participant" in moots as a Harvard Law student in the 1850s and "drew particular attention for his elaborate brief in a losing effort in one case in 1852." Jackson & Cleveland, *supra* note 4, at 221. By the time he was a professor in the early 1880s, however, he seemed to doubt the usefulness of the exercise, choosing to conduct no moots in his courses. *See* Bruce A. Kimball, *Students' Choice and Experience During the Transition to Competitive Academic Achievement at Harvard Law School, 1876–1882*, 55 J. LEGAL EDUC. 163, 196 (2005).

began implementing Langdell's model, for example, the number of moot courts supervised by faculty declined from approximately thirty-two to a mere fifteen.[20] Citing heavy teaching loads resulting from an expanded curriculum, the Harvard faculty voted to suspend moot court for the 1879–80 academic year.[21] Students increasingly preferred participating in the moot courts run by Harvard's student clubs, and some faculty questioned the value of faculty-run moots.[22] Although a couple of professors persisted in using moots as a pedagogical tool, ultimately the pressures and demands of an expanded formal curriculum won out, and Harvard completely discontinued faculty-run moot courts in 1897.[23]

At the beginning of the twentieth century, Harvard instituted a student-run moot court program with two basic components.[24] First-year students participated in appellate moot court competitions supervised by a cohort of faculty-selected third-year students known as the Board of Student Advisors.[25] Meanwhile, second-year students represented their law clubs in what became known as the Ames Moot Court Competition. Although those law clubs no longer exist, the Ames Moot Court Competition continues to this day.[26] Other law schools followed, adding formal, student-run moot court activities to their curricula.

Beginning after World War II, moot court slowly became an inter-law-school sport, with teams from one law school competing against teams from another. The National Moot Court Competition bills itself

20. Kimball, *supra* note 19, at 195–96.

21. *Id.* at 196.

22. *Id.*

23. *Id.* at 196–97.

24. Harvard L. Sch. Bd. of Student Advisers, *History of the BSA*, HARVARD L. SCH., https://orgs.law.harvard.edu/bsa/history/ (last visited Feb. 8, 2023). The Harvard faculty's view of these moot court activities in 1910 seems oddly familiar today. First, the faculty seemed to see moot court as a consolation prize for those students who did not perform well enough in the first year of law school to earn a high-class rank. Second, the faculty found appellate moot court more intellectually valuable than trial practice, which it saw solely as "a relief to the tedium of serious work." THE HARVARD L. SCH. ASS'N, *supra* note 17, at 145.

25. Distinguished alumni of the Board of Student Advisers include United States Supreme Court Justice Anthony Kennedy. Harvard L. Sch. Bd. of Student Advisers, *History*, HARVARD L. SCH., https://orgs.law.harvard.edu/bsa/history/ (last visited Feb. 8, 2023).

26. Harvard L. Sch. Bd. of Student Advisers, *Ames Competition*, HARVARD L. SCH., http://https://orgs.law.harvard.edu/bsa/ames-competition/ (last visited Feb. 8, 2023).

as one of the oldest moot court competitions.[27] Created by the president of the New York City Bar Association, the first competition was held in 1950 when twelve teams from different schools engaged in a mock appellate argument over the legality of "rainmaking."[28] The Jessup International Law Moot Court Competition followed in 1960.[29] The number of external competitions has increased exponentially over the past two decades, with over 200 intercollegiate competitions across the world covering a variety of subject areas.

Over the years, the pendulum has swung from moot court as an exclusively student-run endeavor back to increased faculty involvement in and oversight of moot court programs. Now, virtually every law school has some form of moot court program that includes some combination of required courses, elective courses, and extracurricular student organizations and teams.

III. Why Have a Moot Court/Legal-Skills Competition Program?

If you are involved in moot court or other legal-skills competitions—and most especially if you are seeking funds from your college, alumni, or other sources to support those activities—you will need to answer the question, "Why moot court?" With law schools perpetually facing diminishing resources and increasing financial demands, you will be called upon to defend why your institution should devote some of those resources to organizing a moot court competition, sending students to a competition in a distant city, providing a stipend to an adjunct or full-time professor to run a moot class or program or to coach a team, or to pay you.

The rich history and entrenched traditions of moot court at most schools will be on your side, and because most people still identify pub-

---

27. N.Y. City B., *The National Moot Court Competition*, https://www.nycbar.org/member-and-career-services/law-students/national-moot-court (last visited Feb. 8, 2023).

28. *National Moot Court Competition*, Wikipedia (last modified Jan. 8, 2023 at 2:21 PM) https://en.wikipedia.org/wiki/National_Moot_Court_Competition.

29. *Jessup History*, Int'l L. Students Ass'n, http://www.ilsa.org/jessuphome (last visited Feb. 8, 2023).

lic speaking as among their greatest fears, it remains fairly easy to justify the need to train lawyers who are more comfortable speaking in front of groups. And recent additions and amendments to the ABA Standards after the past two decades, including an experiential-education requirement and a professional-identity-formation requirement, make your argument even easier: moot court programs can play a role in fulfilling both of those core objectives.

Even leaving aside those requirements, though, moot court and other legal-skills competitions provide invaluable experiences that nothing else in the law school curriculum, even in the clinical setting, can offer. Moot court, of course, trains budding attorneys in many of the same skills students gain through legal-skills courses: legal writing, research, oral advocacy, legal analysis, and critical thinking. The emotional and psychological rush of competition can mirror what students will experience in real-life litigation. But moot court and other legal-skills competitions also provide students with hands-on, experiential training in other skills essential to good lawyering. Unlike clinical courses and other live-client experiences, however, moot court provides that training in a relatively low-risk environment. Students can make mistakes and experiment with different strategies and professional personae in a setting where the consequences—injuries to personal pride, disappointing team members, losing a round or a competition—are relatively minimal but still significant enough to make an indelible impression. Also unlike in most clinical settings, students participating in moot court generally stand alone at the podium during oral argument, unable to seek assistance from or be "rescued" by anyone during difficult questioning. Furthermore, by keeping these potential learning outcomes in mind as coaches, professors, and administrators, we can help our students get the most out of their moot court experiences.

A. Moot court can help satisfy new ABA Standards.[30]

Since 2014, the ABA has amended its accreditation standards to add two requirements that moot-court activities can help to satisfy: (1) the

30. As most readers of this text already know, law schools can be accredited at either the national or state level. But the overwhelming majority of states require applicants to have a degree from a nationally accredited law school to sit for the bar exam and be ad-

experiential-education requirement, and (2) the professional-identity-formation requirement. Moot court activities can have a role in meeting both requirements.

1. EXPERIENTIAL EDUCATION REQUIREMENT

First, in 2014, the ABA added Standards mandating that law schools require students to complete "one or more experiential course(s) totaling at least six credit hours," before graduation.[31] Under the Standards, experiential courses can include law clinics or externships, but they also can include simulation courses—courses that provide "substantial experience not involving an actual client, that is reasonably similar to the experience of a lawyer advising or representing a client or engaging in other lawyering tasks in a set of facts and circumstances devised or adopted by a faculty member."[32] To meet this Standard, a simulation course must:

1. [I]ntegrate doctrine, theory, skills, and legal ethics, and engage students in performance of one or more of the professional skills identified in Standard 302;
2. [D]evelop the concepts underlying the professional skills being taught;
3. [P]rovide multiple opportunities for performance;
4. [P]rovide opportunities for student performance, self-evaluation, and feedback from a faculty member . . . ;
5. [P]rovide a classroom instructional component . . . ;
6. [P]rovide direct supervision of the student's performance by the faculty member.[33]

The reference to Standard 302 means that experiential courses also must meet at least one of the following learning outcomes: knowledge of substantive and procedural law; legal research, analysis, problem-solving,

mitted to practice. The American Bar Association sets the standards for national accreditation.

31. 2022–2023 Standards and Rules of Procedure for Approval of L. Schools Standard 303(a)(3) (Am. Bar. Ass'n, amended 2022).

32. *Id.* Standard 304(b).

33. *Id.* Standard 304(a).

and oral and written communication; exercise of professionalism and ethics; and other professional skills necessary in the legal profession.[34]

As discussed in more detail in other sections of this chapter, in many respects, most moot-court courses, competitions, or competition teams fall squarely within the definition of a simulation course that meets the experiential requirements:

- Moot courts give students the chance to practice their writing and oral advocacy skills through a fact pattern that is not related to an actual client, as described in Standard 304(b);
- In researching and writing the brief and practicing oral argument with feedback from moot judges, students learn an area of substantive law, become more familiar with procedural law, and hone their analysis, reasoning, research, and advocacy skills, as required by Standard 304(a)(1) and Standard 302;
- Moot courts provide multiple opportunities for performance through weeks of oral-argument practices and at the competition itself, as required by Standard 304(a)(3) and 304(a)(4).

Direct, ongoing faculty involvement in the moot court activity increases the likelihood[35] that a moot-court course, competition, or competition team meets all the Standards' requirements for an experiential simulation course:

- A faculty-member coach who participates in several practices and competition rounds and provides feedback on student performance can help meet Standard 304(a)(4), which requires faculty feedback, as well as Standard 304(a)(6), which requires "direct supervision of the student's performance by a faculty member";
- The program or an individual faculty member or coach can design periodic, short reflection assignments designed to

---

34. *Id.* Standard 302.

35. Naturally, the authors of this Handbook cannot guarantee that following these suggestions will ensure that your moot court activity meets the ABA Standards.

encourage students to engage in self-evaluation as required by Standard 303(a)(4).[36]

The biggest obstacle to a moot-court activity meeting the requirements for a simulation course may be the "classroom instructional component" requirement under Standard 304(a)(5). The Standards do not provide guidance, through official Interpretations or otherwise, as to what a "classroom instructional component" entails. A moot-court class that meets weekly almost certainly meets this criterion. Whether something short of a formal, weekly class might suffice remains an open question. It might be, for example, that online instructional modules on best practices in oral argument and brief writing might help meet this requirement. Lectures from faculty members expert in the area of substantive law implicated by the problem might help as well.

At minimum, however, moot court programs can tailor courses and competitions to meet the experiential-education requirement. And moot court in general meets many of the goals embodied in that requirement's criteria.

2. PROFESSIONAL IDENTITY FORMATION REQUIREMENT

More recently, in 2022, the ABA adopted a requirement that all law schools "provide substantial opportunities to students for ... the development of professional identity."[37] The ABA defines "professional identity" as "what it means to be a lawyer and the special obligations lawyers have to their clients and society."[38] The ABA notes that "developing professional identity requires reflection and growth over time" and recommends that students "have frequent opportunities during each year of law school and in a variety of courses and co-curricular and professional development activities."[39]

As discussed in detail later throughout this chapter, moot court activities can help satisfy that requirement by providing myriad opportuni-

36. Such a reflection also comports with the requirements imposed by Standard 305.

37. 2022–2023 Standards and Rules of Procedure for Approval of L. Schools Standard 303(b) (Am. Bar. Ass'n, amended 2022).

38. *Id.* Interpretation 303-5

39. *Id.* Interpretation 303-6.

ties for students to explore and reflect upon the values and guiding principles fundamental to law practice.

B. Moot court helps students build skills in collaboration and teamwork.

As studies illustrate, teamwork and collaboration are key lawyering skills.[40] Successful lawyers must collaborate effectively with other attorneys in the same office, in other offices, in other firms, and in client's offices. Sometimes attorneys engaged in complex litigation or transactional matters work on various teams, often collaborating with members of different professions. New lawyers could be leading teams of paralegals, other support staff, and even other attorneys very early in their careers. Legal employers include teamwork and collaboration among the criteria for evaluating attorneys. Clients identify these skills as crucial.

Although collaboration and teamwork are integral to successful law practice, legal education offers few opportunities to learn and develop these skills. Fortunately, moot court is one of those opportunities. Most interscholastic moot court competitions, and several internal competitions and courses,[41] require students to work in pairs or in teams of three or four. Each team then submits a joint brief, which requires the students to research, write, and work collaboratively. Participants need to allocate responsibility, develop systems for holding themselves and each other accountable, and edit and critique each other's work. They also must work productively with students with different personalities, skill levels, and strengths. Students must develop and exercise interpersonal capacities like effective communication, listening skills, conflict resolution strategies, negotiation, appreciation of diversity, and diplomacy. Moot court participants can also learn and practice more nuanced people skills like honoring others' contributions, hearing and reconciling different points of view, and avoiding "groupthink." Better teamwork in the

---

40. Neil Hamilton & Verna Monson, *Teamwork Skills Are Critical for Effective Lawyering*, MINNESOTA LAW. (Apr. 13, 2012), https://minnlawyer.com/2012/04/13/teamwork-skills-are-critical-for-effective-lawyering/; Gerald Lebovits, Drew Gewuerz, & Christopher Hunker, *Winning the Moot Court Oral Argument: A Guide for Intramural and Intermural Moot Court Competitors*, 41 CAP. U. L. REV. 887, 895 (2013).

41. As noted in Chapter Three, a significant number of internal competitions and courses require students to submit individual briefs.

moot court setting means a better brief, a better competition outcome, and better future lawyers.

C. Moot court helps students build confidence in their skills and independent judgment.

Most interscholastic moot court competitions, and some internal competitions and courses, prohibit participants from receiving much or any feedback from their professor or coach on their written work product before it is submitted.[42] Some competitions do allow faculty to provide input, but limit that assistance to the type a senior attorney might provide a junior attorney in practice—mere consultation and oversight, not the detailed written and in-person comments on analysis, organization, and style that students are accustomed to receiving from legal-writing professors. Drafting an appellate brief under those circumstances can be a terrifying but ultimately empowering experience for students. Many students come to appreciate how much they have learned through their legal educations and what they can now do on their own. A brief written under these circumstances becomes a powerful writing sample, illustrating to a future employer what a student can do with little to no guidance.

Drafting the brief independently also serves as a dress rehearsal for practice, forcing students to develop time-management skills, self-monitoring, and long-term planning strategies. Students participating in an extracurricular moot court competition must balance their brief-writing schedule with their other academic obligations. Further, rather than being nudged in the right direction in their research, analysis, or organization by a helpful comment from a professor, moot court students must make those judgments on their own.

---

42. Of course, most students participating in moot court classes, particularly those offered or required in the first year of law school, receive significant written and in-person feedback on their briefs and oral argument from professors, teaching assistants, members of the moot court board, or some combination of the three. The same is true of many internal competitions.

D. Moot court fosters nimble thinkers.

Even attorneys who never set foot in a courtroom must articulate their legal reasoning and analysis orally on a regular basis. Whether explaining legal advice to a client, negotiating an agreement with opposing counsel, reporting the results of a research assignment, or responding to queries from supervising attorneys, lawyers must think quickly and articulate their analysis logically and systematically. A student who learns to respond calmly and effectively to questions from a moot court judge can carry that skill into litigation or appellate practice, or into any area of law they choose to pursue.

Moreover, moot court problems generally present engaging intellectual exercises that may not come along every day in regular law practice. Competition administrators strive to design problems that raise novel or controversial legal issues. Competitors, particularly those who advance to elimination rounds, frequently argue before prominent academics, attorneys, and judges.[43] And competitors then receive feedback on those arguments from some of the top performers in their chosen field.

E. Moot court helps students exercise critical thinking skills and develop professional judgment.

F. Scott Fitzgerald once said that the "test of a first-rate intelligence" was "the ability to hold two opposed ideas in mind at the same time and still retain the ability to function."[44] Although participating in moot court doesn't automatically confer a first-rate intelligence, the structure of many moot court competitions requires participants to see issues from opposing perspectives and develop intellectual agility. Although participants generally brief only one side of the case, most competitions require participants to present oral arguments on both sides.

Some argue not only that this is unrealistic—no attorney will ever argue both sides of the same case—but also that it encourages students to see legal issues as abstractions divorced from emotion and from the

43. Lebovits, Gewuerz, & Hunker, *supra* note 40, at 895.

44. F. Scott Fitzgerald, *The Crack Up*, Esquire Mag. (Feb. 1, 1936), https://classic.esquire.com/article/share/97a6b0a8-ba1c-4b7b-aa64-0d08dd9fb952?source=nl&utm_source=nl_esq&utm_medium=email&date=010621&utm_campaign=nl22576403&utm_term=ESQ_Esquire_Membership_CLASSIC_PAID.

obligation to represent the interests of a client.[45] Although this position may have merit, a good professor or coach can create a more client-focused experience by encouraging the students to think through the practical and human issues the problem poses (which will also, incidentally, improve the student's oral argument). Moreover, the benefits of requiring students to argue both sides of the issue significantly outweigh any possible drawbacks. The exercise requires students to learn the arguments on each side thoroughly, to appreciate the strengths and weaknesses of each argument, and to exercise independent professional judgment about the persuasiveness of each point or sub-point. This not only helps to train attorneys who anticipate and effectively defuse counterarguments, it also can help students develop the professional judgment to assess the strengths and weaknesses of a case and advise a client accordingly. Further, none of this prevents students from retaining the capacity to believe wholeheartedly in the rightness of their side or their cause, and, in fact, many students and attorneys alike find that playing the devil's advocate role helps them refine their primary argument.

F. Moot court deepens learning in substantive areas.

Legal educators have long recognized that moot court not only teaches advocacy and argumentative skills but also helps students learn substantive areas of law more effectively. In the Inns of Court, the lessons learned through lectures and readings were often cemented through the moots. Similarly, student participation in one of the many specialty interscholastic moot court competitions can be an excellent complement to a certificate program or a law school's signature area of specialization.[46] Not only does oral argument keep students engaged and interested, the prospect of facing difficult questions from the bench creates a powerful incentive to learn the legal issues thoroughly. Students preparing for an internal or external competition immerse them-

---

45. *See* Alex Kosinski, *In Praise of Moot Court—Not!*, 97 COLUM. L. REV. 178, 185–86 (1997).

46. LSU L. Ctr. Advoc. Programs, *supra* note 1. Specialty moot court competitions range from the National Health Law Moot Court Competition to the Adoption & Child Welfare National Moot Court Competition to competitions on public international law, evidence, intellectual property, civil rights, and a variety of different areas of substantive law.

selves in the relevant area of law for months to anticipate and address any imaginable question on the topic. As others writing on this topic have noted, not only is fear of failure a powerful incentive to deep and thorough learning, but also students electing to participate in an interscholastic moot court competition do so by choice, and thus are more motivated to internalize the material to compete and win.[47]

G. Moot court is a chance to practice professionalism.

Life isn't fair, and neither, sadly, is lawyering. Even when the law, facts, and even justice seem to be on their sides, lawyers may lose cases. Deals may fail despite their merits and the attorney's best efforts. As a matter of professionalism and ongoing mental health, lawyers need to deal with loss and unfairness constructively. Moot court can be an excellent rehearsal for that inevitable challenge. Much as an attorney may draw a bad panel at the circuit court, a moot court advocate could draw a hard-scoring bench at a competition. Sometimes moot court judges are not as prepared as they could be. Sometimes scoring seems brutally unfair.[48] Sometimes other competitors behave unprofessionally. Learning to deal with those circumstances gracefully is excellent preparation for the emotional demands of sometimes contentious law practice. Indeed, the very flaws inherent in the artificial moot court setting can become a virtue in this context, particularly with thoughtful and constructive coaching.

Similarly, moot court offers an opportunity for students to build and rehearse their professional identities. The Carnegie Report exhorted law schools to foster students' exploration and development of their professional identities—to allow law students to observe different models of lawyering and professionalism, to "try on" different professional identities, and to reflect on that process.[49] And, of course, as discussed earlier

---

47. Paula Gerber & Melissa Castan, *Practice Meets Theory: Using Moots as a Tool to Teach Human Rights Law*, 62 J. Legal Educ. 298, 299 (2012).

48. As an article astutely noted, "To the extent that moot court is subjective and unjust, our response is, 'Welcome to the real world,' a world in which lawyers must strive to improve those things that are good, not discard them altogether." Lebovits, Gewuerz, & Hunker, *supra* note 40, at 894.

49. William M. Sullivan et al., The Carnegie Foundation for the Advancement of Teaching, Educating Lawyers: Preparation for the Profession of Law

in this chapter, the American Bar Association recently added an explicit requirement that law schools provide all law students with "substantial opportunities" for "the development of a professional identity."[50] Often, law schools try to accomplish these ends through clinical experiences and externships, but moot court can also provide opportunities for students to find their own unique lawyering style and voice and to reflect on issues of ethics and professionalism that may arise.

Many moot court programs require students to observe and critique live or recorded appellate arguments. This exercise can be particularly effective if the coach or professor selects arguments delivered by advocates who have different but equally effective styles, keeping in mind diversity of race, ethnicity, sex, gender expression, disability, and more. Ideally, students would be able to see themselves reflected in the examples. The coach or professor could then encourage the students to experiment with different styles and techniques to find the "advocacy persona" that will be most effective for each individual student. The coach or professor should take care to select diverse examples that represent the rich range of effective advocates; students should be able to see themselves reflected in the examples. Many moot court programs also require students to consider and debate professionalism issues particular to appellate practice and to reflect on the type of advocates they want to be.

H. Moot court is a networking opportunity.

Whether students participate in an internal moot court competition arguing against their classmates before panels of local attorneys, or whether they travel to another city to face students from law schools across the country, students can connect with future colleagues and even potential employers. Many moot court advisors have stories of students who received summer or even permanent job offers after impressing a panel of attorneys or judges with skilled oral argument. When it comes to intramural moot court competitions, particularly in smaller legal markets, often the same judges return year after year, and sometimes former competitors return as judges. The competition itself becomes a

---

135 (John Wiley & Sons, Inc. 2007).

50. *See* Standard 303(b), *supra* note 37 and accompanying text.

network that can lead to recommendations, jobs, and client referrals. Even in far-flung interscholastic competitions, many students meet other competitors or judges who become their colleagues, mentors, and clients. Many competitions have banquets or other events designed to optimize these networking opportunities.

I. Moot court is a law-school rite of passage.

Nearly every lawyer can recall their first law-school oral argument, and most have humorous anecdotes or cautionary tales to share from the experience. Toni Young, the Director of Moot Court, Appellate Advocacy, and Legal Writing & Research at the University of California College of Law, San Francisco, calls moot court a "sport for lawyers,"[51] and there is much truth to that characterization.[52] Students on moot court teams work together intensely for months, drafting the brief, practicing oral argument, and sharing in each other's triumphs and disappointments. Often the friendships and camaraderie that develop stay with those students throughout their professional careers. Lest we forget, Bill and Hillary Clinton were moot court partners at Yale Law School. Three years after winning the William Minor Lile Moot Court Competition at the University of Virginia Law School, Ted Kennedy was elected to the U.S. Senate. His moot court partner, John Tunney, joined him there in 1971.[53] Past winners of Harvard's Ames Moot Court Competition include United States Supreme Court Justice Harry Blackmun, Massachusetts Governor Deval Patrick, California Supreme Court Justice Matthew Tobriner, Harvard Law Professor Cass Sunstein, and former child actress and member of the California State Legislature Sheila Kuehl.[54]

---

51. *Sports for Lawyers: UC Law SF Moot Court*, Univ. of Cal. Coll. of L., San Francisco, https://www.uchastings.edu/2015/06/03/sports-for-lawyers-uc-hastings-moot-court/ (last visited Feb. 10, 2023).

52. Others characterize the moot court team as "essentially the law school's football team carrying the law school's flag onto the field." Lebovits, Gewuerz, & Hunker, *supra* note 40, at 894.

53. *Remembering Sen. Ted Kennedy '59: Law School Mourns Exceptional Alum*, U. of Va. Sch. of L., (Aug. 26, 2006) https://www.law.virginia.edu/news/2009_fall/kennedy.htm (last visited Feb. 10, 2023).

54. *Ames Moot Court Competition*, Wikipedia (last modified Sep. 3, 2022, 2:11 PM), https://en.wikipedia.org/wiki/Ames_Moot_Court_Competition (last visited Feb 10, 2023); Harvard L. Sch. Bd. of Student Advisers, *Past Winners of the Ames Competition*,

And future United States Supreme Court Justices Sandra Day O'Connor and William Rehnquist were partners in Stanford Law School's moot court competition.[55]

J. And, of course, more legal writing never hurt anyone.

The value of an additional, intensive legal-writing experience cannot be overstated. Good writers become great writers through repetition. Although most schools require at least five credits of instruction in legal writing or "lawyering skills,"[56] virtually every law student could benefit from an additional practice-oriented legal-writing experience. And even though students receive minimal (if any) faculty feedback on drafts of the moot court brief, nothing prevents a faculty advisor from providing significant written feedback after the brief is submitted.

The moot court experience also teaches students in a very tangible way the consequences of poor brief-writing. Although oral argument judges do not see individual student briefs, in most competitions, the brief does stay with the student in a very real sense: the brief score makes up a percentage of the round score—sometimes as much as a third or a half of the point total—for at least the initial oral argument rounds. Even if students significantly outperform their briefs in oral argument, it's very difficult, if not impossible, to overcome a poor brief score. Many competitions "seed" oral argument rounds by brief score, so that teams with lower brief scores compete against teams with higher brief scores. Thus, a student who "wins" a round in oral argument could still lose—and lose rather badly—because of a low brief score. Such a hard lesson, particularly where it affects peers on a team, can resonate even more than a poor grade.

---

https://orgs.law.harvard.edu/bsa/past-winners/ (last visited Feb. 8, 2023). Hurrah for Zelda Gilroy!

55. Nina Totenberg, *O'Connor, Rehnquist and a Supreme Marriage Proposal*, NPR (Oct. 31, 2018 5:00 AM), https://www.npr.org/2018/10/31/662293127/a-supreme-marriage-proposal (last visited Feb. 10, 2023).

56. 2020–21 Surv. Comm., *ALWD/LWI Legal Writing Survey, 2020–2021: Report of the Individual Survey*, Ass'n of Legal Writing Dirs. & Legal Writing Inst. 17–18 (2020–21), https://www.alwd.org/images/resources/2020-2021-ALWD-and-LWI-Individual-Survey-report-FINAL.pdf.

In short, the moot court experience is about much more than oral advocacy. Participating in moot court, whether through a class, an internal competition, or an external competition, provides law students the opportunity to build and practice key lawyering skills in an environment where the consequences are meaningful but manageable.

CHAPTER 2

Administering a Moot Court/ Legal-Skills Competition Program

THIS CHAPTER WILL HELP YOU TO:

- **Gain a big-picture overview of some of the key aspects of running a successful moot court program;**
- **Understand the various components that may be part of a typical moot court program;**
- **Understand the variety of ways schools structure moot court programs and gain insights into the different priorities and considerations that may inform that structure;**
- **Understand and be able to implement best practices in populating and managing a student-run moot court board;**
- **Understand and be able to implement best practices in developing budgets and fundraising strategies for a moot court program and identifying considerations that may affect those practices;**
- **Understand and be able to implement best practices in successfully developing and managing relationships with alumni.**

I. Overall Organization and Bylaws

A moot court or legal-skills competition program comprises a variety of components and can be structured in myriad ways depending on the size, culture, focus, and structure of a given law school. Most programs, however, include some number or combination of the following components:

1. Student teams that compete in interscholastic moot court competitions;
2. Student teams that compete in other interscholastic legal-skills competitions;
3. One or more internal moot court competitions;
4. A student-run moot court board;
5. One or more moot court or appellate advocacy courses; and
6. Faculty advisors.

Structures vary widely. Although one cannot say that there are as many different programmatic structures as there are law schools, programs certainly vary enough that it is difficult to generalize. At most law schools, however, moot court and the school's other advocacy-skills programs have a close relationship with the legal-writing department. Some schools run moot court through the legal-writing or legal-skills program, using faculty from that department as directors or advisors. A school with a large, extremely well-developed advocacy skills program may run that program as a separate entity, headed by a faculty director whose sole responsibility is to oversee advocacy classes and internal and external legal-skills competitions.

Still other schools have no central moot court administration, but rather staff different portions of the program through different parts of the law school. For example, a school might have a moot court class, internal competition, student moot court board, and one or more competition teams under the umbrella of the legal writing program. That same school might also have a team for the Pace Environmental Law Competition supervised by its environmental law center, a team for the Native American Students Association Competition supervised by its Federal Indian Law faculty, and a team for the National Veterans Law Competition supervised by the faculty overseeing a veterans' law clinic. And still other schools have programs that are evolving—growing, shrinking, or simply changing—with different aspects of the program moving into or out of the purview of a central moot court or advocacy skills administration.

Having all moot court programs run by a faculty director and student moot court board presents some advantages:[1]

- First, having all moot court programs run by a faculty director and student moot court board helps ensure that those with experience, knowledge, and expertise about moot court programs are running the show.
- Second, generally, students gain more from the moot court experience if everyone involved in that experience believes in its value. As a rule, law faculty who devote their careers to advocacy skills training hold that belief, and the same is likely true of students who elect to become members of a moot court board. The same cannot reliably be said, however, of faculty who focus primarily in other areas.
- Third, this type of administration likely allows broader and fairer student access to moot court and other advocacy skills opportunities. The school has one central source of information for students interested in participating in a moot court competition. It also has one central source of information about the students who are interested in competing or whose skills and interests make them particularly well-suited for a particular team. If a promising advocate fails to win a spot on one external competition team, the board or director has the power to offer that student a spot on another team. If a student does well in an internal competition, the board or director will take note and can direct that student to external competition opportunities.
- Fourth, a collaboration between a member of the skills faculty and the student moot court board allows for a system of checks and balances that may enhance the

1. Many think that an "independent moot court board" that decides "who will join the board, who will be officers of the board, in which competitions the team will compete, who will compete in them, and who will argue which issues" is the sign of a quality moot court program. *See, e.g.*, Gerald Lebovits, Drew Gewuerz & Christopher Hunker, *Winning the Moot Court Oral Argument: A Guide for Intramural and Intermural Moot Court Competitors*, 41 Cap. U. L. Rev. 887, 943 (2003).

likelihood that students from diverse backgrounds, including students who do not fit the conventional stereotypes about what makes a "good" lawyer or oral advocate, have equal opportunity to participate and shine. Having a variety of voices participate in team selection, for example, increases the likelihood of diverse perspectives. Students often bring a different—more current—generational and cultural perspective. And a faculty director engaged with the broader legal-skills community who knows best practices in selection, scoring, or coaching methodologies can mitigate the impact of implicit bias or antiquated notions of advocacy style.[2]

- Fifth, fundraising for an entire moot court or advocacy program rather than just for an individual specialty team can present advantages, including more and higher-dollar naming opportunities, for example.
- Sixth, the program can take advantage of efficiencies of scale, including possible access to support-staff time, funds, and informational resources. The central moot court administration can be a repository of knowledge about, for example, the rules and quirks of different external competitions, or best practices in teaching advocacy skills. A central moot court administration might maintain a database of potential practice-round judges along with their areas of expertise and the dates they have served, and it might make sure that volunteers are not overtaxed and that they are officially and appropriately acknowledged for their service.

---

2. For more information on diversity issues in moot court and the legal profession, see Marcus Lind-Martinez, *Latinidad, White Supremacy, and Reforming First-Year Moot Court Competitions to Confront Racial and Ethnic Bias*, 23 Harv. Latinx L. Rev. 125, 125–27, 141 (2020) (providing a first-hand account of racial and ethnic biases in moot court competitions and providing guidance to ensure anti-racist instruction); Angela Mae Kupenda, *Simply Put: How Diversity Benefits Whites and How Whites Can Simply Benefit Diversity*, 6 Seattle J. for Soc. Just. 649, 668 (2008) (discussing how student organizations, such as moot courts and journals, tend "to maintain a status quo of whiteness"); Mairi N. Morrison, *May it Please Whose Court?: How Moot Court Perpetuates Gender Bias in the "Real World" of Practice*, 6 UCLA W. L.J. 49 (1995); Dave Giles, *Legal Profession Must Evolve in Step with the World Around Us*, 35-WTR Comm. Law. 2, 2–4 (2020) (providing information on the diversity gap in the legal workforce and how diversity moot court competitions can be used to fill that gap).

On the other hand, several compelling reasons support having some aspects of the moot court program—certain external competition teams, for example—run primarily by other parts of the law school:

- If the school's purpose in sending students to a particular external competition is to enhance student learning in a specific area of substantive law, it might be more effective to have the faculty who specialize in that area of substantive law oversee the recruitment and selection of participants and the coaching of the team. This may be particularly true if this area of substantive law is one for which your law school is or wants to be nationally known, or where your school has a certificate program or emphasis in that area.
- Moreover, funds may be available to faculty teaching in a particular area of law—a grant, endowment, or donation, for example—that, because of the stated purpose of the grant, endowment, or donation, are not available to the central moot court administration.
- Some moot court competitions require students to be active participants in activities or organizations relevant to the subject matter and objectives of the competition.[3] In that situation, often the relevant student organization is best situated to recruit competitors and coaches and to ensure student compliance with any idiosyncratic rules or requirements consistent with the educational mission of the competition.

---

3. The National Native American Law Students' Association Moot Court Competition, for instance, requires students to be "active" members of their local NALSA chapter and have an interest in advancing the mission of the organization. NNALSA Moot Court Rules Committee, *National Native American Law Students Association Annual Moot Court Competition Official Rules* (As Amended November 2022), Rule 4.2, available at https://static1.squarespace.com/static/632a44209ed09b07936efaa5/t/63d2c4e0855f6a3ffbf153ed/1674757345725/2023+Moot+Court+Rules+%28Amended+November+2022%29.pdf (last visited Jan. 30, 2023). To be eligible to compete, an interested student must submit a letter from the local chapter's president or secretary. *Id.* If there is no local chapter, the student must become a member of the national organization, submit a personal letter attesting to her commitment to the organization's mission, and submit a letter from someone in her law school's faculty or administration vouching for that student's involvement and commitment. *Id.* at Rule 4.3.

Probably the best structure for a moot court program is one in which an independent, central moot court administration, including a student moot court board and legal writing / legal skills faculty, works closely with the substantive law faculty to run a program that maximizes all of the potential learning outcomes listed in Chapter One. Although some external competition teams might be selected and coached by substantive law faculty, that faculty should coordinate with the moot court administration to identify interested and talented students and to make sure that all students have access to information about the opportunity. And the moot court administration should take advantage of the expertise of the substantive law faculty by recruiting them as advisors, team coaches, and oral-argument practice judges.

Academic politics, priorities, and financial constraints being what they are, this level of cooperation may not be possible at every law school. But you can keep these goals in mind and work toward them as you have opportunities.

A. Bylaws and other governing documents

Many law schools dictate some aspects of the moot court program's structure and administration through provisions in the faculty bylaws. The bylaws may cover selection criteria for the board and for competition teams, the number and identity of competitions to which the law school sends student teams every year, mechanisms for authorizing students to represent the school at competitions the school does not ordinarily attend, and even criteria for certain awards. The online appendix includes some model bylaws, handbooks, and contracts you might consider adapting to your school's needs.

Incorporating key provisions about your moot court program into the faculty bylaws presents some advantages. Most faculty bylaws include sections about law review and other student-run academic publications. Including moot court and other legal-skills competitions puts them on the same footing. It also helps maintain stability and continuity in a program during times of transition—when a new director is hired, for example, or when the law school's dean and central administration changes.

That said, you should be judicious about which policies, and how much detail, you include in bylaws. Bylaws are difficult to change because they often require a vote by the entire faculty as well as review and approval by a faculty subcommittee. For this reason, when you are drafting or revising bylaws, you want to include only those aspects of your program that are unlikely to change (and especially those aspects that you do not wish to change).

Many moot court programs draft and adopt their own codes, rule books, or bylaws. These are separate from the faculty bylaws, and amendments often require only the permission of the program director or a vote by the board (so long as the amendments do not affect the school's overall curriculum). Such bylaws can and should be significantly more detailed than any related provisions in the faculty bylaws. Some topics these bylaws might address include:

- The board's duties, composition, and structure;
- Any board committees or subcommittees and their duties;
- Any board officers and their duties;
- Member selection procedures;
- Procedures for selecting members of external competition teams;
- Procedures to safeguard diversity, equity, and inclusion in member selection;
- Procedures for selecting which external competition teams the school will participate in;
- Eligibility requirements for participating in external competitions;
- Requirements for and expectations of competitors;
- Travel and reimbursement policies;
- Whether and when students receive academic credit or financial compensation for participation on the moot court board or on external competition teams; and
- Procedures for addressing violations of the bylaws.

Even if you do not have a full set of program rules or bylaws, you should memorialize in writing your board members' rights and obligations. A good practice is to have board members sign an agreement at the beginning of their term of service, acknowledging their tasks and responsibilities and documenting any consequences for failing to fulfill those responsibilities. Some programs have board members sign a "contract," particularly if those board members are receiving units or monetary compensation for their service. Although you may not always enforce a breach of this document—particularly if the students are not receiving academic units or financial compensation—the mere act of having your board sign it can impress upon them the gravity of their responsibilities.

Some programs impose a minimum hour requirement on their board members and require board members to keep track of their hours during their board service. Not only does this mechanism promote accountability and full board participation, recording time on a regular basis is an excellent experience for those board members who will go into private law practice after law school. And, of course, if students do receive academic credit for board service, their timesheets help document the program's compliance with the credit-hour standards set forth in ABA Standard 310.[4]

B. Assembling and managing a moot court board

Most schools have some form of student moot court board—whether it is called a moot court honor society, a board of advocates or board of barristers, moot court council, or some other title[5]—that is involved in administering some aspect of the school's moot court program. Moot court boards have existed in the United States for almost as long as moot court programs have. The University of Mississippi School of Law's Moot Court Board, for instance, has existed for over 140 years.[6] Harvard Law School's Board of Student Advisers has been involved in teaching Harvard Law students legal research, writing, and advocacy for over 100 years.[7] At many schools, board membership confers significant prestige. Students list it on their resumes, and some schools even include it as an honors designation in the graduation program.

---

4. *2022–2023 Standards and Rules of Procedure for Approval of Law Schools, Chapter 3: Program of Legal Education*, Am. Bar. Ass'n, at Standard 310, https://www.americanbar.org/content/dam/aba/administrative/legal_education_and_admissions_to_the_bar/standards/2022-2023/22-23-standard-ch3.pdf.

5. Darby Dickerson, *In re Moot Court*, 29 Stetson L. Rev. 1217, 1218 n.6 (2000).

6. *Id.* at 1224.

7. Harvard L. Sch. Bd. of Student Advisers, *About the BSA*, Harvard L. Sch., https://orgs.law.harvard.edu/bsa/ (last visited Jan. 31, 2023); Harvard L. Sch. Bd. of Student Advisers, *History of the BSA*, Harvard L. Sch., https://orgs.law.harvard.edu/bsa/history/ (last visited Jan. 31, 2023).

Assembling and managing a moot court board presents both opportunities and challenges for the responsible faculty member, but well-run moot court boards shift much of the administrative burden and responsibility for the success of the program to the students. Service on the moot court board also provides students with an invaluable educational and leadership experience; board members often work closely with faculty and with the school's administration.

1. POTENTIAL ROLES FOR A MOOT COURT BOARD

The role of the moot court board varies from school to school. At some schools, the entire moot court program is run by the student board. At others, students run isolated aspects of the program—an internal moot court competition, for example, or the selection and assignment of team members—but the rest is administered by faculty and staff. At many schools, the student board takes a leading role in running many aspects of the program but works closely with a full-time or adjunct faculty member who serves as director and advisor. Some schools have one board that oversees all advocacy-related programs. Others have multiple boards, including perhaps a trial-advocacy board, a negotiation board, a mediation board, a transactional-skills board, and a moot court board.

Most boards play some combination of the following roles:

- Administering one or more internal moot court competitions;
- Administering an external moot court competition hosted by the school;
- Serving as teaching assistants for 1L or 2L legal-writing, appellate advocacy, or moot-court classes;
- Writing moot court problems;
- Handling travel arrangements for teams;
- Mentoring junior moot court participants;
- Serving as coaches or assistant coaches of external competition teams;
- Selecting members of external competition teams;
- Participating on external competition teams;

- Devising and executing fundraising strategies for the moot court program;
- Organizing social, team-building, and visibility-building activities for the moot court program; and
- Representing the moot court program to administration, alumni, faculty, the student body, and other interested constituencies.

The best fit for your school depends on your school's size and culture and on student interest. And, to some extent, the moot court board's role may vary from year to year depending on the personalities and priorities of the students involved; for example, one year, a board may be more involved in fundraising and outreach, whereas another board might be more focused on expanding the number of external competition teams.

The degree of student involvement in each role may also vary. For example, administering an internal moot court competition involves a long list of tasks and responsibilities for a student board, most of which will be discussed in more detail in Chapter Three. Some of those tasks, such as creating and troubleshooting the problem and writing the bench brief, among others, lend themselves naturally to enriching educational opportunities for the students involved. Others, like recruiting local attorneys to serve as judges, may be fine networking opportunities for students and may foster confidence and communication skills, but may be done more efficiently by a moot-court-program director who has numerous and significant contacts amongst the local bench and bar.

You will need to evaluate the benefits and drawbacks of assigning each task to the board and make that decision on a case-by-case basis; the right decision for one school in one community will not necessarily be the right decision for another school in a different area. Moot court programs run with little or no faculty oversight tend to garner less prestige and respect. As an illustration of this, few if any schools with student-run moot court programs will grant academic credit, or credit for satisfying an upper-level writing requirement, for participation in moot court activities.[8]

8. *See* Ass'n of Legal Writing Dirs. & Legal Writing Inst., *Report of the Annual Legal Writing Survey* 25 (2014), available at https://www.alwd.org/images/resources/2014%20Survey%20Report%20(AY%202013-2014).pdf (last visited Jan. 31, 2023).

Assigning a task to the board should not necessarily mean wholesale delegation; the board will be more successful—and the learning experience for the students more productive—if the board receives thoughtful training, guidance, and feedback from a faculty advisor or director. Moreover, vesting too much authority in a student board has the same pitfall that besets all student organizations: the lack of continuity from year to year, the absence of institutional memory, and the steepness of the learning curve. A student board often spends the first half of its tenure learning what it needs to do to accomplish its ends, and a body composed of students who will leave the institution within months or a year is by its very nature ill-situated for long-term planning or program development. Although, as discussed later in this chapter, you can mitigate or eliminate some of these issues through transition planning and other mechanisms, most student-run programs face these limitations to some extent.

Nonetheless, service on a moot court board can be an invaluable educational experience for students, particularly if they are vested with some amount of discretion and independence. The experience of running an internal or external moot court competition, overseeing team recruitment and selection, designing a competition problem, interacting with alumni and guest judges, directing fellow board members, or even just planning and executing an awards ceremony, can help build administrative, supervisory, organizational, leadership, and interpersonal skills.

2. BOARD SELECTION PROCESS AND CONSIDERATIONS IN DETERMINING COMPOSITION

Schools use different methods to select students for the board:

- A tryout, where students submit a written brief and deliver oral argument before a panel of judges (often including a faculty advisor and members of the current moot court board);
- Based on performance in first-year legal writing courses or upper-level appellate advocacy electives;
- Based on overall grade point average;

- Based on performance in one or more intramural moot court competitions;
- Through an application process, with students submitting resumes and writing samples and being interviewed by the advisor, members of the current student board, or some combination;
- Elections;
- Based solely on participation on any external moot court team;
- A combination of some or all of these factors—perhaps GPA, performance in first-year class, and a tryout, or performance in an upper-level class plus score in a competition.

How you select the board depends on several considerations. Most importantly, you will want to consider the board's role and purpose. If board members serve as teaching assistants providing advice and feedback on writing, analysis, and advocacy to junior students, for example, academic performance and teaching ability may weigh more heavily, and you may wish to limit board membership to third-year students. If the success of one or more key components of your program rests on the quality and reliability of your board, you may wish to have a more burdensome application process—and one that allows you a better opportunity to know the applicants as individuals—in an effort to select those students most invested in and committed to your program. In such a case, you may require:

- an application or letter of interest;
- one or more letters of recommendation from relevant faculty or administrators;
- satisfaction of course prerequisites;
- an interview;
- preparation of a writing assignment;
- an oral argument tryout; and
- perhaps even documentation of previous service to your program.

If you need a large board, you may need to have less burdensome requirements.

Your selection process will also affect the prestige of the board to some extent. A more arduous selection process generally means that board membership signifies more than it does if any student who participates in any internal or external competition wins a seat on your board. Marquette Law School, for example, limits candidates for its moot court executive board to students who participated in the honors moot court competition the previous year. Students in that group run for the board, and incoming national competitors vote to select the final board.

a. Criteria for board membership

At minimum, most boards require that members satisfy key prerequisites:

- Satisfactory (or excellent) performance in legal-writing and advocacy courses,
- Some minimum GPA (or a requirement that the student remain in good academic standing, whatever that means at your law school),
- Participation in your school's internal moot court competition, or
- Earlier participation on one of the school's external competition teams.

GPA requirements are often problematic and controversial. On the one hand, requiring a relatively high minimum GPA means that your board will include the students who have been among the highest academic achievers at your law school, which has many advantages. In the frequently elitist atmosphere of legal academia, it helps put your board on more equal footing with law review in terms of prestige and respect within your institution. Moreover, students who earn good grades in law school often—but not always—have stronger writing, reasoning, and organizational skills. On the other hand, many students who perform well in moot court may have blossomed later in law school, may have strengths that a single end-of-semester exam does not showcase, or may have focused more on activities and interests more in line with their overall career goals and passions. And law-school grades as a metric suffer from the same issues of implicit and structural bias as do standardized tests and other commonly used measures of aptitude and achievement.[9] At some schools, moot court board is a way for students to earn recognition even if they do not necessarily rank in the top tier of the class when it comes to grades. The students with the top grades have ample opportunities to participate in enriching extracurricular activities that look good on a resume; moot court should not be reserved solely for those students who will already be getting the best externships, summer jobs, and coveted law review spots. You will need to consider carefully the objectives of your program, the culture of your law school, and the variety of options available to your students before setting a minimum GPA requirement.

Speaking of law review, it is a good idea to build strong relationships with the faculty who serve as advisors for the law review and other student-run scholarly publications, as well as with their editorial boards. Some schools bar their law review members—or at least their 3L editorial boards—from serving on the moot court board or participating on competition teams. This often means that your moot court program misses out on some of the most academically successful, ambitious students. If you can convince your colleagues that students can successfully juggle both moot court and law review, and that such juggling is actually excellent preparation for the demands of law practice, your board will benefit. Not only is it possible to do both law review and moot court, it's possible to succeed in both, perhaps because students who choose to do both develop good time management skills and are motivated and organized.

As always, diversity is important. A diverse board brings diverse perspectives, which improve decisionmaking and enrich the program and

9. Research has shown that students with diverse ethnic and racial backgrounds are considerably more likely to have a lower law school GPA than white students. Alexia Brunet Marks & Scott A. Moss, *What Makes a Law Student Succeed? A Longitudinal Study Correlating Law Student Applicant Data and Law School Outcomes*, 13(2) J. EMPIRICAL LEGAL STUDIES 205, 221, 243–45 (2016). Such disparities may be due to implicit bias of professors possibly infecting non-anonymously graded aspects of classes, such as participation, or non-anonymously graded classes, "such as seminars, clinics, and most skills courses." *Id.* at 45. Similar issues have been observed in graduate and professional tests. *See* Peter Sacks, "How Admissions Tests Hinder Access to Graduate and Professional Schools," 47, issue 39, CHRON. OF HIGHER EDUC. 2–3 (2001) (describing how poorly "graduate and professional tests (such as the LSAT) predict performance in academic settings and beyond," but how well the tests sort candidates along race and class lines).

student experience.[10] Moreover, a more diverse board likely will facilitate a more diverse program overall.

b. Who selects the board?

You also will want to consider who selects the board. Again, different schools take different approaches, which include:

- A faculty director or advisor single-handedly selects the board;
- Current board members select their successors;
- Current board members work closely with faculty advisor to select new board;
- A committee of the current board, which includes the faculty advisor, selects the new board;
- Current board or faculty advisor or some combination of both select officers for incoming board and incoming officers select remaining board members.

Faculty and student collaboration in the selection process generally improves the likelihood of building a functional and effective board. Faculty oversight can increase the likelihood that board members are selected on the basis of their qualifications for the job, their administrative skills, and their ability to work well with others, rather than on their popularity with their fellow students. The best selection processes usually involve the outgoing board—or at least the board's officers or executive committee—working closely with the board's faculty advisors or the program director.

c. When to select your board

When you select your board depends on the board's roles and responsibilities and your membership criteria. Most schools select boards near the end of one academic year to serve in the following academic year. As discussed later in this chapter, you should choose the following year's board early enough to permit time for effective transition communica-

---

10. *See generally* Rebecca K. Lee, *Implementing Grutter's Diversity Rationale: Diversity and Empathy in Leadership*, 19 Duke J. Gender L. & Pol'y 133 (2011).

tion with the departing board.[11] You also should allow time for the new board to elect its officers or executive committee. Some boards begin work over the summer or even late in the spring semester, particularly if they must plan for a fall internal or external competition.

Many law schools limit board membership to 3L students. This policy has some advantages, particularly if your board members have a role in teaching junior students. On the other hand, limiting membership to 3Ls means that each member serves for a maximum of one academic year. This means you lose the opportunity to have 3L board members who already have a year of board experience, and you lose the chance to have your 3L board members train your 2L board members. You also exacerbate the lack of institutional knowledge and experience that can plague student organizations. To reduce this loss of institutional knowledge, some law schools allow students to become active in moot court programs as early as the second semester of first year.[12]

d. Board size

The size of your board will vary depending on a variety of factors, including:

- The size of your student body;
- The role of the board;
- The number of external competitions in which your students participate;
- How many internal competitions your school conducts; and
- Whether your school hosts an external competition.

Board sizes range from as small as four to six members to as large as fifty or sixty members. The smaller the board is relative to the size of the student body, the more prestigious membership becomes. Often, a smaller board means that each individual board member plays an indispensable role in the success of the program. On the other hand, the larger the board, the larger and more ambitious its goals and projects can be. Sometimes, however, a larger board means that a handful of students

11. For example, the board selection process at Indiana University McKinney School of Law begins in mid-to-late February.

12. For example, at Marquette Law School, 1Ls may bailiff in the internal and external competitions that the school hosts, which benefits both the students and the program.

do the vast majority of the work and there is less individual accountability. You can always modify the size of the board from year to year depending on your program's needs, provided that you reserve that flexibility in any faculty or moot court bylaws or rules.

Most boards have one or more officers—usually 3L students—who serve an additional administrative role. Generally, the larger the board, the more officers it has. A small board may merely have a president, and that role may largely be honorary and signify more about a student's popularity than about that student's administrative ability. A larger board may have an active set of officers with significant authority and administrative responsibilities, and those officers may even receive a monetary stipend or academic credit for their service.

As with board selection, your process for choosing board officers depends on your objectives. At some schools, the faculty director or advisor selects the officers. This has some advantages: you can choose students you know and whom you have reason to believe you can trust to do the work required. On the other hand, such a selection process often creates a stigma of favoritism. At other schools, the board elects its own officers. Although this process risks electing the most popular, rather than the most capable, candidate, it also enhances board autonomy, which can foster a board that takes more ownership and responsibility for its own objectives. A board can also mitigate the "popularity contest" aspect by having the faculty advisor and outgoing board interview the potential new officers to narrow the field of candidates before the election.

e. Board-to-board transition

You can improve continuity, institutional knowledge, and long-range planning on your board if you design a robust board-to-board transition process at the end of the year. Some components of that transition process might include:

- A series of meetings between the outgoing and incoming boards—or, at minimum, between the outgoing board officers and incoming board officers—at the end of the school year to permit the outgoing board to share the wisdom of experience, advise the incoming board on policies and decisions, and communicate about ongoing projects or plans;

- A handbook maintained in both hard copy and electronic form to pass from board to board;
- A detailed transition memorandum prepared by the outgoing board president each year to help maximize accumulated wisdom, allow for the successful completion of multi-year projects or implementation of long-term initiatives, and minimize the learning curve for the new board.

3. OTHER FEATURES OF YOUR MOOT COURT BOARD

Aside from determining your board's size, responsibilities, selection criteria, and selection process, you may also have the opportunity to make other decisions that will affect the nature and quality of the board's experience, which can also impact the actual and perceived nature and quality of your program.

a. Academic credit and other "perks" of board service

Schools differ on how students are rewarded for participating on a moot court board. Different approaches include:

- Providing small financial stipends for board members or, more often, for board officers;
- Awarding academic credit for board service. Generally, that credit is ungraded, and the number of units varies from one unit of credit per year of service to two units of credit per semester. As with the stipends, some schools provide credit only to board officers (or provide additional credit to board officers); other schools provide equal academic credit for all board members.

In determining whether board members should receive financial compensation, academic credit, or neither, you should consider the size of your board, the nature of each board member's responsibilities, and the difficulty of administration. To award academic credit, you likely need approval from your law school's curriculum committee and full faculty. Those entities will consult the American Bar Association's accreditation standards in determining whether particular activities warrant academic credit. It is easier to lobby for academic credit if board members engage in significant research and writing activities, such as drafting bench briefs or problems. You might also compare your board's duties with the responsibilities of other students who receive academic credit or financial compensation, such as participants on scholarly publications. Finally, a faculty advisor who seeks academic credit for board members should prepare a syllabus that includes, at minimum, learning objectives and concrete criteria for awarding or denying credit.

Regardless of whether your board members receive academic credit or compensation, recognition is crucial to the prestige and success of your moot court program. As this text echoes in other chapters, the law school should celebrate all moot court successes equally and jointly at one end-of-the-year banquet or awards ceremony where all students who participated in any form of moot court competition—internal or external, supervised by the central moot court administration or by substantive law faculty—are invited, along with all faculty and staff involved. Students who excel in moot court should be recognized at commencement in a manner commensurate with students who serve on academic publications.[13]

b. Physical facilities and other infrastructure

Dedicated space—both physical and virtual—can help facilitate board tasks and information sharing and create a feeling of value, investment, and prestige.

- *Physical facilities.* Ideally, the moot court board will have physical space at the law school for meetings, storage, staging of materials for competitions and other activities, and collaborative work. Your options are constrained, obviously, by the facilities available at your school. Some law schools that have been constructed or renovated recently have board facilities adjacent to the moot courtrooms. Even small office space near your office, near the offices for your law review or journal, or near offices for other student organizations will suffice. Ideally, this office would include a dedicated computer and printer.

---

13. Gerald Lebovits, Gewuerz & Hunker, *supra* note 1, 943.

- *Virtual components.* An easier and less expensive way to foster collaboration and facilitate continuity is to take advantage of the many online options. Document storage systems like Google Drive, Sharepoint, or Box can serve as repositories for board rules, significant correspondence, an exercise and bench brief archive, lists of judge contact information, competition rules and materials, presentation slides, and other useful materials. Many different types of software permit real-time group drafting and editing. Platforms like Slack, GroupMe, Discord, and others allow users to create private group messages and send notifications directly to users' phones. These platforms facilitate organized team collaboration and accountability while also maintaining a record of communications. Establishing dedicated email addresses for key board officers can make it easier for long-term contacts to reach the right person and can provide storage for vital contact information in the email's address book, making it easier to send mass emails—perhaps through a listserv. Your school's IT department may have other suggestions.

II. Funding

No moot court program can exist without funding: money to send teams and advisors to external competitions, money for copying and supplies, and money for awards and celebrations. Some programs are fully supported by law school funds. Most programs cobble together funding from a variety of sources: some law school funds, some grants and subsidies from university sources, fundraising, and some monies from other outside sources.

A. Creating a budget

Although the budgeting process varies from school to school, ultimately the law school's administration determines the dollar amount allocated to your program. Because you know your program's expenses, however, you may have some input in determining that dollar amount, or at least you can use the previous year's budget as a model. Even if you have no voice in determining the ultimate dollar figure, you and your board will be responsible for allocating those dollars to your different programs and activities.

Generally, budgets are set before fiscal year-end, which at many schools is June 30. If your student board has budgeting responsibilities, you will need to have your board estimate and allocate the following year's budget before the end of the academic year. For example, the 2023/24 board will allocate the moot court budget for the 2024/25 school year. If you have some input into the overall budgeting process, you will want to communicate your proposed budget—with detailed documentation of why you need each dollar—to those handling the overall budgeting process as long before their budget deadlines as you can.

Budgeting, of course, requires a significant amount of planning. Ideally, you will want some "wiggle room" in your budget to account for unanticipated expenses, emergencies, new competition opportunities, or other contingencies. In reality, and especially with ever-overtaxed law school finances, you will need to plan for and enumerate every expense that you can possibly anticipate.

Your budget will need to account for the expenses associated with:

- Sending teams to the regional and national rounds of external competitions;
- Any internal competitions;
- Any external competitions your school hosts;
- Costs for new and replacement equipment—like microphones and webcams—needed to participate successfully in virtual competitions (see Chapter Six for more on this);
- Social events and awards ceremonies for your board and program participants;
- Any moot-court alumni functions;
- Any faculty and staff salaries;
- Any stipends for coaches or advisors;
- Any stipends for board officers; and
- Any costs associated with fundraising for your program.

1. EXTERNAL COMPETITIONS

Other than any faculty salaries—which may or may not form part of your budget—the largest portion of your budget will be allocated to sending student teams to external moot court competitions. Air and even car travel are increasingly expensive, and many external competitions take place in cities where lodging, meals, ground transportation, and taxes can best be described as exorbitant. In developing the travel portion of your budget for external competitions, you will want to budget for:

- one hotel room (plus taxes and fees) for every two students of the same sex,[14] allowing for an extra room in case you do not have a team that neatly divides into same-sex pairs;
- one room for any coach or faculty member accompanying the team;
- if the team will be flying to the competition, the cost of airfare and any necessary ground transportation;
- funds for ground transportation between the hotel and the competition location, if necessary;
- if the team will travel by car, funds for vehicle rental or mileage;
- funds for parking at your home airport;
- if the team is driving, for parking costs at the competition location;
- funds for meals not provided by the competition host.

Keeping good records of each year's expenses will make it easier to develop the next year's budget.

Very few, if any, competitions still require teams to submit hard copies of their briefs for overnight delivery; check competition rules to ensure that you need not include funds in your budget for printing, copying, binding, and mailing. But virtually every external competition

---

14. If funds are tight, as they usually are, you may wish to have a detailed, written travel policy (if your school does not already have one) that requires students to room together if they are of the same sex. You should provide this written travel policy to students as soon as they join the program. This policy should contain explicit provisions that permit flexibility to accommodate nonbinary students and students who need their own rooms for various reasons, which may include disability, parental status, or other factors.

charges teams a registration fee, so you will want to allocate funds to cover those expenses for each team you send.

Many competitions change at least some of their regional locations each year, so you will want to budget for the priciest cities in terms of transportation, hotel, and per diem. Moreover, if you can, you should include funds in your budget to cover the costs of a team advancing to the national round of a competition. You want to avoid needing to negotiate for additional funds on the spot or, worse yet, forcing a successful team to scramble for its own funding to travel to nationals (talk about a morale killer!). Another option is to ask your school's administration to commit to pay the expenses of any teams advancing to national rounds from other law school funding sources.

Be sure to communicate your school's travel and reimbursement policies to your students in writing as early as possible, preferably in the board bylaws, in a student handbook, or on a dedicated page in your school's course-management software. Many schools require students and faculty to seek and obtain authorization from a central administration before traveling. Many schools require students to pay certain costs, like hotels, ground transportation, and meals, up front, and the school will reimburse those costs later. Other costs, like airfare, the school may pay directly. The school may book and prepay hotel room, tax, and fees by purchase order, check, or credit card. Where students will be reimbursed for out-of-pocket costs, make sure your students know precisely what documentation the school requires and how, when, and to whom to submit that documentation.

2. INTERNAL COMPETITIONS

By contrast, internal moot court competitions are relatively inexpensive, although not without cost. Your expenses may include:

- designing and printing letterhead;
- printing and copying costs for any materials you circulate in hard copy to competitors;
- printing and copying costs for materials you circulate to judges;

- possible postage or mailing costs for materials you circulate to judges (although most programs now communicate with judges by email and telephone to save on these expenses);
- refreshments for judges during oral argument rounds or team practices;
- parking expenses for judges;
- travel costs for any out-of-town judges;
- any website expenses;
- any token gifts for judges; and
- any costs associated with offering continuing legal education credit to your oral argument or team-practice judges.

Some of these costs may be offset by donated materials, but you should still account for them in your budget.

3. HOSTING EXTERNAL COMPETITIONS

Schools that host external moot court competitions generally try to cover all competition expenses through the registration fees they collect from participants and through sponsorships. This strategy is not always feasible, however, particularly when starting a competition or hosting one for the first time. Expenses your program may incur in hosting an external moot court competition include:

- advertising;
- any physical awards you confer;
- any mailing costs for recruiting judges, sponsors, and donors;
- any food or drink you provide at the competition;
- any parking costs;
- any website expenses, including administration of the registration website;
- costs associated with offering continuing legal education credit to oral argument judges;
- printing and copying costs for any materials you need to circulate to competitors or judges; and
- designing and printing letterhead, if you choose to do so.

4. SOCIAL EVENTS/AWARDS CEREMONIES

Ideally, your program or board would host at least one special event each year to honor the students who excelled in moot court or provided particular service to the program during that academic year. An event like this can be conducted for relatively minimal cost and can pay dividends later in alumni loyalty. Your costs for this event would vary depending on where you held it, the nature of the event, and the number of attendees. You may be able to do a very nice awards reception with appetizers and non-alcoholic beverages in a room at your law school for a fairly modest amount; a sit-down banquet at a local restaurant, banquet center, or resort will cost you significantly more. Your budget for an event like this should include any costs for space rental, linens, catering, and cleaning.[15] You will also want to include money in your budget for the physical awards, whether to cover the cost of engraving new names in a plaque that remains at the law school, to purchase individual plaques for the winners of certain honors, to print certificates for other honorees, or to buy and engrave gavels for your entire board. Gavels are a lovely tradition; they are relatively inexpensive to purchase and engrave, and many former board members display their moot court gavels in their law offices for years.

5. ALUMNI ASSOCIATION EVENTS

If you have—or start—a moot court alumni association, you should try to budget for at least one association event each academic year. As with your student events, your costs will vary depending on your ambitions. You can mitigate cost and perhaps enhance the effectiveness of your event by partially combining your alumni event with your student awards ceremony. Or you can share costs with your school's overall alumni relations effort by holding your event in conjunction with your school's annual alumni weekend or homecoming festivities.

---

15. You can, of course, defray the costs of such an event by charging students for tickets. This likely will, however, decrease attendance and may cost you some goodwill in the long run.

6. OTHER EXPENSES

Your program may have other expenses that you will need to allocate. Faculty salaries—or stipends paid to faculty or students who serve as advisors or coaches to moot court teams—may come out of your overall budget. Some programs pay nominal stipends to key officers of their moot court boards. You may also want or need to include funds in your budget for incidental costs related to fundraising, including printing, postage, list management, website management, and other items. If you can, it would be wonderful to include funds in your budget for volunteer and alumni appreciation gifts, whether they be plaques or just little items with your law school or moot court program's logo on them to present to your competition judges and other volunteers.

Some years, your program may incur fewer expenses than in others. One or more teams may opt to attend a virtual competition instead of an in-person competition, for example. A competition that traditionally holds an in-person event may need to be virtual for a year or two and then return to in-person arguments. You may have a year when, for whatever reason, you do not field a team for a particular competition. The size of a particular incoming class may be smaller than usual, resulting in fewer students interested in participating in moot court activities. In budgeting, be sure to look at multiple years of expense history and continue to request adequate funding to provide your program options and opportunities. And, of course, as prices rise, continue to reevaluate your budget to account for anticipated changes.

B. Fundraising

If you are involved in moot court or other legal-skills competitions, at some point you will want or need to raise funds. Whether you need money to pay registration and travel expenses to send a team to an additional competition, other sources of funding have fallen victim to budget cuts, or you just want to have some additional money for awards or other incidentals, some strategic fundraising can be extremely helpful to your program, but it is not without its challenges.

The first and most important rule of moot court fundraising is that you must obtain permission from the law school's administration before initiating any fundraising efforts (and sometimes from the main university administration). Your dean and development officers spend an enormous amount of time and effort planning and executing fundraising strategies for your school. Undercutting their fundraising efforts with your own may be the easiest way to alienate the powers-that-be at your law school. Imagine their annoyance when they have spent months or years cultivating a potential donor only to have you step in and make an ask for your program before they have the opportunity to close the deal on a larger gift for the entire school.

The best practice is to develop a strong, cooperative working relationship with your administration and development department. Learn how your school's alumni relations, publicity, public relations, and fundraising organs are structured and how responsibility and roles are allocated. Some schools have separate alumni relations, development, advancement, and public relations offices. Others coordinate all those functions under one administrator who supervises several individuals operating in discrete fundraising, alumni relations, communications, and other roles. Identify the person or people with whom you should be communicating about your fundraising activities and communicate with those people clearly and consistently. If you click with that person, you might do some of that communicating over lunch now and again. Fundraising is all about building relationships, and your first and most crucial relationships are within the four walls of your school.

You can fundraise in several ways, but probably the most lucrative vehicle is to make some sort of direct or indirect ask to an individual, group of individuals, or organization, either by letter, email, or in-person visit. Often this ultimate ask is the culmination of a series of communications. For example, you might create a quarterly "moot court news" email that you send to alumni, local judges and attorneys who have volunteered for your program in the past, and other potential supporters. That email could give the recipients updates on moot court coaches and faculty, results of internal and external competitions, upcoming events such as awards ceremonies or alumni gatherings, and other information about your program. At the end of that email, you would include your direct contact information and a link to donate to your program. When you send thank-you letters to judges or attorneys who have volunteered for your program—which you should do as soon as possible after they volunteer—you should include a brief note letting them know to contact you if they wish to become more involved in your program. Some schools send periodic—even weekly—communications to alumni and others with connections to the school. You can ask to have your program featured in that publication at key points during the year, like in mid-April after most competitions have concluded, and perhaps right after an internal competition.

You can also go the more direct route, sending a letter or email directly to alums, local attorneys, local or regional firms, and even local businesses that serve the law school or the legal community, asking for a donation to your program. Having well-trained, well-prepared board members make carefully scripted follow-up calls to individual targets can significantly enhance your return. Again, you may need to have your development office or someone in your communications or alumni-relations office approve any solicitation materials you send to the public. Be sure you follow the protocols set by your institution.

Many schools have prominent local alums or law firms fund student awards. For example, you might have a local firm fund an award for the best brief in your internal moot court competition, or a local alum might create an award in the name of his late father to honor the winners of your internal moot court competition.

A note about terminology: in soliciting and obtaining monies to support your program, you should recognize key distinctions between gifts, donations, sponsorships, and endowments, even if just to make sure that you are using the right vocabulary:[16]

- *Gifts or donations.* A gift simply entails giving some amount of money or property to an individual or organization. A gift becomes a donation when the recipient of that money or property is a qualified charitable organization. Gifts and donations may be one-time events or they may be repeated periodically over time. Generally, gifts or donations can be used at any time and for any purpose—to send a team to a competition, to fund your annual awards banquet, or to pay other costs of your program—unless the donor places explicit restrictions on the gift. Gifts and donations have different tax consequences, and your donor should consult

16. Note, however, that you cannot and should not advise donors explicitly about the tax or other legal consequences of their charitable giving!

an accountant or other tax professional for further advice. A donor who gives a gift or donation generally expects no measurable benefit in return.

- *Sponsorships.* A sponsorship means that an individual or company provides money or property in return for some form of valuable acknowledgement, whether that be naming rights or other advertising. For example, a legal publisher may sponsor the food at your annual awards ceremony in return for signage acknowledging the sponsorship, or a local law firm may sponsor an external moot court competition in return for having the competition named after the firm and mentioned in all advertising and promotional materials. This type of transaction may have different tax consequences for the giver; again, the giver should consult a tax advisor.
- *Endowments.* An endowment is a fund composed of gifts, donations, and bequests. The principal in that fund must remain intact, but the interest may be used to fulfill a specified purpose, such as to provide ongoing funding for an award, attendance at a competition, or even an entire moot court program. Generally, endowments require some minimum amount of principal to be worthwhile. You will want to work closely with your development department and the law school's administration when discussing the possibility of forming an endowment to benefit your program, but endowments can be an incredibly stable ongoing source of funding.

Certainly, your board can try to raise money by holding traditional fundraisers like bake sales or other food sales, car washes, auctions, tournaments, and other events. Your board may already have a tradition of, for example, selling tacos at lunchtime at new-student orientation, holding a student-and-faculty talent show at a local bar every March, or auctioning lunches with local attorneys and judges. These types of fundraising activities—especially when done well—have the added benefit of raising visibility for your program within the law school and making participation in your program seem like a fun way to be more involved in day-to-day law school life. You will want to make sure that you know what types of approvals and permissions are required to conduct these sorts of activities, particularly if they take place off the law school campus. Some of these activities may implicate insurance, tax, or other issues, and you will want to make sure you follow all applicable rules and procedures.

Although less common, grant funding may be available to supplement your program's funding, particularly if an aspect of your program furthers defined goals of your university, a private entity, or a government agency. It may be worth chatting with your development team and any people at your institution knowledgeable about grant research and writing. Note that grants generally impose significant reporting and administration obligations, so you will want to be sure you have the staffing bandwidth to meet those obligations.

Any fundraising you do will affect your budgeting. If you are lucky, your school will not require you to raise some fixed percentage of your budget each year but instead will permit you to raise money for expenses, activities, and competitions beyond those covered by the funds the school provides. For instance, you may be permitted to raise money to send teams to new competitions, or you might rely on fundraising to cover expenses for an awards banquet or alumni event. Some programs are able to obtain sponsorship for their annual moot court banquet or for individual competition teams.

C. Enlisting alumni support

Alumni can enrich your moot court program financially but also in myriad other ways. Alumni in active litigation or appellate practice are excellent sources of problem ideas and materials, or even just for input on problem selection. Alumni often make excellent, and very invested, competition and practice argument judges. And alumni can be advocates for your program with your school's administration and with other potential supporters.

A vibrant moot court program can be an asset to alumni relations, and you should actively promote it as such to your administration. Alumni involved with the moot court program—whether as oral-argument judges, brief scorers, financial sponsors of moot court teams, or otherwise—are intimately and personally engaged with and invested in their alma mater and its current students and faculty. They are more likely to donate not just to your program but to the law school because they see tangible evidence of what the school is contributing to the legal profession, and because they feel emotionally connected to the school's current students and activities. Graduates who perhaps did not have the best feelings about the school's administration or faculty might nonetheless feel intense loyalty to a moot court program that gave them a chance to shine or created a sense of community in what may have seemed to them to be a large, impersonal, or uncaring law school. Further, inviting diverse alumni back to your school as brief scorers and judges could encourage more diverse students to participate in moot court. Volunteer to speak about moot court to your school's alumni board; most board members are looking for ways to connect with students and be involved with the school.

Creating loyal alumni, of course, hinges in the first instance on creating satisfied graduates and maintaining a relationship with those graduates. Your most reliable moot court boosters will be graduates who had happy and valuable experiences as participants in your program. Make students feel their talents and contributions are recognized and valued while they are on your teams, in your classes, and on your board, and they will be more appreciative and engaged alumni. The best way to do this is to make sure participation in your program is a valuable learning experience for each and every student, which is, after all, the ultimate goal of your program and of this book. The more that you can make all students feel they were treated fairly and honestly by your program, the more likely you are to have happy alums.

You cannot make the most of these positive feelings, however, unless you remain connected. Before the end of each academic year, be sure you collect accurate contact information for all your 3L board and team members. Memorialize that information in a spreadsheet immediately; information is of no use to you if you cannot locate it. Each year, verify and update that information. At least once a year, contact those alumni who remain geographically close to your law school and ask them to judge a team practice or competition oral argument round. If you conduct or participate in virtual competitions, of course, you can cast that net wider and include all alumni. Make sure all moot court alumni receive any newsletters or email updates your program sends, and make sure they all have your personal contact information and an easy clickable link that allows them to donate directly to your program.

If your school does not already have a moot court alumni association, you should strongly consider working with your development or alumni relations office to develop one. Ideally, you would hold at least one moot court alumni association event each year, perhaps in conjunction with your school's reunion weekend or homecoming events, or perhaps together with your student moot court awards or banquet. This association not only can be a tool for fundraising but also can raise the profile and prestige of your program within and outside your institution.

Continued alumni support depends, in part, on showing your alumni donors and volunteers that you appreciate and value their input and support. Something as small as a thank-you letter signed by you or your moot court board president can mean the difference between a one-time volunteer stint and ongoing loyalty and support. You might contact your development office to see if there are any logo-emblazoned toys or tchotchkes that you can share with oral-argument judges; even a pencil or lapel pin bearing your law school's insignia can delight volunteers and make them feel special and appreciated. If you cannot cadge items from within your institution, it might be a worthy budget item that will pay dividends well beyond the investment. Even a quick email updating preliminary-round judges on the overall results of the competition makes those volunteers feel invested in the process.

You will want to make sure, of course, that your communications are professional, well-written, and reflect positively on your program. Although you may want to delegate some of this work to your student board, you will want to conduct careful final review and revision before anything representing your program reaches alumni and other supporters. Do not be surprised to receive return emails expressing pleasure that this or that competitor won an award; a well-run moot court program will create alumni who feel personally invested in the success of individual students. Reward your loyal alumni by making them feel like treasured insiders, and they will remain reliable volunteers and donors for years to come.

As moot court director or advisor, it is also important for you to become or remain involved and visible in your local bar association, specialty bar associations, and other avenues for networking with local and regional attorneys and judges. The more that alumni and other interested parties see you—the face of your school's moot court program—as a part of the local legal community, the more receptive individual alumni will be to your requests for their time, thought, and treasure. Giving back to the local legal community by offering free continuing-education programs on advocacy, brief-writing, or other areas in which you have expertise may further endear you to potential volunteers, advocates, and donors for your program.

III. Conclusion

Although there may be as many ways to organize and run a moot court program as there are programs, employing some of these "best practices" when it comes to governance, composition, and management of your moot court board, budgeting and fundraising, and alumni relations will help your program, and the students who participate in it, thrive for years to come.

CHAPTER 3

Managing an Internal Moot Court Competition

THIS CHAPTER WILL HELP YOU TO:

- Build a framework for an internal moot court competition, including the creation of—
  - the competition's format;
  - the competition rules;
  - the simulated case that the competitors will address in their briefs and oral arguments;
  - the scoring rubrics that the judges will use to assess the competitors' briefs and oral arguments;
  - the bench memo that will guide the brief judges and the oral-argument judges during the assessment process; and
- Put the competition framework into action, including—
  - recruiting and preparing brief judges and oral-argument judges;
  - orienting the competitors;
  - communicating with judges and competitors;
  - managing the brief-scoring process;
  - managing the oral arguments; and
  - rewarding the competitors.

Introduction

Most law students' moot court experience begins in an internal appellate advocacy competition in which they compete against classmates at their school. Some schools use this competition to observe and select advocates and coaches for the teams that the school sends to represent it in external moot court competitions.[1] Others use the competition to select students to serve on the school's moot court board.[2]

Yet an internal competition's main goal is to teach students foundational lawyering skills such as legal research, persuasive legal writing, oral advocacy, case development, professionalism, legal ethics, effective collaboration, and analytical thinking. Because an internal competition's goal is to teach these skills, the competition should be built and conducted in a way that promotes that goal.

With this goal in mind, this chapter provides a blueprint for organizing and running an internal competition. Much of the advice discussed here also applies to Chapter Five, which discusses planning and conducting external moot court competitions, and to Chapter Six, which discusses planning and conducting virtual moot court competitions.

I. Building the Framework

As an internal competition administrator, you must begin by building the framework for your school's internal competition. In this first phase of competition planning, you should create the following competition components:

- the competition's format and rules;
- the problem that the competitors will be assigned;
- the rubrics that the competition judges will use to score the competitors;

---

1. *See, e.g.*, *Staton Intramural Competition*, IU Robert H. McKinney Sch. L., http://www.mckinneylaw.iu.edu/practice/moot-court/intramural-competition/index.html (last visited Feb. 8, 2023) (noting that the competition is used in part to select external team participants and moot court board members).

2. *Id.*

- the bench brief that you will use to educate the competition judges about the competition problem; and
- the competition website.

A. Creating the competition format and rules

You should begin your work by choosing your internal competition's format. After you've chosen that format, you should use it to create the rules that will govern the competition.

1. THE COMPETITION FORMAT

When you choose a format for your internal competition, you will have two key questions to answer:

- How should your competition fit into your school's curriculum?
- What components should your competition contain?

a. How should the competition fit into your school's curriculum?

The curricular fit that you choose for your school's internal competition will depend on the structure of your school's overall curriculum. It may also depend on your school's location unless you plan to hold a virtual competition.

i. A course for first-year students

The competition may be a mandatory or an elective course for first-year students. Under this curricular plan, the competition may be integrated with the students' first-year legal writing course, which typically focuses on written and oral advocacy at some point and thus serves as a natural curricular fit with the competition.[3] For example, in a first-year, two-semester legal writing course in which persuasive writing and oral

---

3. *See, e.g.*, *Moot Court Program and Competitions*, Boston U. Sch. L., http://www.bu.edu/law/experiential-learning/moot-court (last visited Feb. 8, 2023); *Legal Research and Writing Curriculum*, Chi.-Kent C.L. Ill. Tech, http://www.kentlaw.iit.edu/academics/jd-program/legal-research-and-writing-program/curriculum#firstyear (last visited Feb. 8, 2023).

advocacy are taught during the course's spring semester, the 1L competition may also be staged in that semester as part of the course.[4]

ii. A for-credit course or extracurricular activity for upper-level students

Instead of being offered as a first-year course, an internal competition could be offered as an upper-level mandatory or elective course, perhaps in conjunction with an appellate advocacy course.[5] For instance, some law schools have a legal-writing curriculum that requires coursework beyond the first year, such as a three-semester program,[6] or a curriculum that requires coursework during all three years of school.[7] In these programs, an internal competition could be integrated with a third-semester legal writing course that occurs during the students' second year. Or the competition could be offered as an upper-level elective course for all 2Ls and 3Ls, either in conjunction with or independent of an upper-level advocacy course.[8]

Yet another option is to offer the internal competition as an elective extracurricular activity for upper-level students. This type of competition could be offered as an optional "add-on" to an upper-level course, such as an appellate advocacy course, but without academic credit.

iii. Multiple internal competitions

A school may also decide to stage multiple internal competitions. For example, a school might hold one competition open only to first-year students and a second competition for upper-level students.[9] One com-

---

4. *See, e.g.*, *id.*

5. *See, e.g.*, *Dean's Cup*, Duke L., http://law.duke.edu/students/orgs/mootcourt/deans/ (last visited Feb. 8, 2023).

6. *See, e.g.*, *Legal Writing Program*, Vt. L. & Graduate Sch., https://www.vermontlaw.edu/academics/centers-and-programs/legal-writing-program (last visited Feb. 8, 2023).

7. *See, e.g.*, *Legal Research and Writing Curriculum*, Chi.-Kent C.L. Ill. Tech, *supra* note 3.

8. *See, e.g.*, *Practical Skills Training, Eugene Gressman Moot Court Competition*, Seton Hall L., https://https://law.shu.edu/students/academics/legal-skills-training/index.cfm (last visited Feb. 8, 2023).

9. *See, e.g.*, *Moot Court Honors Program*, U. Ill. Chi. L., https://law.uic.edu/academics/jd/honors/moot-court/ (last visited Feb. 8, 2023) (holding the 1L Moot Court Competition for first-year students and the Dean Fred F. Herzog Moot Court Competition for upper-level students).

petition could also focus on an area of law that the school has developed a reputation for, such as health law.

iv. The impact of your school's location

Unless you plan to hold a virtual competition,[10] your internal competition's curricular fit may depend on your school's location. For example, if your school is in a small community or rural area, your pool of competition judges from the local legal community will probably be small. In that case, you probably will need to draw most of your judges from within your school to ensure that you have enough judges for the competition. Therefore, you might choose to integrate your competition with your school's legal writing course so that the professors who teach that course may double as competition judges.

b. What components should your competition contain?

When moot court is mentioned to law students, some of them envision arguing before a mock appellate panel composed of faculty, practitioners, student moot-court-board members, and even real judges. And indeed, oral advocacy is an important lawyering skill; though appellate courts hear oral arguments less often than they once did,[11] appellate judges value oral arguments,[12] particularly in appeals involving complex issues or weighty policy implications.[13] What's more, lawyers must use their skills as oralists in settings other than appellate proceedings, whether they are arguing a motion to a trial court, giving an opening statement or a closing argument to a jury, or presenting an oral report to

---

10. See Chapter Six for advice on administering a virtual competition.

11. *See* Richard E. Finneran, *Wherefore Moot Court?*, 53 Wash. U. J.L. & Pol'y 121, 121–22 (2017) (describing the decline in number of oral arguments in federal courts).

12. *See* Robert M. Casale, *Does Oral Argument in the Supreme Court Really Matter?*, 85 Conn. Bar J. 323, 326 (2011) (noting that the U.S. Supreme Court's justices use oral argument "to augment their decision-making and to facilitate consensus-building" among them); Margaret D. McGaughey, *May It Please the Court—Or Not: Appellate Judges' Preferences and Pet Peeves About Oral Argument*, 20 J. App. Prac. & Process 141, 144 (2020) ("[A]lthough oral argument changes the outcome of an appeal only between ten and twenty percent of the time, it alters the [judges'] reasoning more frequently.").

13. *See* Hon. Joseph W. Hatchett & Robert J. Telfer III, *The Importance of Appellate Oral Argument*, 33 Stetson L. Rev. 139, 140 (2003) ("[T]he cases that make it to oral argument typically are the ones that raise 'important' or complex issues or include facts that are so complex that the judges or justices on the appellate panel reviewing the briefs encounter enough difficulty that they require clarification.").

other attorneys or to clients.[14] Accordingly, an effective internal competition will require the competitors to give multiple oral arguments so they may gain oral advocacy experience.

i. A briefing requirement

Real appeals, however, are usually decided on the parties' briefs.[15] Thus, internal competitions often include a briefing requirement.[16] This requirement not only reflects real appellate practice, but also provides students with a vehicle by which they can practice and refine their skills in analytical writing and persuasive writing.

Yet depending on the circumstances, a briefing requirement may not always be feasible or even desired in an internal competition. For instance, your school might decide to use the competition to focus on oral advocacy. This may be the case if, before the competition, the competitors were given multiple opportunities to learn and hone brief-writing skills in other courses or clinical experiences.

Further, logistical constraints, such as a short timetable for the competition, may not provide the competitors with enough time to research and write briefs. Or your competition's sole purpose might be to place students on external competition teams. In this case, you might decide to ask each competitor to submit a writing sample to the national-team coaches instead of requiring each competitor or team write a full brief.

If you decide not to require briefing in your internal competition, you might consider basing the competition problem on a live appeal and giving the competitors access to the briefs filed in the live case. This approach will help competitors to prepare for oral argument because they'll be able to see the arguments for their client and their opponent in the briefs. Or you might structure your internal competition so that the

---

14. Jennifer Kruse Hanrahan, *Truth in Action: Revitalizing Classical Rhetoric as a Tool for Teaching Oral Advocacy in American Law Schools*, 2003 BYU EDUC. & L.J. 299, 302 (2003).

15. *See* McGaughey, *supra* note 12, at 141 (noting that "only one fifth of cases in the federal courts of appeals are decided on the basis of both briefs and oral arguments"); Stanley Mosk, *In Defense of Oral Argument*, 1 J. APP. PRAC. & PROCESS 25, 25 (1999).

16. *See, e.g.*, *Legal Research and Writing Curriculum*, CHI.-KENT C.L. ILL. TECH, *supra* note 3.

competitors argue a brief that they wrote for a previous class, such as an appellate advocacy class.[17]

If your internal competition includes a briefing requirement, the competition should begin with a briefing period, during which the competitors research and write their briefs, just as they would in a real appeal. This period should commence with the release of the competition problem, which should include the record of proceedings upon which the competitors' briefs and oral arguments are based. Ideally, the problem will be an open-universe problem, which will require the competitors to conduct research and gather authorities to support their briefs and oral arguments, rather than a closed-universe problem, in which the competitors are given the authorities. By setting the problem in an open universe, you will give the competitors an opportunity to develop their legal-research and legal-analysis skills.

ii. An oral-argument requirement

After the competitors have submitted their briefs by the briefing deadline, the oral-argument stage of the competition should take place. If the competition is integrated with the school's first-year legal writing course, the competition is likely the competitors' first opportunity to learn oral advocacy skills. To allow the competitors to get their "sea legs" before the competition's oral rounds begin, you might allow the competitors to participate in practice oral arguments before moot court board members or faculty, who will give feedback to the competitors. These practice rounds should not be scored and thus should not count toward the competitors' advancement in the competition. Further, you could assign each competitor a 2L or 3L coach who assists the competitor through the oral-argument process.

If the competition is an upper-level elective, you could forego practice oral arguments and coaching assignments because the competitors likely will have learned oral advocacy basics in a previous course or clinical experience. Still, upper-level students benefit from repeatedly practicing their lawyering skills and from frequent mentoring. Thus, you might require the competitors to complete short review sessions on ad-

---

17. *See, e.g.*, *Samuel M. Fegtly Moot Court Competition*, U. Ariz. James E. Rogers C.L., https://law.arizona.edu/fegtly-moot-court (last visited Feb. 8, 2023).

vanced advocacy skills. Then, you might assign the competitors student coaches who oversee practice oral arguments for the competitors.

Competitors should argue the case multiple times. They should argue at least once for the party whom they were assigned to represent, which is called arguing "on brief," and at least once for the opposing party, which is called arguing "off brief." Having the competitors switch sides of the argument from round to round will spur them to think carefully about the weaknesses of their client's case, which is something any lawyer must do to be an effective advocate. Specific recommendations on how to conduct the briefing and oral-argument stages of the competition will be discussed in the next section on drafting competition rules, and in Part II of this chapter on managing the competition process.

2. THE COMPETITION RULES

Once you've established the competition's format, you'll need to write the rules to implement that format. These rules should be consistent, transparent, and fair. You should also give them to the competitors well before the competition so that the competitors have plenty of time to read them and to ask you questions about them. Examples of internal competition rules are included in the online appendix, which is linked in the front matter of this book.

At a minimum, an internal competition's rules should cover eight subjects:

- the competitors;
- the briefs;
- the oral arguments;
- competitor conduct and decorum;
- protests;
- scoring;
- plagiarism; and
- outside assistance.

a. Who is eligible to compete, and will they compete individually or in a team?

The rules should state who is eligible to compete. For example, if the competition is integrated with the students' first-year legal writing course, only 1Ls will be eligible to compete. But if the competition is an elective course or elective extracurricular activity reserved for students who have completed their first year, only upper-level students will be eligible. The elective competition's prerequisites might even include the completion of foundational courses, such as an advanced persuasive writing course or an appellate advocacy course. Further, if the competition requires specialized knowledge of a particular area of the law, the competition rules might limit eligibility to only those students who have taken courses in that area of the law or who have work experience or clinical experience in that area of law.

The rules also should address whether competitors will compete individually or as part of a team. In team-based competitions, each team usually consists of two people. However, because appellate courts usually discourage multiple lawyers representing the same client from splitting oral argument time,[18] requiring competitors to compete individually might be the ideal model. This is especially true if the field of competitors is small, where staging oral arguments and coordinating brief scoring will not require as much effort as would be necessary with a large field of competitors. Moreover, a competition that requires students to compete individually prevents teams with one weak competitor and one strong competitor from advancing in the competition based on the strong competitor's performance. And an individual-based competition furthers the goal of providing individual instruction in lawyering skills to the competitors because the judges are forced to focus their scoring and feedback on each competitor rather than on each team.

That said, at some schools, many students participate in the school's internal competition. In that case, it's probably better for the students to compete as part of a two-person team, with each student tackling a separate legal issue on their client's behalf. Conducting a large internal competition on a team basis decreases the number of oral arguments to be heard, which eases the burden on the competition administrators.[19]

---

18. *See, e.g.*, Sup. Ct. R. 28(4) ("Only one attorney will be heard for each side, except by leave of the Court.... Divided argument is not favored.").

19. Even when a competition is conducted on a team basis, the rules may be written to require the judges to individually evaluate each competitor. By using this scheme, the competition's focus remains on individual performance rather than on team performance. For example, at Indiana University Robert H. McKinney School of Law, each internal competition competitor has a teammate but writes their own brief, which is

b. What requirements will apply to the briefs?

The competition rules should also address who is to research and write the briefs; the briefs' form, arrangement, and content; and the timing and logistics of brief submission.

i. Which competitor or competitors will research and write the brief?

If your competition will require students to compete in teams, those rules must address which competitor or competitors will research and write the briefs. Because one purpose of an internal competition is to teach legal research and persuasive writing, the rules ideally will require all competitors to research and write the briefs.

Yet this requirement usually poses a problem if the competitors are participating in teams but being assessed individually; the brief scorers may be unable to evaluate each competitor's individual performance if the team members co-authored their briefs. To avoid this problem, the rules could require each team member to write a separate brief on only one of the two issues presented in the competition problem. If the competitors submit their own briefs on their own issue, the brief scorers will be able to individually evaluate the competitors' writing skills.

ii. What should be the briefs' form, arrangement, and content?

The rules should address the briefs' form, arrangement, and content. Thus, the rules should discuss—

---

scored on its own merits. Further, each competitor is scored on an individual basis during the preliminary oral argument rounds of the competition even though they have a teammate. At the end of the preliminary oral rounds, the competitors who place in the top 32 competitors based on their brief and oral-argument scores advance to the competition's elimination rounds, where the competitors' brief scores are no longer considered, and advancement is on a team basis. Teams for which both members advanced to the elimination rounds remain intact; competitors whose teammate did not advance to the elimination rounds are paired with a new partner. The team with the higher combined oral argument score at the end of each elimination round wins the round. *Staton Intramural Competition*, IU U. Robert H. McKinney Sch. L., *supra* note 1.

- the typography requirements for the briefs (such as permissible fonts and margins);[20]
- the word limit or page limit for the briefs;
- the sections that must be included in the briefs, such as the questions presented, the statement of the case, the summary of the argument, and the argument; and
- the order in which those sections should appear in the brief.

For your convenience, you might even wholly or partially adopt the briefing rules of your state's appellate courts. Indeed, this adoption could serve as a valuable "head start" for students who intend to enter appellate practice in your state.

iii. How may the competitors identify themselves in the briefs?

The rules should discuss how the competitors may identify themselves in the briefs. If the competition administrators are concerned about impartiality in the brief-scoring process, the rules might require competitors to identify themselves only by an advocate number that has been randomly assigned to them by the administrators. This requirement preserves the competitors' anonymity and thus prevents brief judges from potentially being biased for or against a particular competitor.[21]

iv. When and how should the competitors submit their briefs?

Finally, the rules should state the date, time, and method by which the competitors must submit their briefs. When determining the briefing period's length, you should consider the competitors' skill level. Most

---

20. For comprehensive tips on good typography principles in legal writing, see MATTHEW BUTTERICK, TYPOGRAPHY FOR LAWYERS (2d ed. 2018) (also available at http://typographyforlawyers.com/).

21. *But see* Marcus Lind-Martinez, *Latinidad, White Supremacy, and Reforming First-Year Moot Court Competitions to Confront Racial and Ethnic Bias*, 23 HARV. LATINX L. REV. 125, 130–31 (2020) (arguing that anonymous brief-scoring in moot court may perpetuate the myth of a color-blind society by preventing judges from seeing competitor names that mark those competitors' racial or ethnic identity, thus depriving the law school and the legal community of an opportunity to confront and constructively address the myth and its deleterious effects on the legal system).

first-year students will need more time to research and write an appellate brief than third-year students will. Thus, while a four-week briefing period might suffice for an upper-level student, a 1L competitor might need at least five weeks.

As for the method of submission, allowing the competitors to submit their briefs through an online portal is probably the most convenient method. This method also reflects the trend of electronic-filing requirements in today's appellate courts.[22]

c. What requirements will apply to the oral arguments?

Because oral argument is a key part of any moot court competition, the rules must address this topic. Particularly, the rules should describe the overall format of the competition's oral-argument stage and the format of each oral argument.

i. How should the competition's oral-argument stage be organized?

In most moot court competitions, the oral arguments are staged in a tournament format. Under this format, the arguments begin with a series of preliminary rounds designed to narrow the field of competitors to the elite advocates, who then move on to compete in a single-elimination phase.[23] If the field of competitors is small, the rules may require the preliminary rounds to be conducted in a round-robin format, under which each competitor/team argues against every other competitor/team.[24] But the field of most competitions is too large to make a round-robin format feasible. In that case, the preliminary rounds may instead require each competitor/team to argue at least twice.[25]

---

22. *See, e.g.*, IND. R. APP. P. 68 (requiring attorneys to electronically file all documents submitted to Indiana's appellate courts); WIS. STAT. § 801.18 (phasing in mandatory e-filing for Wisconsin's courts).

23. *See, e.g.*, *Staton Intramural Competition*, IU ROBERT H. MCKINNEY SCH. L., *supra* note 1.

24. *See, e.g.*, *Moot Court Board of Appellate Advocacy*, FIU L., https://law.fiu.edu/academics/experiential-learning/competition-teams/moot-court/ (last visited Feb. 8, 2023).

25. *See, e.g.*, *Dean's Cup*, DUKE L., *supra* note 5 (requiring two, three, or four preliminary-round arguments depending on the number of competitors); *Staton Intramural Competition*, IU ROBERT H. MCKINNEY SCH. L., *supra* note 1 (requiring four preliminary-round arguments).

The competition rules should also discuss whether competitors are expected to argue on both sides of their issue during preliminary and elimination rounds.[26] Though the most common practice is to require competitors to argue both sides, a few internal competitions have competitors argue only on brief.[27] While this practice may better reflect the real-world representation of a client, in moot court it presents logistical issues that may outweigh the benefits.[28] Further, arguing only on brief may create a disadvantage for the competitors who must argue the side of the case that the judges may perceive as the weaker side.

Oral argument matchups—determining which competitors will argue against one another in the preliminary rounds—may be assigned at random[29] or according to a seeding system. For instance, the matchups for the first preliminary round may be based on brief score, with competitors with high brief scores pitted against competitors with low brief scores. Specific methods of matching and seeding the competitors for oral arguments are discussed in more detail in Part II of this chapter.

After the preliminary rounds, most moot court competitions move on to a single-elimination tournament that culminates in a final round in which the two best competitors or teams vie for the competition championship.[30] If the competition includes such a knockout phase, the rules must address which competitors or teams advance from the preliminary rounds to the elimination rounds. Whether a competitor or team advances to the elimination phase is usually determined by ranking the competitors or teams based on their performance in the preliminary rounds.

This ranking may be determined in one of two ways. Under the first method, a winner is declared for each preliminary-round argument. At

---

26. *See, e.g.*, *id.* (requiring advocates to argue both sides of the case).

27. *See, e.g.*, *Dean's Cup*, Duke L., *supra* note 5 (requiring advocates to argue only the side that they briefed).

28. Allowing teams to argue a single side all the way through a competition requires adjustments in seeding and requires resolving how to handle a final round if both teams have argued the same side. For most programs, these complications are probably not worth the lesson to be gained from arguing one side all the way through the competition.

29. *See, e.g.*, *Julius H. Miner Moot Court Competition*, Nw. Pritzker Sch. L., https://wwws.law.northwestern.edu/academics/curricular-offerings/practice/mootcourt/juliusminer/documents/miner-rules.pdf, at 3 (last visited Feb. 8, 2023) (requiring that advocates be randomly paired for the first two preliminary rounds).

30. *See, e.g.*, *id.* at 5.

the end of the preliminary rounds, the competitors with the best win-loss records advance to the elimination rounds.[31] Under the second method, the competition administrators do not declare a winner for each preliminary-round argument. Instead, each competitor receives a score for each preliminary-round argument. At the end of the preliminary rounds, the competitors with the highest total or average scores through the preliminary rounds advance to the elimination rounds.[32] Specific options for determining competitor advancement to the elimination rounds are discussed in Part II of this chapter.

If the competition contains a knockout phase, the rules must also address the method used to determine which competitor wins an elimination round. Some competitions determine who wins the round based on a combination of the competitors' brief and oral-argument scores, with the competitor with the higher combined score winning the round.[33] Other competitions give the round to the competitor with the higher oral argument score.[34] Still other competitions have the judging panel vote on the winner of the round, giving the round to the competitor who wins a majority of votes from the panel.[35]

Because real appeals are won or lost based largely on the parties' briefs,[36] a scheme that includes the competitors' brief scores to determine an elimination round's winner is ideal. But such a scheme may not be logistically feasible depending on other factors, such as whether the briefs will be scored in time for the competition administrator to include them in the elimination-round scoring. Specific options for determining who wins an elimination round are discussed in Part II of this chapter.

---

31. *See, e.g.*, *id.*

32. *See, e.g.*, *Staton Intramural Competition*, IU Robert H. McKinney Sch. L., *supra* note 1 (using highest average scores).

33. *See, e.g.*, *Julius H. Miner Moot Court Competition*, Nw. Pritzker Sch. L., *supra* note 29, at 5; *Tullis Moot Court Competition*, LSU L., https://www.law.lsu.edu/advocacy/files/2022/08/2022-Tullis-Competition-Rules.pdf, at 7 (last visited Feb. 8, 2023).

34. *See, e.g.*, *Staton Intramural Competition*, IU Robert H. McKinney Sch. L., *supra* note 1.

35. *See, e.g.*, *Dean's Cup*, Duke L., https://law.duke.edu/sites/default/files/mootcourt/Competition-Rules-2021-a11y.pdf, at 11 (last visited Feb. 8, 2023) (leaving it to the judges' discretion to choose the final round's winner).

36. Hatchett & Telfer, *supra* note 13, at 139.

ii. How should each oral argument be organized?

As to each oral argument, the rules must dictate the sequence in which the competitors will argue and the argument time that will be allotted to each competitor.

The oral argument sequence should mirror the sequence that one would normally see in a real oral argument. Under this sequence the appealing party argues first. Then the responding party argues, followed by rebuttal time for the appealing party.

In competitions in which the competitors argue as a team, the competitors are usually required to argue in sequence. Put differently, the first advocate for the petitioner/appellant argues, followed by the second advocate for the petitioner/appellant.[37] Then the first advocate for the respondent/appellee argues, followed by the second advocate.[38] And if the petitioner/appellant team wishes to give rebuttal, the rules in most competitions prohibit the team members from splitting their rebuttal argument; only one member of the team gives rebuttal.[39]

The time allotted for each competitor's argument also varies from competition to competition. In many competitions, each competitor is given ten to fifteen minutes to argue, including any rebuttal time reserved.[40] But less time certainly may be allotted if the circumstances require it. For example, if the internal competition's purpose is to select teams for external competitions or to select members of the school's moot court board, shorter argument times of ten minutes with a two-minute rebuttal for the petitioner/appellant may be appropriate. This shorter argument time may be sufficient to allow the external-team coaches to evaluate a competitor's skills for placement on a team while minimizing the time spent on what is essentially a tryout.

---

37. *See, e.g., Staton Intramural Competition*, IU Robert H. McKinney Sch. L., *supra* note 1.

38. *Id.; but see, e.g., Internal Moot Court Arguments*, Santa Clara U. Sch. L., https://law.scu.edu/mootcourt/arguments/ (last visited Feb. 8, 2023) (requiring both advocates who are arguing the first issue to give their oral arguments before the advocates who are arguing the second issue).

39. *See, e.g., Tullis Moot Court Competition*, LSU L., *supra* note 33, at 6.

40. *See, e.g., id.* (allotting 10 minutes per advocate); *Dean's Cup*, Duke L., *supra* note 35, at 9 (allotting 15 minutes per advocate); *Internal Moot Court Arguments*, Santa Clara U. Sch. L., *supra* note 38 (allotting 15 minutes per advocate); *Julius H. Miner Moot Court Competition*, Nw. Pritzker Sch. L., *supra* note 29, at 4 (requiring at least 12 minutes per advocate).

If the competitors are arguing in teams, the rules may provide some flexibility to the team members as to how much time each advocate may argue.[41] For example, if the rules allot thirty minutes per team, the rules might allow advocates to divide their allotted time as they see fit as long as each advocate argues for at least ten minutes.

Finally, because the oral arguments must be timed, the rules should discuss who will keep time for each oral argument. The timekeeper usually functions as the bailiff for the argument, calling the court to order at the argument's beginning and announcing the names of the judges who are presiding over the argument. You may furnish the bailiff for the competitors from a pool of volunteers, or you may require the competitors to furnish their own bailiffs. You could also have members of your moot court board serve as bailiffs.

d. What conduct and decorum must the competitors observe?

Because moot court oral arguments should mirror real appellate oral arguments, the rules for any internal competition should discuss the competitors' conduct and decorum. Specifically, the rules should cover topics such as promptness and should impose a penalty for competitors who arrive late for an oral argument without a bona fide excuse. Similarly, the rules should admonish competitors to show respect to the judges and their fellow competitors both during oral argument and in their briefs. The rules might also state that any improper conduct or failure to observe decorum may result in proceedings against the competitor under the school's honor code, provided of course that these violations in fact fall under the honor code.

e. How may the competitors lodge protests?

Unfortunately, events may arise during an internal competition that cast doubt on the competition's fairness. Therefore, the competition rules should provide competitors with the opportunity to protest any improprieties that cast such a doubt. To serve this end, the rules should set forth the types of improprieties that may be protested, the procedures for lodging a protest, who will review and rule on a protest, and how that decision-maker should review and rule on a protest.

---

41. *See, e.g., id.*

As for the types of improprieties that may be protested, the rules should focus on improprieties that cause harm to a competitor. For instance, an oral argument judge's impartiality may be questioned because the judge is a family friend of a competitor that the judge is judging. Or perhaps a mathematical error occurred during the scoring process that caused a competitor to lose a round. The rules should allow protests of these sorts of events and should include a few specific examples to help define events that might qualify for a protest.

As for the procedures for lodging a protest, the rules should state with whom a protest should be lodged. The most logical entity with whom a protest should be lodged is the competition administrator, such as a faculty advisor or the student moot court board charged with running the competition. The timing of the protest should also be covered by the rules, perhaps giving competitors a limited period after the impropriety has come to their attention to protest that impropriety. And finally, the rules should discuss how the party responsible for ruling on the protest will go about doing its job. As one example, the rules may require the decision-maker to find that the impropriety harmed the protesting competitor before the decision-maker orders remedial action, such as rehearing the oral argument in which the harm occurred.

f. How will the briefs and oral arguments be scored?

i. Basic scoring rules

The competition rules must transparently discuss the scoring of the competitors' briefs and oral arguments. At a minimum, the rules should cover the following scoring matters:

- the point scale on which judges will score briefs and oral arguments (for example, a one-hundred-point scale);
- the penalties to be assessed for formatting violations, such as a violation of the word limit or page limit;
- the penalties for briefs that are submitted after the submission deadline;
- the weight afforded to each competitor's brief scores and oral argument scores for the purposes of determining whether the competitor advances through the competition;

- tie-breaking measures to determine the winner of an oral argument round that ends in a draw; and
- the form and timing of the feedback that the brief judges and oral-argument judges will give to the competitors.

Specific advice about scoring, tie-breaking measures, and judge feedback is provided later in this chapter.

ii. Rules that address how the number of judges impacts scores

In some competitions, multiple judges score each brief, and the final brief score given to the competitor is the average of the judges' scores for that competitor.[42] If this is the case in your competition, the rules should discuss how many judges will score each brief and whether any judge's score will be dropped when determining a competitor's average brief score. For instance, to promote parity among competitors, the highest and lowest brief scores for each competitor might be dropped in arriving at an average brief score for that competitor. This drop-the-highest-and-lowest-score system could also be applied when determining a competitor's average oral argument score for a given round.

You may not, however, be able to recruit multiple judges to score each brief. If your competition rules permit each brief to be scored by only a single judge, the likelihood increases that the judges' subjective views will affect the fairness of the scoring. Because of this, your competition's rules might require the reassessment of any brief whose score significantly departs from the mean brief score. For example, the rules might require a second judge to rescore any brief whose score is more than two standard deviations from the mean brief score.[43]

iii. Rules concerning the scoring weights given to brief scores and to oral argument scores

Another important consideration in scoring is the weight that will be given to the brief scores and the oral argument scores in determining

42. *See, e.g., Julius H. Miner Moot Court Competition*, Nw. Pritzker Sch. L., *supra* note 29, at 2 (requiring at least two judges per brief).

43. For a basic discussion of standard deviation, see *Standard Deviation and Variance*, For Dummies, https://www.dummies.com/article/academics-the-arts/math/statistics/standard-deviation-and-variance-147351/ (last visited Feb. 8, 2023).

whether a competitor or team wins a preliminary round or an elimination round. In some competitions, the brief scores are factored into the competitors' advancement only in the preliminary rounds.[44] In other competitions, the brief scores are factored into the competitors' advancement through the elimination rounds, too.[45] Which option you choose is up to you, though a system that factors in the brief scores through all oral argument rounds reflects real appellate practice more than a system that includes those scores only in the preliminary rounds.

In competitions that factor briefs into the scoring of each round, the oral argument score for each competitor is often weighted more heavily than the brief score—for example, 60 percent for oral argument and 40 percent for the brief.[46] If your rules require brief scores to be factored into the competitors' advancement from round to round, the weight you assign to each component is up to you. But an equal weighting (50 percent brief, 50 percent oral argument) is more reflective of the weight given to those components in a real appeal. In fact, if internal-competition briefs and oral arguments were weighted in the same proportions as those used by real appellate courts, the brief would probably be given significantly more weight than the oral argument.[47]

g. How will competitor plagiarism be addressed?

The rules certainly must prohibit plagiarism in the briefs. Specifically, the rules should require the competitors to give appropriate credit to the source of any words or ideas that did not originate from them. Further, the rules should state the penalties for plagiarism, such as point deductions and possible sanctions for academic misconduct.

In framing plagiarism policies, rule drafters should be thoughtful about how to address the use of generative artificial intelligence, and specifically large language models like ChatGPT. Using AI to draft sec-

---

44. *See, e.g.*, *Staton Intramural Competition*, IU Robert H. McKinney Sch. L., *supra* note 1.

45. *See, e.g.*, *Julius H. Miner Moot Court Competition*, Nw. Pritzker Sch. L., *supra* note 29, at 5; *Tullis Moot Court Competition*, LSU L., *supra* note 33, at 7.

46. *See, e.g.*, *Staton Intramural Competition*, IU Robert H. McKinney Sch. L., *supra* note 1.

47. *See* McGaughey, *supra* note 12, at 143 (noting that according to a survey of nineteen state and federal appellate judges, "all agreed that the most important part of the appellate process is not oral argument, but the briefs").

tions of a brief can constitute plagiarism in a couple of different ways. Large language models draw on banks of information that include text initially drafted by others, and some models memorize that material and then plagiarize when generating text.[48] Further, regardless of whether the AI tool itself plagiarized, by inserting that text into a brief, students present material they did not draft as if it were their own work.

That said, artificial intelligence has been a part of legal education and law practice for decades. Unless you expect competitors to conduct legal research exclusively through physical books and plan to ban the use of spell-check and other similar tools, rules cannot impose a blanket ban on the use of AI. But rules certainly should address the extent that competitors can use specific types of AI tools—tools that generate legal documents and draft large blocks of text for the user, for example. Because the technological landscape evolves so quickly, avoid naming specific products; rules should focus instead on the types of tasks the tools accomplish for the user. Also, think carefully about how to enforce any such rules consistently and fairly. As the technology evolves, so do methods to detect the use of that technology. But as those detection methods evolve, so do tools to evade those methods.

As with all rules governing moot court competitions, provisions addressing the use of generative AI tools should focus on the ultimate goals of (1) maintaining fairness and a level playing field among competitors, (2) preserving the educational value of the experience, and (3) training ethical, professional, competent future attorneys. As generative AI tools become part of day-to-day law practice, and as access to those tools becomes more commonplace among law students,[49] the goal of training students competent in the use of those tools may outweigh concerns about "cheating" by using those tools.

---

48. *See* Jooyoung Lee, Thai Le, Jinghui Chen, and Dongwon Lee, *Do Language Models Plagiarize?*, https://arxiv.org/pdf/2203.07618v1.pdf (last visited May 30, 2023).

49. For example, online legal-research platforms likely will include some generative AI tools in the resources most law students can access for free. As of this writing, Lexis-Nexis has announced Lexis+ AI, which incorporates a tool that purports to "generate winning briefs and quality contract clauses with remarkable speed, ease, and precision." *Lexis+ AI*, Lexis-Nexis, https://www.lexisnexis.com/en-us/products/lexis-plus-ai.page (last visited May 30, 2023).

h. How much outside assistance may the competitors receive?

Finally, the rules must address who may help the competitors prepare their briefs and oral arguments. And if outside assistance is permissible, the rules must define the boundaries of that assistance.

The extent of outside assistance may depend on whether the competition is integrated with the competitors' first-year legal-writing course or is an upper-level experience. If the competition is part of a first-year legal-writing course, the rules might permit professors who are teaching the course, and any student moot court board members who are administering the competition, to mentor the competitors. The rules might allow this because the competition is probably the first time that the competitors are learning written and oral advocacy. So the rules might permit professors or moot court board members to read and critique brief drafts before the briefs are due. Similarly, the rules might permit faculty or student board members to stage practice oral arguments with the competitors before the oral rounds begin. If, however, your competition is an upper-level elective and the competitors have already had basic advocacy training, you may want to limit the extent and types of outside assistance to promote individual achievement and a spirit of competition among the competitors.

Even if the competition rules allow the faculty and student moot court board to help competitors, the rules should limit the types of assistance that competitors may receive. The rules should prohibit teams from sharing written work—such as outlines, drafts, or notes—with other teams before the briefs are due to ensure that each team's brief is the product of that team's own work. Further, the rules should prohibit competitors from observing other competitors' oral arguments so that they won't gain an unfair advantage by learning questions that the judges might ask or arguments that other competitors might make. This rule, however, could be relaxed during the competition's knockout phase for competitors who have already been eliminated from the competition. Finally, the rules might state that if a competitor gives or receives any impermissible outside assistance, the competitor may be subject to proceedings under the school's honor code, provided that such a violation falls under the honor code.

B. Creating the competition problem

Creating the competition problem is a critical and challenging aspect of managing an internal moot court competition. The problem usually includes the record of proceedings upon which the students' briefs and oral arguments are based. If the problem is to be valuable, it must foster the lawyering skills that the competition is designed to teach. Moreover, the problem should provide the competitors and the judges with a realistic and engaging experience that they will look back on positively.[50] This means that the creators of the problem must take great care in constructing it.

To create a valuable competition, you must consider the following:

- whether the problem will be an open-universe problem or a closed-universe problem;
- who will write the problem;
- which attributes and components the problem should have;
- where to look for problem topics;
- how the problem's factual scenario should be created;
- which jurisdiction the problem will be set in; and
- whether you should borrow or purchase the problem.

1. SHOULD THE PROBLEM PRESENT AN OPEN UNIVERSE OR A CLOSED UNIVERSE?

You must consider whether the problem will be an open-universe problem, which will require the competitors to conduct research and gather their own authorities, or a closed-universe problem, in which the relevant authorities will be provided to the competitors. Recall that the core purpose of an internal competition is to foster the learning of key lawyering skills. Thus, the ideal competition problem is an open-universe problem, which gives the competitors an opportunity to develop their legal-research, legal-analysis, and advocacy skills.[51]

---

50. Michael Vitiello, *Teaching Oral Advocacy: Creating More Opportunities to Teach an Essential Skill*, 45 SETON HALL L. REV. 1031, 1040 (2015).

51. *See* Diana J. Simon, *Focused and Fun: A How-To Guide for Creating Hypotheticals for Law Students*, 19 SCRIBES J. LEGAL WRITING 161, 168 (2020) (stating that an ideal problem should "teach the students how to conduct research").

However, circumstances may legitimately dictate against an open-universe problem. For example, the competitors may have a short timeframe in which to prepare their briefs and thus may not have sufficient time to conduct research for their supporting authorities. Perhaps the students received extensive training in legal research before the competition, so you may not need to emphasize legal research as a key objective of the competition. Or perhaps you want make it easier for the judges to learn the law by limiting the number of authorities that they must become familiar with.

In these situations, you may opt for a closed-universe problem. If you use a closed-universe problem, provide the competitors with the authorities that they may use in their briefs and oral arguments. These authorities may be provided in a list or cited in the lower-court opinions that are included in the problem.

If the problem is an open-universe problem, the record of proceedings in the problem ought to cite some of the key authority to provide a springboard for the competitors' research. For example, you could cite these authorities in the trial court order that the parties are appealing. Or you could simply give the students the list of authorities separately from the record.

2. WHO WILL CREATE THE PROBLEM?

Schools have different models for creating the competition problem. Some schools place the responsibility of problem writing in the hands of a student moot court board that is running the internal competition. A school could adopt this model because it wants to give the students an opportunity to learn how an appellate record is assembled. Or perhaps the school wants to give the students more training in legal research, analysis, and writing, all of which are part of creating an internal-competition problem. Other schools—for example, schools that integrate their internal moot court competition with their first-year legal writing course as discussed above—place the responsibility for writing the problem solely in faculty hands or in the hands of an alumni or practitioner advisory group.

a. Faculty members write the problem.

While there are sound pedagogical reasons for having students write a competition problem, faculty-written problems are ideal for two reasons. First, faculty who advise moot court programs usually have experience as practitioners, which means that they are familiar with the typical contents of an appellate record. Thus, they know which materials should go into the competition problem and understand the impact of the appellate standard of review on the parties' arguments. Second, because faculty problem writers are teachers, they know the pedagogical goals that should be achieved through a skills-based exercise like moot court. This is particularly so if the professor in question is teaching skills-focused courses that require the professor to frequently design simulation-based assignments. As a result, such a faculty member is likely able to tailor the competition problem to those goals.

If, however, you are a faculty member charged with writing the problem and have no appellate practice experience, you should seek help from other faculty or from practitioners who do. You may ask the faculty supervising the school's law clinic for advice and assistance. Or you could explore assembling a board of advisors composed of practitioners—perhaps alumni of your school—with whom you may consult or even co-write the problem, especially if those practitioners are experts in the legal issues that the problem will present to the competitors. And even if you have appellate practice experience, you may still want to ask others for assistance in writing the problem, particularly during the editing process.

b. Students write the problem.

As mentioned, some schools place problem-writing responsibility in the hands of their student moot court board.[52] If the board members are earning academic credit for their board service, they may even be required to write the competition problem to earn that credit.

If students are to write the problem, faculty should closely supervise those students because the students probably won't have teaching or appellate practice experience. While the students will likely have participated in a moot court competition before joining the moot court board,

52. This is the system in place at Indiana University Robert H. McKinney School of Law, where a subcommittee of the school's moot court board writes the problem.

this experience is usually insufficient to prepare them to write a valuable problem.

If you are the faculty member who will supervise the students who write a competition problem, you should consider adopting five measures in supervising them:

i. Work with a manageable number of students.

If the moot court board is composed of a large number of students, consider assigning a smaller group within the board—perhaps three to four students—to create the problem, provided that all board members are not required to write a problem to receive academic credit for their board activities. Assigning a smaller group to write the problem may help to avoid the "too many cooks spoil the soup" phenomenon that tends to arise when a large group of people is assigned to work on a small set of involved, highly focused tasks.

ii. Train the students properly.

Set up training sessions with the board members to discuss how to create an effective moot court competition problem. If board members are required to attend class sessions as part of their board service, set aside some of these class sessions to discuss problem writing. And give the board members examples of good moot court problems with the admonition that those examples are not "one size fits all" templates into which the students may simply plug the record that they wish to construct for their competition problem.

iii. Provide the students with a list of problem topics.

As a faculty member, you likely will be well versed in writing problems. Therefore, you should do the initial legwork in finding a problem topic for the competition provided that you have the time to do so. For example, you might provide the students with a "short list" of three or four possible problem topics. The students can then conduct preliminary research on those topics and present their findings to you, including any topic preferences and any challenges presented by each topic. You can then choose the final problem topic. The benefit of this method is that it gives the students a degree of autonomy while allowing you to retain a measure of control over the process.

iv. Establish a drafting schedule with strict editing deadlines.

Ensure that the problem-writing process begins well before the competition is scheduled to begin. Researching and writing the problem typically takes much longer than the students anticipate, so imposing a rigorous set of editing deadlines is important. You should schedule regular status meetings with the board members charged with writing the problem to ensure that their work is on schedule and to address any issues that arise during the writing of the problem before those issues morph into bigger problems.

v. Use a "back-to-front" process.

Consider implementing a "back-to-front" process for the problem's creation. Specifically, consider instructing the students to write the lower court order or orders being appealed before they write the relevant pleadings, transcripts of evidence, and motions upon which the order or orders are based. By doing this, the students might get a better sense of the problem's "big picture," which may in turn help them to maintain the proper focus as they create the record of proceedings.

3. WHAT ATTRIBUTES AND COMPONENTS SHOULD THE PROBLEM HAVE?

Whether the author of the problem is a professor, a student-run moot court board, or a practitioner, that author must consider what precisely will go into the problem. An effective problem will have four main characteristics:

- It will look like a real appellate record;
- It will be interesting;
- It will be balanced; and
- It will be manageable for the competitors and judges.[53]

---

53. *See* Simon, *supra* note 51, at 165 (noting that hypotheticals presented to students should "sound real"); Vitiello, *supra* note 50, at 1040 (emphasizing that a good moot court problem is "balanced," "sufficiently interesting," and "realistic").

a. The problem should approximate a real appellate record.

Because the ultimate goal of a good moot court competition is to develop lawyering skills in a simulation-based experience, a good competition problem will give the competitors an experience similar to the experience that a lawyer would encounter in a real case. This means that, to a certain extent, the problem's contents should approximate a real appellate record. The problem should include not only the lower court order or orders being appealed but also real-world materials such as transcripts of evidence, discovery responses, pleadings, motions, and documentary evidence.[54]

These materials do not need to be as voluminous as the materials that might be found in a real appellate record. Indeed, the problem should not be so voluminous that it would discourage competition judges, who are very busy people, from taking the time to read the problem, therefore leaving those judges unprepared to judge the competitors.

In short, the problem ought to be substantial enough that it forces the competitors to sift through the record for relevant information[55], just as any appellate attorney would do, yet succinct enough that judges will not be hard-pressed to find the time to read the problem before judging the competitors.

b. The problem should be interesting.

Appellate attorneys occasionally face boring cases. In fact, law students should understand that they will have to tackle uninteresting cases throughout their legal careers.

Yet because teachers should try to actively engage their students to promote learning, an effective moot court competition problem will be interesting to the competitors. An interesting problem also helps the judges who score the competitors' briefs and oral arguments. Put yourself in the judges' shoes. These judges might be scoring multiple briefs or oral arguments. An engaging problem is more likely to hold judges' attention while they evaluate the students, and it might give them more

---

54. *See* Vitiello, *supra* note 50, at 1039 ("The skill that is perhaps the most important and unique to the appellate litigator is that of developing and working with the record on appeal.").

55. Simon, *supra* note 51, at 166.

incentive to thoroughly prepare to carry out their judging duties. In turn, this preparedness will likely lead to more constructive critiques from the judges to the competitors.

What sorts of moot court problems do students and judges find interesting? Problems that require the competitors to base their arguments on public policy will often deeply engage competitors and judges. For example, problems in external moot court competitions sometimes involve a split of authority. Problems based on a split of authority provide fertile ground for policy arguments. And to create policy arguments, competitors usually must commit to a deeper level of analytical thinking than the thinking they will have to do to create arguments for a moot court problem that involves only the simple application of an established rule of law to a set of established facts.

Other competition problems that tend to be interesting are those based on statutory construction issues and constitutional issues. The major external moot court competitions typically have competition problems that focus on these areas because most competitors will have received some instruction in these topics. Again, these issues often require a heavy focus on public policy. This focus promotes the deep level of analytical thinking that many students tend to find challenging yet interesting and that they need to cultivate to become successful practitioners.

Problems that focus on areas of the law that the students have covered during their first year of school, such as tort law, criminal law, and contract law, can also provide the basis for an interesting problem, especially if the problem writer is an expert in the topic. You might even consider conducting a "specialty" internal competition that focuses on an area of law that your school is known for and that might have been a motivating reason for students to attend your school. For example, if your school has a center for intellectual property law, a specialty internal competition might focus on trademark law.

Problems that involve extremely divisive social issues, such as abortion, or issues that might be personally upsetting to the competitors or judges, such as child abuse and rape, should be avoided. While these sorts of issues may provide for lively arguments and the discussion of weighty policy justifications, the emotions involved in debating these topics might distract and even distress the competitors and the judges.[56]

c. The problem should be balanced.

In real appeals, the issues presented by the parties are sometimes not evenly balanced; one party may have substantially stronger arguments for one or more of the issues on appeal than the other party has. And in fact, our students should learn that they'll occasionally have to represent clients whose arguments are likely losers and, thus, they'll need to become skilled at minimizing the weaknesses of their client's case.

But an effective moot court problem is as evenly balanced on the issues as possible. Severely "lopsided" problems might encourage the competition judges to award lower scores to competitors who are assigned to argue the clearly weaker side of the case, even when the judges have been instructed that they are not to let their personal opinions about how the case ought to be decided impact their scores. Or conversely, the judges might feel sorry for the competitors arguing the tougher side and award them higher scores than might be justified.

Creating an evenly balanced problem is difficult even for the most experienced problem writers. This creation requires a painstaking consideration of the arguments for both parties, which necessitates a firm grasp of the relevant authorities and the kinds of facts and policies that could be marshaled in each party's favor. It also requires a recognition that it's nearly impossible to create a perfectly balanced problem. Often, arguments for one side of the case will have inherent strengths or weaknesses that the arguments for the other side will not have.

The problem writer should examine the authorities, legal doctrines, public policy justifications, and facts that support each party's arguments. The problem writer might even list these items side-by-side in a sort of "argument ledger" to see whether one side of the ledger is too "stacked."

The problem writer should also ensure that the relevant precedent contains enough detailed reasoning to give the competitors on each side enough material to work with in their arguments. For example, if your

56. *See* Simon, *supra* note 51, at 167 (noting that while students may face distressing issues in practice, professors should want the students' focus "to be on learning how to write effectively").

problem involves a split of authority, it will function well only if the authority on both sides of the split contains thorough reasoning. If authority on one side of the split contains sparse reasoning, this may put competitors arguing for that side of the split at a disadvantage, thus throwing the problem out of balance.

Still, the problem writer should recognize that achieving balance is not simply a numbers game in which each side of the ledger has to balance out precisely. Rather, the key is to ensure that one side of the ledger doesn't overwhelm the other side. Some reasonable imbalance in a moot court problem might provide the competitors with the opportunity to practice the skill of minimizing the weaknesses of their client's case. To provide this opportunity, the facts, policy justifications, or evolving societal norms discussed in the problem might be more favorable to one party, while the law might be more favorable to the other party.

d. The problem should be manageable for the competitors and the judges.

After they become practitioners, law students will undoubtedly have to deal with complex and challenging legal issues on their clients' behalf. Clients will usually seek their help precisely because of their expertise in dealing with those issues.

But as competitors in a moot court competition, law students are still relatively new to the skills of analyzing legal issues and persuading judges. Indeed, a moot court competition's core purpose is to give the students a setting in which to learn, practice, and refine those skills. If the competitors are assigned a problem that presents legal issues beyond their capabilities as novices, most competitors will flounder rather than flourish, thus defeating the competition's pedagogical purpose.

Therefore, an effective moot court competition problem includes legal issues that the competitors will find challenging yet manageable given their skill level. Furthermore, the problem should have a procedural posture that the competitors will easily understand. Indeed, a manageable problem is also helpful for the judges, who will probably find it easy to learn and understand. And if the judges can easily grasp the problem, they will probably be more likely to focus on the substance of the competitors' arguments—the most important part of an argument—rather than on the competitors' argument style.

When considering manageability, problem writers should keep in mind where the students are in their law school careers. If the competition is part of the competitors' first-year legal-writing course, a problem that involves issues the students have encountered in their first-year courses should be manageable for them. If, however, the competition is an upper-level elective, a problem that involves legal issues covered in widely taken upper-level courses, such as Evidence, should be manageable for the competitors.

This is not to say that an effective problem will never cover advanced legal issues. Indeed, problems with complex yet manageable legal issues may complement what the competitors are learning in other classes and provide them with opportunities to become interested in new areas of law. So first-year competitors might reasonably be assigned a problem involving federal constitutional issues as long as those issues are narrowly drawn. To cite one example, a problem writer might present as an issue the constitutional validity of the police's "stop and frisk" of a passenger riding in a suspect's automobile.[57] The writer, however, could keep this issue narrow by limiting the competitors to using authority from only one jurisdiction to support their arguments.

As to the procedural posture of the problem, the students' progress in their law school career should once again be considered. Procedural postures such as summary judgment, dismissal under Rule 12(b)(6), and a jury verdict after a full trial will likely be covered during the students' first year of school. A competition problem that involves appeals in these settings will likely work well, particularly when the standards of appellate review presented by these settings will likely have been discussed during the students' first year. But avoid procedural postures such as cross-appeals, or orders that the students probably haven't discussed in Civil Procedure.

4. WHERE MAY PROBLEM TOPICS BE FOUND?

Selecting a problem topic is among the most time-consuming parts of problem creation. How does a problem writer go about finding legal issues that the writer can craft into an interesting, well-balanced prob-

---

57. *See* Brendlin v. California, 551 U.S. 249 (2007); Maryland v. Wilson, 519 U.S. 408 (1997).

lem that may be tailored to the competitors' skill level, especially when the writer must usually sort through numerous topics before arriving at a good one?

a. Talk to colleagues.

Consider asking colleagues from the academy, the bench, and the bar if they know of any interesting legal issues percolating in the courts. For instance, another professor may have published an article covering a circuit split that might serve well as the foundation for a competition problem. Or a local trial court judge may have presided over a case that involved engaging legal issues.

b. Consult legal periodicals.

Legal periodicals are another helpful source of problem ideas. National and local print periodicals, such as bar association magazines and legal newspapers, often have regular columns devoted to up-and-coming legal issues.[58] Many of these publications also offer online subscriptions for their readers' convenience. Similarly, law reviews and law journals frequently feature articles on topics that might make excellent competition-problem topics, such as circuit splits.[59]

c. Consult online sources.

Online sources besides periodicals are also fertile ground for cultivating problem-topic ideas.

i. Ask for ideas on listservs and discussion forums.

Consider asking for problem-topic ideas on professional email listservs and discussion forums that you subscribe to, such as those sponsored by faculty organizations or bar associations. These sources, like the Legal Writing Institute's Online Community,[60] are excellent spring-

58. For instance, the *ABA Journal* has a regular column entitled "The National Pulse" that covers emerging legal issues.

59. *See, e.g.*, Chloe Cornett, Comment, *Lights, Camera, Action … As Long As You Live in the Proper Circuit: An Analysis of the Circuit Split Concerning Civilians' First Amendment Right to Record Police Officers*, 25 SMU SCI. & TECH. L. REV. 237 (2022).

60. The Legal Writing Institute Community (LWIC) is open only to legal writing professionals. For information on how to subscribe to the LWI listserv, visit https://lwic.mobilize.io/.

boards for problem ideas because they have subscribers from across the country who frequently deal with novel and interesting legal issues.

ii. Read law blogs.

Law blogs provide incisive and insightful commentary from legal experts on current legal issues. Thus, you might visit them for potential problem topics. Some blogs focus on particular legal issues or topics, such as appellate advocacy,[61] sentencing law,[62] constitutional law,[63] or circuit splits.[64] Others discuss only the goings-on of the U.S. Supreme Court.[65] Still others cast broad nets and aggregate all kinds of general legal news.[66]

iii. Listen to legal podcasts.

Finally, consider subscribing and listening to legal podcasts for problem ideas. Because there are many podcasts to choose from, you might begin by listening to podcasts with that focus only on issues presented to the U.S. Supreme Court[67] or those that feature legal scholars who explore current legal issues in depth.[68]

5. HOW SHOULD THE PROBLEM'S FACTUAL SCENARIO BE CREATED?

To create your competition problem's factual scenario, you may choose one of the following three options as your approach:

---

61. *See, e.g.*, App. Advoc. Blog, https://lawprofessors.typepad.com/appellate_advocacy/ (last visited Feb. 8, 2023).

62. *See, e.g.*, Sent'g L. & Pol'y, https://sentencing.typepad.com/sentencing_law_and_policy/ (last visited Feb. 8, 2023).

63. *See, e.g.*, Const. L. Prof. Blog, https://lawprofessors.typepad.com/conlaw/ (last visited Feb. 8, 2023); The Volokh Conspiracy, https://reason.com/volokh/ (last visited Feb. 8, 2023).

64. *See, e.g.*, Sunday Splits, https://www.sundaysplits.com/blog (last visited Feb. 8, 2023).

65. *See, e.g.*, SCOTUSblog, http://www.scotusblog.com (last visited Feb. 8, 2023).

66. *See, e.g.*, How Appealing, https://howappealing.abovethelaw.com/ (last visited Feb. 8, 2023).

67. *See, e.g.*, Amicus, https://slate.com/podcasts/amicus (last visited Feb. 8, 2023).

68. *See, e.g.*, Yale L.J. Podcast, https://podcasts.apple.com/us/podcast/the-yale-law-journal-podcast/id989854020 (last visited Feb. 8, 2023).

- You may write the facts from scratch.
- You may borrow facts from a live appeal.
- You may use real cases as a foundation for the problem's facts.

a. Write the facts from scratch.

Writing a competition problem's facts from scratch can be fun. Indeed, if you choose this method of problem writing, it allows you to tap into your creativity as a writer, which is one of the best parts of being a teacher. It also gives you a lot of flexibility in making the problem interesting and balanced for the competitors because you can adjust the facts as you see fit. And it can provide you with opportunities to learn new areas of law, which will enrich your teaching.

b. Borrow the facts from a live appeal.

But writing facts from scratch is time consuming, especially when a live case might provide a good scenario for the competition problem. In a live appeal, you have a ready-made record of proceedings at your disposal. Therefore, you may simply obtain a copy of the record from the live case, perhaps change the parties' names, and then assign that record as the problem, thus saving the time required to create the story behind the appeal.

Yet using a live appeal creates a greater risk of academic misconduct. Students may be able to find the parties' briefs, which are often available online. Then the students may copy the arguments from those briefs and paste those arguments into their own briefs.

Further, the live case might be decided during the competition. This puts the competitors and the judges in the awkward position of possibly knowing about but having to ignore the court's opinion on the very issues that the competitors are arguing.

c. Use real cases as a foundation for the problem's facts.

Perhaps the ideal method of creating the factual scenario for a competition problem is to consult real cases to provide a foundation for the problem's scenario, but to alter the facts of that foundation substantially enough that the problem essentially becomes a "new case." For example, the writer might consult facts from cases at both ends of a legal issue's spectrum—say, cases finding that a particular stop and frisk of a suspect is constitutional, and other cases finding that the same stop and frisk is unconstitutional—and craft a similar set of facts that falls somewhere into the factual "middle ground" of those cases. While this method will require more time than simply borrowing a live appeal for the problem scenario, it will provide you with the ability to adjust the facts as needed to ensure that the problem is well balanced and fair for the competitors.

6. IN WHICH JURISDICTION SHOULD THE PROBLEM BE SET?

As for the jurisdiction in which you will set your problem, you have two choices:

- You may set the problem in a fictional jurisdiction; or
- You may set the problem in a real jurisdiction.

a. Set the problem in a fictional jurisdiction.

Some moot court competitions are set in a fictional jurisdiction. This setting is usually imposed to provide the competition administrators with flexibility. More specifically, a fictional jurisdiction contains no binding authority. Accordingly, every legal issue presented in the appeal is an issue of first impression. Further, because the competitors are not bound by any legal authority in arguing the issue of first impression, they will be on relatively equal footing when making their arguments. And if the competition administrators wish to base the problem on a statutory construction issue, using a fictional jurisdiction gives them the ability to draft their own statute rather than relying on an existing statute. The administrators can write the statute so its language doesn't clearly favor one competitor over the other.

Yet the flexibility provided by a competition set in a fictional jurisdiction may also create challenges. The lack of binding authority may force the problem writer to create binding authority, such as the authority that sets forth the standard of appellate review. This sort of authority would be readily available if the problem were set in a real jurisdiction, which would save the problem writer time in writing this component of the problem. And some of the richness and simulation of reality that stems from setting a problem in a real jurisdiction is lost if the competition is set in a fictional jurisdiction.

b. Set the problem in a real jurisdiction.

If you wish to retain a richness and simulation of reality in the problem yet still want to focus the problem on an issue of first impression, you might search for a real jurisdiction that has not yet considered the issue. For instance, a circuit split sometimes involves a circuit that hasn't yet jumped into the fray. So if you want to use that circuit split as the basis for the competition problem but maintain the competition issue as an issue of first impression, you could set the problem in a circuit that had not yet addressed the issue.

c. Should you borrow or purchase a problem?

What if you simply don't have time to research and write an internal competition problem? In that case, you may ask colleagues at other law schools to share a problem from their internal competitions. As in a search for a problem topic for a problem created from scratch, you might visit faculty email listservs or online discussion forums to ask for a problem. Or you could purchase a problem packet that is sold commercially. *The Moot Court Casebook*, which is published every year by the moot court board at New York University School of Law, is one example.[69]

If you borrow or purchase the problem, you must update it to ensure that the legal issues presented in the problem are still live issues. And to prevent academic misconduct, you should change the names of the parties involved in the problem. You should also consider altering the problem's facts to ensure that competitors make novel arguments.

C. Creating scoring rubrics

The competition judges need guidance on how they are to assess the competitors' briefs and oral arguments. This guidance is important because the judges' assessment of the competitors will tell the competitors which lawyering skills they have sufficiently mastered and which skills they need to improve.

69. *Casebook*, NYU L. Moot Ct. Bd., https://www.nyumootcourt.org/casebook/ (last visited Feb. 8, 2023).

Accordingly, you, as an internal competition administrator, must create scoring rubrics for the brief and oral argument judges. These rubrics must include—

- the brief-writing skills and oral-argument skills to be assessed;
- the scoring weights and ranges that will be allocated to each assessment category; and
- an opportunity for the judges to provide detailed and constructive feedback to the competitors.

Sample scoring rubrics are included in the online appendix.

1. BRIEF-SCORING RUBRICS

To create the brief-scoring rubrics, you will need to consider the following things:

- which brief-writing skills the rubric should assess;
- which weights you should assign to the rubric's scoring categories;
- which components you might include in the rubric to prompt the judges to give relatively objective scores; and
- whether the rubric should include space for written feedback.

a. What skills should the brief rubric assess?

A good appellate brief should convey the party's contentions on appeal in a clear, concise, thorough, and persuasive manner.[70] Perhaps the most logical way to determine whether an internal competition brief does this is to structure the brief-scoring rubric according to the brief's components. In most appellate courts, a brief must contain the following components, each of which might give rise to a separate scoring category in a brief-scoring rubric:

---

70. For a comprehensive discussion of what an effective appellate brief should contain, see generally Mary Beth Beazley, A Practical Guide To Appellate Advocacy (6th ed. 2022).

- *The cover page.* This category should address whether the cover page—
  - contains the proper cause number;
  - lists the correct parties;
  - uses the correct title (e.g., "Brief of Appellant"); and
  - identifies the competitor by name or by ID number if the briefs are submitted anonymously.
- *The tables of contents and authorities.* This category should address—
  - whether the tables list all brief sections and authorities; and
  - whether the tables list the correct page numbers for the pages of the brief on which those sections and authorities may be found.
- *The questions presented (also called the statement of the issues).* This category should address—
  - whether the questions presented have included the key legal principles and key facts from the case; and
  - whether the questions presented are written persuasively—that is, whether they are written in a way that suggests to the court the conclusions that the advocate wants the court to reach.
- *The statement of the case (also called the statement of facts).* This category should address whether the relevant facts of the client's case are presented to the court as a persuasive narrative. More specifically, this scoring category should gauge whether the statement of the case includes—
  - the legally relevant facts;
  - facts that might subtly generate emotional appeal for the client; and
  - the relevant procedural history of the case.[71]
- *The summary of the argument.* This category should address whether the brief provides a clear and concise summary of

71. In some competitions, the legally relevant facts and the procedural history are contained in separate sections of the brief. If this is the case in your competition, your brief-scoring rubric might include separate scoring categories for each section.

the main arguments in the brief rather than merely rehashing the point headings found in the argument.

- *The standard of appellate review.* This category should assess whether the brief has correctly stated the applicable standard or standards of appellate review.
- *The argument.* This category should assess the organization and substance of the brief's argument. More specifically, this category should assess whether the argument—
  - is logically and persuasively organized on large-scale and small-scale levels;
  - clearly and completely states the relevant law;
  - includes the most relevant and important authority; and
  - clearly, completely, and persuasively explains how and why the law supports the advocate's contentions on appeal.
- *The conclusion.* This category should assess whether the brief clearly and succinctly states the relief that the advocate seeks from the court.[72]

Some of the scoring categories that should go into the brief-scoring rubric will not fit neatly under a particular section of the brief. These scoring categories include the following:

- *Format.* This category should assess whether the brief uses the fonts, margins, and spacing required by the competition rules.
- *Citation.* This category should assess whether the brief contains citations to the record and to the authorities that are—
  - precise in that they contain pinpoint references;
  - properly formatted under the applicable legal citation manual;
  - provided where required; and
  - accurate.

---

72. *See, e.g.*, Fed. R. App. P. 28 (stating the sections that briefs submitted in federal appeals must contain). Some competitions also require the briefs to contain a jurisdictional statement. If this is the case in your competition, your brief-scoring rubric might include a separate scoring category for this section.

- *Writing mechanics.* This category should assess whether the brief—
  - is written concisely and clearly;
  - contains proper grammar, style, and usage; and
  - adopts an assertive yet respectful tone.

b. What weights should the brief rubric assign to the rubric's scoring categories?

In a real appeal, the court will be most concerned with the substance of the parties' arguments on the merits. For this reason, the brief's argument section should be the most heavily weighted category in the brief-scoring rubric, making up at least 45 to 50 percent of the overall score. As for the remaining scoring categories, the statement of the case section and the summary of the argument section should be weighted more heavily than the others because these two sections are fairly heavy on content.

c. How may the brief rubric be set up to yield relatively objective scores?

Without question, judging moot court briefs is a subjective process. Usually, judges will come from different practice backgrounds and will have different practice experiences.

Because of these differences, the judges will have varied perspectives on what is effective advocacy and what is not. Based on these biases, some judges might give the advocates' briefs unreasonably low scores or unreasonably high scores.

Therefore, you should build objectivity into the brief-scoring rubrics while recognizing that achieving total objectivity in the scoring process is impossible. To prompt the judges to score the competitors' briefs objectively, you should include the following components in the rubrics:

- a minimum total score—in other words, the lowest brief score that the judges may give to the competitors; and
- a recommended scoring range for each competency level that the competitors may achieve.

You might also consider whether the rubrics should require the judges to impose a scoring curve on the briefs that they will score.

i. Require a minimum total score.

You should set up the rubrics so that the scoring categories generate a minimum total score. For example, if a rubric is set up on a one-hundred-point scale, the rubric's scoring categories might be set up to yield a minimum total score of fifty points.

ii. Include a recommended scoring range for each competency level.

The rubrics should include a recommended scoring range for each competency level that the competitors may achieve. For instance, if the brief-scoring rubric is set up on a one-hundred-point scale, the rubric might contain instructions to the judges that—

- a *poor* brief should fall into the fifty- to fifty-nine-point range;
- an *unsatisfactory* brief should fall into the sixty- to sixty-nine-point range;
- an *average* brief should fall into the seventy- to seventy-nine-point range;
- a *good* brief should fall into the eighty- to eighty-nine-point range; and
- an *excellent* brief should fall into the ninety- to one-hundred-point range.

iii. Should you use curved scoring?

In some national competitions in which each judge scores multiple briefs, the judges are given a curve to follow when they give brief scores. While this method might be used in an internal competition, the judges in an internal competition may not end up scoring every competitor's brief. Instead, each judge might be assigned to score only a handful of briefs.

Thus, under this type of brief-scoring system, the judges will be unable to compare each brief against all the others. And if the judges are required to apply a curve to only a small set of briefs, the judges may end up giving unreasonably harsh or unreasonably good scores to the briefs in their set because the judges' only frame of reference when imposing the curve is a set of briefs that is too small to accurately represent a true curve. Hence, under this system, imposing a curve on the judges might not be workable. A curve may be applied more fairly, however, when each judge will assess every brief submitted in the competition.

d. Should the brief rubric include space for written feedback?

Finally, a good brief-scoring rubric will give the judge space in which to give written feedback to the competitors whose briefs the judge is scoring. You might even permit the judges to write comments in the briefs' margins. This feedback is particularly important if the internal competition is tied to the competitors' first-year legal-writing course because the competition might be the first time that the competitors are learning and applying persuasive writing skills. Thorough feedback will help them to know which skills they have mastered and those that they need to continue working on.

2. ORAL-ARGUMENT-SCORING RUBRICS

To create the oral-argument-scoring rubrics, you will need to consider the following things:

- which oral-argument skills the rubric should assess;
- which weights you should assign to the rubric's scoring categories;
- whether the rubric should limit the range of scores that the judges may submit; and
- whether the rubric should include space for written feedback.

a. What skills should the oral-argument rubric assess?

A good oral advocate will convey their arguments clearly, thoroughly, and logically. This advocate will also welcome questions from the bench and provide direct, thorough, and well-reasoned answers to those questions. Additionally, the advocate will do the foregoing things persuasively by evincing a sense of conviction and enthusiasm for the client's case and by avoiding annoying or distracting mannerisms. And finally, the advocate will use proper decorum during the oral argument, affording respect to the advocate's opponent and to the bench.[73]

To assess whether an oral advocate has these attributes, an oral-argument-scoring rubric for an internal competition may be broken down into the following general categories:

- *Substance and organization.* This scoring category should gauge how well the competitor knows their case and how effectively they convey their arguments on the merits. More specifically, this category should assess—
  - how well the competitor knows the record and the relevant legal authority;
  - whether they convey their contentions clearly, thoroughly, and logically; and
  - whether their argument is well organized.
- *Answering questions from the bench.* This category should assess whether the competitor directly and thoroughly answers questions from the bench. More specifically, this category should gauge whether—
  - the competitor stops talking and listens carefully when a judge asks a question;
  - the competitor's answer responds to or evades the question;
  - the competitor sufficiently explains their reasons for the answer;
  - the competitor tries to engage the entire bench with the answer; and
  - the competitor smoothly moves back into their argument after answering the question.
- *Advocacy tone.* This category should assess whether the competitor uses the proper tone in conveying their arguments. More specifically, this category should gauge

73. For a thorough discussion of good oral-advocacy skills, see generally James D. Dimitri, *Stepping Up to the Podium with Confidence: A Primer for Law Students on Preparing and Delivering an Appellate Oral Argument*, 38 Stetson L. Rev. 75 (2008); Stephanie A. Vaughan, *Experiential Learning: Moving Forward in Teaching Oral Advocacy Skills By Looking Back at the Origins of Rhetoric*, 59 S. Tex. L. Rev. 121 (2017).

whether the competitor's arguments are backed with a sense of conviction and enthusiasm.

- *Mechanics.* This category should assess the effectiveness of the competitor's forensic performance. More specifically, this category should assess whether—
  - the competitor maintains sufficient eye contact with the judges;
  - the competitor is overly reliant on notes;
  - the competitor's speaking pace is appropriate;
  - the competitor speaks loudly enough and clearly;
  - the competitor displays any annoying or distracting mannerisms, such as shifting back and forth on their feet at the lectern.
- *Decorum.* This category should assess whether the competitor maintains proper decorum during the oral argument. More specifically, this category should focus on whether—
  - the competitor manages their allotted time effectively;
  - the competitor displays the appropriate level of deference to the bench;
  - the competitor is respectful to opposing counsel;
  - the competitor's speech and mannerisms are appropriately formal, such as whether the competitor stands up straight or slouches; and
  - the competitor behaves appropriately while sitting at the counsel table—for example, whether the competitor is attentive while opposing counsel is arguing.

b. What weights should the oral-argument rubric assign to the rubric's scoring categories?

Because a real appellate court would be most concerned with the substance of the party's arguments on the merits, the oral argument's substance and organization ought to be the category that receives the most weight in the oral-argument-scoring rubric. Close behind this category in weight should be the category that focuses on how effectively the competitors answer questions from the bench. This should be so because the main reason many appellate courts set oral argument is because they wish to ask the parties questions about their positions.[74] The third most heavily weighted category should be advocacy tone because tone plays a key role in oral argument. The categories of mechanics and decorum should be given the least weight to avoid having the oral argument judges become unduly focused on style over substance.

c. Should the oral-argument rubric limit the range of scores that the judges may submit?

Because the scoring of oral arguments is likely to be just as subjective as the scoring of the briefs, the oral-argument-scoring rubrics should contain required ranges to promote objectivity in scoring. So like the brief-scoring rubrics, the oral-argument-scoring rubrics should be set up so the scoring categories generate a minimum total score that cannot fall below a certain point value. Moreover, like the brief-scoring rubrics, the oral-argument-scoring rubrics might include a recommended range for each competency level that the competitors may achieve. You could use the same recommended ranges for competency levels that you used in the brief-scoring rubric.

d. Should the oral-argument rubric include space for written feedback?

You might also provide space in the oral-argument-scoring rubric for written feedback. For practical purposes, however, you may want to forego this option because competition oral arguments are usually on a strict schedule, requiring the oral argument judges to complete their score sheets quickly. A more efficient option is a post-argument period for oral feedback from the judges about the competitors' oral arguments.

D. Creating the bench brief

Internal competition judges come from different backgrounds and varying levels of practice experience. Some may be experts in the competition problem's topic; others might have only general knowledge about the topic. And other judges may be students who are still relatively new to the law despite having previous moot court experience.

---

74. Hon. Jacques L. Wiener, Jr., *Ruminations from the Bench: Brief Writing and Oral Argument in the Fifth Circuit*, 70 TUL. L. REV. 187, 199–200 (1995).

Regardless of how familiar the judges are with the problem's topic, they need a tool to educate themselves about the aspects of the problem with which they aren't already familiar. This is where a bench brief comes into play.

1. THE BENCH BRIEF'S PURPOSE AND CONTENT

A bench brief is a confidential document that educates the competition judges about the competition problem and the relevant law so that the judges are prepared to score briefs and hear oral arguments. The bench brief usually provides an overview of the issues raised in the competition problem, the arguments that the competitors may make, and the legal authorities that the competitors should use to support their arguments.

A good bench brief will contain the following components:

- a cover page containing a confidentiality statement;
- a preliminary statement about the bench brief's purpose;
- a statement of the legal issues that the competitors will argue;
- a summary of the case's relevant facts and procedural history;
- a summary of the arguments for each side and issue;
- a detailed discussion of the arguments for each side and issue; and
- a list of sample questions that the judges might ask the competitors.[75]

a. The cover page and confidentiality statement

A bench brief usually begins with a cover page. This cover page typically contains the competition's name and the case's caption. The caption should list the parties on appeal and the court before which the appeal is pending.

The cover page's most important feature is the confidentiality statement. This statement should conspicuously note the following things:

75. The bench brief may also include a table of contents and a table of the relevant authorities.

- that the bench brief is intended only for the competition administrators and judges;
- that the bench brief's contents should not be disclosed to anyone other than the competition administrators and judges;
- that the viewing or sharing of the bench brief by or with competitors violates the competition rules and may result in a competitor's elimination from the competition;
- that anyone other than a judge or competition administrator who comes into possession of the bench brief should return it immediately to the competition administrators; and
- that the unauthorized disclosure of the bench brief violates the school's honor code (provided of course that the code deems this disclosure a violation).

b. The preliminary statement

Normally, the bench brief's cover page is followed by a preliminary statement about the bench brief's purpose. Because this purpose is to give only a general overview of the case presented in the competition problem, the preliminary statement might emphasize that the bench brief isn't intended to provide an exhaustive treatment of all arguments that the competitors might make or all authorities that might be relevant to the problem.

c. The statement of the issues

The bench brief should clearly state the legal issues raised in the problem. This issue statement should also summarize what is not at issue, particularly if the parties could have raised issues that aren't presented in the problem.

d. The summary of relevant facts and procedural history

A bench brief usually summarizes the facts that the parties will use to support their arguments and the relevant procedural occurrences leading up to the appeal. Because some judges might want access to the record of proceedings from the problem, you may also want to attach the record as an appendix to the bench brief.

e. The summary of arguments

A bench brief normally summarizes the arguments that each competitor will likely make. This summary's purpose is to orient the judges to the detailed discussion of the arguments that will follow. The summary of arguments usually focuses only on the strongest arguments for each competitor and is typically presented according to party and issue. Normally, the arguments for the petitioner/appellant are summarized first, followed by the arguments for the respondent/appellee.

The summary of arguments is also a good place to include a disclaimer noting that the competitors may make arguments not included in the bench brief, and that the judges should independently evaluate the merits of those arguments. This disclaimer might also admonish the judges not to penalize competitors for making arguments not included in the bench brief if those arguments are logical and firmly based on the relevant law and facts.

f. The detailed discussion of arguments

The summary of arguments should be followed by a detailed discussion of the arguments. This section of the bench brief will be significantly longer than the summary of the arguments. But in drafting both sections, it is important to remember the bench brief's purpose of educating the judges about the relevant legal authority and the likely arguments in the case.

Thus, the bench brief's detailed discussion of the arguments should explain only the most likely arguments that each side will make, including any distinguishing counterarguments. As in the bench brief's summary of the argument, the detailed discussion of arguments should set forth the arguments according to party and issue.

Moreover, this section of the bench brief should summarize the authorities that the competitors most likely will rely on and discuss how the competitors should use those authorities to support their arguments. Only on the most important authorities should be included.

Summaries of constitutional provisions, statutes, and administrative regulations should point the judges only to the relevant parts of those authorities. Case summaries should briefly highlight each case's facts, holding, and reasoning.

g. Sample oral argument questions

Finally, a bench brief may include a list of sample oral argument questions for the judges. These sample questions may be organized by side and issue.

The list of sample questions should be relatively short. Ideally, the sample questions should be designed to prompt further questions from the judges, not to be perceived by the judges as an exclusive list to which the judges will be limited.

Because the judges' assessments of the competitors' arguments should focus mostly on the competitors' substantive knowledge, the sample questions should focus on the merits of the issues presented in the competition problem. Avoid including sample questions that judges tend to ask when they are unprepared, or questions that address simple stylistic concerns about oral arguments, because these questions rarely add value to the competitors' educational experience. For example, if the standard of appellate review is not raised as an issue in the competition problem, don't include in the list of sample questions, "What is the standard of appellate review?"

2. THE BENCH BRIEF'S LENGTH AND FORMAT

Whether the competition judges are attorneys or real judges, they are busy people. For this reason, the longer a bench brief is, the less likely the judges are to read it. This, in turn, is bad for the competitors because it means that some judges will not be adequately prepared to do their jobs. Therefore, make the judges' jobs as easy as possible; as a general rule, a bench brief should be no longer than fifteen to twenty pages, excluding any appendices.[76]

Also, make the bench brief easy to read by using reader-friendly formatting. Avoid artsy fonts and, if possible, use 1.15 to 1.5 line spacing. Moreover, use headings and subheadings for the bench brief's sections and sub-sections to allow the judges to easily navigate the document. And consider providing the bench brief to the judges in Portable Docu-

76. This recommendation provides only a general guideline. Internal competitions involving more complex problems may certainly warrant a bench brief that is longer than fifteen to twenty pages. But keep in mind that judges are unlikely to immerse themselves in a long bench brief.

ment Format (PDF). One benefit of this format is that it will allow you to embed internal hyperlinks in the document that will permit the document's reader to navigate it quickly and easily.[77]

3. DRAFTING AND EDITING THE BENCH BRIEF

Begin drafting the bench brief as soon as the competition problem is finalized, and complete it well before the judges need to use it to score briefs and judge oral arguments. Whoever wrote the competition problem—whether that be faculty, practitioners, the moot court board, or some combination of these people—should write the bench brief because the problem writers will be familiar with the best arguments and the most relevant authorities. If students are writing the bench brief, faculty who are supervising those students should consider using the same oversight measures that were suggested previously for the problem-writing process.

Careful editing of the bench brief will improve its usefulness to the judges. Consider assigning the editing to people who did not write the bench brief, such as moot court board members who are responsible for aspects of the competition besides problem creation, and to faculty or practitioners who are unfamiliar with the competition problem and relevant authority. These editors should pay particular attention to the clarity, concision, and cohesiveness of the bench brief.

An example of an internal competition bench brief is provided in the online appendix.

E. Creating a competition website

A well-run internal competition will have a user-friendly website that the competitors and perhaps the judges will have access to. Creating this website will require you to answer two questions:

- What components should the website contain?
- What tools should you use to build the website?

---

77. For an overview of good document-design principles, see generally Butterick, *supra* note 20; Ruth Anne Robbins, *Painting with Print: Incorporating Concepts of Typographic and Layout Design into the Text of Legal Writing Documents*, 2 J. ALWD 108 (2004).

1. WHAT COMPONENTS SHOULD THE COMPETITION WEBSITE CONTAIN?

Your competition's website should contain a library for competition materials and channels of communication that you, the competitors, and the judges may use.

a. Create a library for competition materials.

The competition website should provide a virtual library for important competition materials for the competitors and the judges. This library should include the competition rules and the competition problem. It might also contain the competition schedule, the bench brief for the judges (secured, of course, from competitor access), score sheets, and links to digital forms that the judges or the competitors may have to complete (e.g., contact information, availability for oral arguments, etc.)

Each piece of information in your website's library may be contained on a separate webpage, on a single webpage as a list of hyperlinks, or in a combination of these two. For example, you could create separate webpages for competitor materials and judge materials. And on each page, you could feature links to those materials. On the page for judge materials, you could secure the links so that only users with a password could access the linked material.

b. Create channels for communicating with competitors and judges.

Your competition's website should include channels that you may use to communicate with the competitors and the judges. These channels might include the following—

- a page for announcements where you can post information that all participants need to see;
- a discussions page or an FAQ page where you can answer questions posted by competition participants in a threaded format;
- an instant-messaging application that may already be included with the digital tools that you will use to create the website; and

- a link to the email address for the competition administrators (for example, the email address for the moot court board).

2. WHAT TOOLS SHOULD YOU USE TO BUILD THE COMPETITION WEBSITE?

Building the competition website is a responsibility that you may delegate to your school's information-technology staff, or it's one that you may undertake yourself.

a. Ask your information-technology staff to build the website.

You could ask your school's information-technology staff to create a page or a series of pages on the school's main website to serve as your competition's website. At a minimum, most law schools have a webpage that contains basic information about the school's advocacy program and the competitions that the program is involved in, including any internal moot court competitions.[78]

b. Do it yourself by using your school's learning management system.

Though your school's IT staff is a great resource for creating a competition website, you may find it more efficient or convenient to use the digital tools that your school's faculty uses to create course websites. The most accessible tool will be the learning management system that your school or university has adopted. These systems include applications like Blackboard,[79] D2L Brightspace,[80] Canvas,[81] and TWEN.[82] They usually provide user-friendly templates for creating and organizing a simple

---

78. *See, e.g.*, *Legal Skills Competitions*, U. Ariz. James E. Rogers C.L., https://law.arizona.edu/legal-skills-competitions (last visited Feb. 8, 2023); *Moot Court*, IU Robert H. McKinney Sch. L., https://mckinneylaw.iu.edu/practice/moot-court/index.html (last visited Feb. 8, 2023); *Moot Court Overview*, Marq. U.L. Sch., https://law.marquette.edu/programs-degrees/moot-court-overview (last visited Feb. 8, 2023).

79. Blackboard, https://www.blackboard.com/ (last visited Feb. 8, 2023).

80. D2L, https://www.d2l.com/ (last visited Feb. 8, 2023).

81. Canvas, https://www.instructure.com/canvas (last visited Feb. 8, 2023).

82. TWEN, https://lawschool.westlaw.com/twen (last visited Feb. 8, 2023).

website; tools for securely hosting online libraries of course materials; and secure channels for virtually communicating with the website's users, such as instant messaging. For instance, Canvas's course templates have a ready-made page that instructors may use to store files. These files may then be hyperlinked in other pages that an instructor creates with the course template.[83]

Additionally, many of these learning management systems allow you to integrate external online tools that you may find useful in running a competition, such as YouTube, Zoom, and Google's suite of applications.[84] For example, if you've recorded a video of an oral-argument demonstration for the competitors, the external tools integrated into your learning management system may allow you to embed that video in the competition website that you've created.

c. Do it yourself by using other digital applications.

Your university may not allow people without a university technology account to use the school's learning management system. This may include competition judges who are not faculty members. Thus, some or perhaps all of your competition's judges may not have access to a website created with your university's learning management system.

If this is so at your school, you must explore other online tools for sharing competition materials with judges and for communicating with judges. For instance, to share competition materials, you could use a cloud-storage and file-sharing application for which your school has given you a free account, such as Google Drive,[85] Microsoft OneDrive,[86] or Dropbox.[87] With these applications, you may create secure online folders for competition materials and securely share links to those folders and materials with the judges.

Instead of using a learning management system for communicating with judges, you may use older but reliable communication methods,

---

83. *Files*, Instructure Community, https://community.canvaslms.com/t5/Instructor-Guide/tkb-p/Instructor#Files (last visited Feb. 8, 2023).

84. *See, e.g.*, *External Tools Available in Canvas*, U. Info. Tech. Servs., https://kb.iu.edu/d/aaka (last visited Feb. 8, 2023).

85. *See, e.g.*, *Storage at IU*, U. Info. Tech. Servs., https://uits.iu.edu/services/software-and-platforms/storage (last visited Feb. 8, 2023).

86. *Id.*

87. Dropbox, https://www.dropbox.com/ (last visited Feb. 8, 2023).

like phone calls, text messages, and email lists or groups. To promote efficiency, you could combine all these media into one online platform by using a centralized, instant-messaging application designed for professional or organizational communications, such as WhatsApp[88] or Slack.[89]

II. Managing the Process

Once the preliminary work has been completed, it is time to get the competition up and running. This section provides tips on managing the internal competition process, including—

- recruiting and preparing judges;
- conducting competitor orientation;
- administering the brief scoring;
- conducting the oral arguments; and
- handling announcements and awards.

A. Recruiting and preparing judges

Many complaints about internal competitions concern the quality of the judging.[90] Sometimes, this criticism is justified. Indeed, it's not unusual for some judges to come to oral arguments unprepared. Unfortunately, this lack of preparedness causes these judges to ask the competitors unhelpful questions during the oral arguments. What's more, because they're unprepared to judge, these judges may unfairly score the competitors and give bad advice to the competitors during the post-argument critiques.

And good judges aren't just needed for the oral arguments. If your competition has a briefing requirement, your brief judges also must be trained to perform their duties. In fact, because brief writing is perhaps

---

88. WhatsApp, https://www.whatsapp.com/ (last visited Feb. 8, 2023).

89. Slack, https://slack.com/ (last visited Feb. 8, 2023).

90. *See* Barbara Kritchevsky, *Judging: The Missing Piece of the Moot Court Puzzle*, 37 U. Mem. L. Rev. 45, 48 (2006) ("One aspect of moot court that is the target of frequent criticism is the lack of competence of many of the individuals who judge the rounds and critique the students' performance.").

the most important appellate advocacy skill that the competitors will be learning, the brief judges must be thoroughly prepared to adequately assess the competitors' brief-writing performances and to give constructive feedback to the competitors.

Therefore, recruiting people who are well suited to judge is one of the most important tasks facing an internal competition administrator. To perform that task, you must—

- decide whom to recruit to judge the competition;
- carry out an effective plan to recruit those people; and
- prepare the judges you have recruited to do their jobs.

1. RECRUITING EFFECTIVE JUDGES

Because an internal competition's main focus is to foster lawyering skills, the competition judges should function as teachers who promote that goal by providing a realistic and constructive experience for the competitors.[91] Hence, you should try to recruit judges who will effectively fulfill these teaching roles.

a. Whom should you invite to judge?

Optimally, your competition judges will be appellate judges and experienced appellate practitioners because they are naturally well suited to assess and critique appellate briefs and oral arguments. But at many schools, this is not a realistic goal; most attorneys have no appellate practice experience, and your school may not be close to any appellate court. In addition, your internal competition may be too large to fill every judge spot with appellate judges and attorneys.

Accordingly, your pool of potential judges needs to be broader. Filling judge spots usually is a formidable challenge—particularly in large internal competitions—so a sizeable judge pool is often necessary. Cast your judge-recruitment net as widely as reasonably possible, keeping in mind that a good judge-training program for your competition is an excellent tool for helping competition judges to fulfill their role as teachers, even if those judges are not appellate practitioners.

---

91. *Id.* at 54.

i. Invite faculty.

Of course, your school's faculty is a good source of judges. If the competition is integrated with another course, the professors who teach that course are unquestionably well suited to judge. They may even be required to judge as part of their teaching duties.

ii. Invite real judges and practitioners.

If appellate judges and attorneys are conveniently at your disposal, certainly target them too. But don't ignore real judges and practitioners whose expertise lies in other areas, especially if they practice in the areas of law on which the competition problem is based.

iii. Invite alumni.

Your school's alumni may be eager to serve as judges, particularly alumni who were on the moot court board or who competed on an external competition team. You might even tell graduating members of your school's moot court board and external competition teams that they "owe" you several years of judging after graduation, provided that those graduates stay in the area after graduation. They may take this admonition to heart and provide a solid base of new judges each year. If your school has a moot court alumni association, its membership is an excellent source of judges as well.

iv. Invite students who are members of your school's advocacy program.

Finally, in some internal competitions, students who are members of your school's advocacy program (such as moot court board members) are required to judge oral arguments. This requirement creates a ready-made pool of competition judges for you. Moreover, these students usually make excellent judges because they normally take their responsibilities seriously and are typically well prepared.

b. What special considerations should you take into account when you recruit brief judges?

If your internal competition includes a briefing requirement, you need to give special consideration to the people you recruit to score the briefs. A key difference between scoring briefs and judging oral arguments is that brief scoring is usually more time-consuming than judging oral arguments and requires the judges to give more detailed feedback than is provided in oral argument critiques.

Thus, people who are experts in giving written feedback and who are willing to invest the time necessary to score the briefs make ideal brief judges. If your competition is integrated with another course, such as legal writing or an upper-level appellate advocacy course, the professors who teach those courses are usually charged with scoring the briefs, and rightly so given their expertise in the topic and experience in giving constructive, detailed feedback. Other faculty such as clinical faculty, faculty whose teaching focus is on lawyering skills, and faculty whose academic focus is on the competition problem's topic are also well suited to score competition briefs.

If faculty are not available to score briefs, you should recruit appellate judges and practitioners if this is logistically possible. You should also consider recruiting practitioners who are experts in the area of law that you chose for the competition problem's topic. However, you should probably not assign students to judge briefs unless they are responsible only for non-substantive tasks, such as checking the briefs for proper format and citation.

2. EXECUTING AN EFFECTIVE JUDGE-RECRUITMENT PLAN

Once you know whom you want to include in your judge pool, you'll need to carry out a plan to recruit those people. The steps that should you take in executing that plan include the following:

- Share the recruiting load with others;
- Start your recruitment efforts early;
- Maintain ties with your alumni and cultivate networks within the legal community;
- Make it easy for the judges to sign up;
- Keep and update a judge database;
- Recruit enough judges to meet your judging needs; and
- Consider offering continuing legal education credit to the judges.

a. Share the recruiting load with others.

Judge recruitment is a labor- and time-intensive process. It might be the most challenging part of running an internal competition. Judge recruitment is most effectively accomplished when both the faculty and the moot court board are involved, especially when the internal competition is large and thus requires a large number of judges. Professors are able to use their contacts with their colleagues in the academy, the bench, and the bar to bring in competition judges, as are moot court board members who have built a network in the legal community through clerkships and internships. In addition, the labor can be divided and thus be made easier than if the faculty advisor or the moot court board were solely responsible for recruiting judges.

b. Start recruiting judges early.

Start recruiting judges well before the competition is scheduled to begin. How far in advance of the competition you start recruiting judges will probably depend on the competition's structure. If the competition includes a brief-writing component and some or all of the briefs will be scored by judges from outside the school, judge recruitment may need to begin as far as twelve to sixteen weeks before the competition commences. Getting this early start ensures that all brief-judge spots are filled before the competition's briefing period ends. But if the competition is only an oral advocacy competition, you might be able to wait until eight to ten weeks before the competition to begin recruiting judges.

c. Maintain ties with your alumni and cultivate networks within the legal community.

You will probably find that the deepest pool of volunteers for your internal competition will come from the legal community that is closest to your school. Of course, this pool will include alumni from your school. You should give special attention to this pool because you'll be drawing from it frequently.

i. Maintain ties with alumni.

Maintaining ties with alumni is a crucial part of recruiting judges, especially the ties that you've created with alumni who were part of your school's advocacy program while they were in law school. Thus, at the end of each academic year, obtain contact information from graduating students who were active on your school's moot court board or internal- and external-competition teams. Social networking apps like LinkedIn[92] and Facebook[93] are good sources for finding recent graduates, especially because legal employers are sometimes slow to notify the legal community about their new hires.

Your school's alumni relations office or development office might also be able to help you track down recent graduates and any other alumni you intend to target. However, you should review law school and university policies on contacting alumni before you contact them because schools often have strict rules governing who may contact alumni and when alumni may be contacted.

You might also consider creating a board of alumni advisors or a moot court alumni association for your moot court program if you don't already have such an organization. Not only can this organization help you to generate student interest in your school's moot court program; it can also help you to network with the alumni in your legal community.

ii. Network within the legal community.

Networking within the legal community is essential when recruiting judges from outside the school, such as practitioners and real judges. Consider initially contacting these people in person or by phone, particularly if a potential judge is someone you know personally. Though in-person conversations and phone calls might be considered old-fashioned, potential judges may appreciate the personal touch and may be more likely to volunteer as a result.

If in-person or phone solicitations fail to garner enough judges to fill all judge spots, consider sending email invitations to practitioners and judges in your school's legal community. If your school is located in an urban area, you may want to consider hand delivering print invitations to targeted law offices, provided that you have the resources to do so.

Just as you might use social media to maintain ties with alumni, so too can you use it to invite members of the legal community to judge in your internal competition. Because many lawyers are on LinkedIn, and

---

92. LinkedIn, https://www.linkedin.com (last visited Feb. 8, 2023).

93. Facebook, https://www.facebook.com (last visited Feb. 8, 2023).

because LinkedIn's focus is professional networking, it might be the first social media platform that you use in your effort to recruit outside judges.

Consider using your state and local bar associations to help you recruit judges, particularly if those organizations have appellate practice sections that can help you target appellate practitioners in your legal community. If your state or local bar association or your legal community publishes print or digital periodicals, such as newspapers, magazines, or electronic newsletters, consider advertising for judges in those forums.

Finally, your school's dean may be able to help you in your networking efforts. Your dean might even have specific practitioners or judges in mind for you to recruit to sit on the panel in your competition's final round.

d. Make signing up to judge easy.

The people whom you invite to judge should be able to register to do so easily. Thus, make it easy for them by directing them to conveniently accessible sign-up sheets. Online survey applications, such as Google Forms,[94] Qualtrics,[95] and Survey Monkey,[96] provide user-friendly tools to create these sign-up sheets. Your university may even offer faculty members a free account for one or more of these applications, or your school's learning management system may have a built-in sign-up-sheet tool that you may use to create registration forms. The judge-registration forms that you create with these apps may then be linked on or embedded in your competition website, or they may be distributed through other online channels such as email.

e. Keep and update a judge database.

After someone agrees to judge, get their contact information, including business or home address, email address, and phone number. Additionally, keep an up-to-date database of potential judges and judges who have previously volunteered. Creating this database can be made easier

---

94. GOOGLE FORMS, https://www.google.com/forms/about/ (last visited Feb. 8, 2023).

95. QUALTRICS, https://www.qualtrics.com/ (last visited Feb. 8, 2023).

96. SURVEY MONKEY, https://www.surveymonkey.com/ (last visited Feb. 8, 2023).

by using one of the online survey applications noted above. Your school's information technology staff might be able to help you use the app to route the judges' contact information to the database and to help you effectively organize the database.

The database may then be passed on to new competition administrators from year to year. Before you pass on the database, make sure that you update it with new contact information if that information changes for any judges. Furthermore, the database may be used to flag any judges who should not be invited back to judge in the future—for instance, judges who were unprepared or were hostile to competitors. Finally, you should counsel any students who have access to the database, such as students on your school's moot court board, that they must keep the information in the database confidential.

f. Recruit enough judges to meet your judging needs.

Because judging is inherently subjective, using multiple judges to score each brief and each oral round may promote a more objective scoring process. However, determining the number of judges needed for each of these two competition components requires a somewhat different approach.

i. How many brief judges do you need to promote objective scoring?

If your competition includes a briefing requirement and is integrated with another course, the professors who teach that course usually are required to score the briefs as part of their teaching duties. These professors likely have extensive experience in grading and critiquing student papers. What's more, they likely are experts in the competition problem's subject matter because they probably wrote the problem. Therefore, they almost assuredly will be more objective and insightful in scoring briefs than an outside brief judge who is not accustomed to assessing student work. So in this situation, recruiting multiple judges to score each brief probably isn't necessary to promote objectivity in the scoring process.

In addition, when only faculty serve as brief judges, only a few people may be necessary to score a large number of briefs, thereby promoting more consistency in the scoring process. For example, if the competition has fifty competitors and two faculty members are teaching the course, these professors can split the workload by each scoring twenty-five briefs.

But if the competition has a briefing requirement and isn't tethered to another course, recruiting multiple judges to score each brief will probably make the brief-scoring process more objective than if only one judge were recruited to score each brief. In this situation, three judges per brief might be necessary to promote objectivity, particularly if judges from outside the school are used. This is because these judges probably won't be accustomed to scoring and critiquing student work.

Under this system, the three judges' scores could be averaged to offset the score of any judge among the three who gave the brief an unusually high or low score. Or, if the competition has a small number of competitors, thus requiring a relatively small number of judges, five judges per brief could be employed to inject even more objectivity into the scoring. That's because under a five-judge system, the highest and lowest brief scores for each brief could be dropped, and the remaining three could be averaged to arrive at the final brief score.[97]

To reduce the number of brief judges that you need to recruit when you have multiple judges score each brief, you may assign each brief judge multiple briefs to score. To determine the number of brief judges needed under this system, you should first determine the number of brief-judge spots that you must fill. Then, you should divide the number of brief-judge spots that you must fill by the number of briefs that each judge will be assigned to score. This will yield the total number of judges required.[98]

You also should recruit auxiliary brief judges to step in in case some judges fail to fulfill their responsibilities. Have them ready to step in before brief scores are due so they'll have enough time to score the briefs and return those scores to you. Faculty usually serve as the best auxiliary

---

97. If you would like to add yet another layer of objectivity to the brief scoring under a multiple-judge system, you could also require the rescoring of any brief whose initial score is more than two standard deviations from the average brief score.

98. For instance, if the competition has twenty competitors and three judges will score each brief, sixty brief-judge spots will be required (twenty briefs x three judges per brief = sixty brief-judge spots). This means that if each brief judge were assigned to score only one brief, sixty judges would be needed (sixty brief-judge spots ÷ one brief per judge = sixty judges). However, if each brief judge were assigned five briefs to score, only twelve brief judges would be needed (sixty brief-judge spots ÷ five briefs per judge = twelve judges).

brief judges because they will be more readily accessible than outside judges.

In the end, whichever brief-scoring system you use will largely depend on the circumstances facing your school. If your school is in an area without ready access to outside judges, it might be best to tie your internal competition to another course so the professors who teach that course can score the briefs. Or if you anticipate having difficulty recruiting good-quality outside judges and you can't have faculty score briefs, you may decide to forego a brief-writing requirement altogether, especially if the competitors have already received brief-writing instruction in previous courses or clinical settings.

ii. How many oral argument judges do you need to promote objective scoring?

In many internal competitions, preliminary-round panels are composed of three judges, and the elimination rounds have panels that are larger—often at least five judges. If the competition is large and requires a large number of judges, you may want to go with three-judge panels to make the judge-recruiting task easier. Whatever number of judges you choose for each panel, that number ought to be an odd number, especially if the winner of any oral round is determined by the panel's majority vote. And in any case, you should never have one-judge panels because one-judge panels jeopardize the fairness of the scoring.

To determine the number of oral argument judges needed, take the number of competitors/teams and divide that number by two to get the number of arguments. Then, multiply the number of arguments by three (or by a larger odd number if you've decided to use more than three judges per argument) to get the number of judge spots that you need to fill. This may not be the actual number of judges that you need because you may be able to use some judges for multiple arguments. So count only the number of judge spots that you must fill, not the number of people that you would need if you were to require each judge to judge only one argument.[99]

99. For example, if the competition includes twenty competitors/teams, there will be ten arguments in each preliminary round. Therefore, if three-judge panels will judge each round, thirty judge spots will need to be filled for each round.

For the preliminary rounds and the elimination rounds before the final round, recruit standby judges to cover unexpected no-shows, to resolve judge/competitor conflicts of interest, and to avoid using the same judge twice for the same competitor/team during the competition. If possible, recruit at least one alternate judge for each oral argument in the competition. Faculty and moot court board members make good alternate judges because they are probably already in the building and are not driving from a distant location.

For the competition's final elimination round, try to recruit appellate judges in your jurisdiction to provide the competitors with a memorable and valuable experience. Persuading members of the judiciary to judge the final round can be a simple task as long as the judges are asked well before the final round. Because last-minute conflicts are common with appellate judges, you may want to schedule at least seven judges, knowing that you will be fine if you end up with only five. Another alternative is to schedule a standby judge or two for the final round. The best standby judges may be those affiliated with the law school, such as the dean or a nationally known scholar who has expertise in the competition problem's topic.

g. Consider offering continuing legal education credit.

Some potential judges may be enticed to volunteer if they are given the opportunity to earn continuing legal education for their judging duties. Some states will offer CLE credit to competition judges. If you're interested in offering judges this credit, check with your state bar association or state commission for continuing legal education for the requirements in your state.

Before your state will award CLE credit to competition judges, it may require you to train the judges in the competition's subject matter. This training may take place in CLE sessions in which you discuss with the judges the legal issues presented in the competition, the logistics of the competition, the judging criteria, and the critiquing of the competitors. What is more, your state likely will require you to distribute written materials in these sessions, such as the competition problem, the bench brief, and the score sheets.

3. PREPARING THE JUDGES

As mentioned above, well-prepared judges are crucial to an internal competition's success. To some competition judges, scoring briefs and judging oral arguments are nothing new. For example, some judges may be faculty who have experience as practitioners and as teachers of advocacy skills. Other judges may be moot court board members who have judged oral arguments before. Still other judges may be local practitioners who have judged for you year after year. You will not need to spend much time preparing these judges for the competition.

Yet many judges are new to the process. Or the competition procedures may have changed in some way compared to the procedures for a previous year's edition of the competition. And of course, each new edition of the competition brings a different competition problem. Hence, judges who return after having judged in a previous edition of the competition will not be familiar with the new procedures or the law involved in the new competition problem.

Therefore, at some point before the judges score briefs and judge oral arguments, you must give them the materials that they'll need to prepare to judge. In the same vein, you should consider holding training sessions for the judges in how they are to fulfill their judging responsibilities.

a. What materials will the judges need to prepare?

Before judging, the judges will need to know the following things:

- the competition problem's substance;
- the arguments that the competitors probably will make in their briefs and oral arguments;
- the competition's format;
- the competition's scoring system; and
- the procedures that they'll need to follow when they judge.

To inform the judges about these things, you should give them the following materials:

- the competition problem, including the record of proceedings;
- the bench brief, which will summarize the issues, the relevant law, and the competitors' best arguments;

- the competition rules, which should familiarize the judges with the competition's format;
- the scoring rubrics, which will show them the criteria upon which the competitors will be assessed; and
- to the extent that the judging procedures are not specifically discussed in the competition rules, a set of written judging guidelines that will give the judges a summary of how they're to do their jobs.[100]

b. How do you effectively disseminate judge materials?

If your competition has a briefing requirement, the judging materials should be distributed to each brief judge as soon as possible after the competitors have submitted their briefs. This timeline ensures that the brief judges have enough time to score the briefs and submit their scores to you. These materials should also be distributed to each oral argument judge at least five to seven days before the oral arguments begin so the oral argument judges have enough time to prepare for these arguments. Ideally, you should digitally distribute the materials to your judges. Consult the tips discussed in Part I on creating a competition website for ideas on digital distribution channels.

Carefully monitor to whom the bench brief is given. Do not distribute the bench brief to moot court board members except for the bench brief's authors, the moot court board presiding officer, and any board members who serve as judges. Minimizing the number of people who have access to the bench brief decreases the risk of the brief falling into the wrong hands, either intentionally or unintentionally. Remind students who have access to the bench brief not to make personal copies of it and not to leave hard copies lying around the law school. And remind them not to post the bench brief in unsecured online forums, such as social media.

100. As an example of written judging guidelines, the Legal Writing Institute's Model Oral Argument Judging Guidelines are included in the online appendix.

c. Should you hold training sessions for the judges?

i. In-person and synchronous-online training sessions

In addition to giving the judges written judging materials, you may offer them an in-person training session. In this session, you might discuss the competition problem's subject matter, the competition's procedures, and the scoring process for briefs and for oral arguments.

You may repeat the training session at different times for the judges' convenience, especially if you believe that you won't be able to get all judges to attend a single session. Or you could offer it as a synchronous online session for everyone's convenience, using a videoconferencing application such as Zoom.[101] You could even offer the session as a hybrid experience, giving the judges the option of attending in-person or attending online.

If you hold an in-person training session, you should keep extra hard copies of the written judging materials on hand in case some judges have misplaced their materials before the session. If the session includes CLE credit, you may have to monitor attendance because you may have to verify the attendees' participation in the session in order for them to receive CLE credit.

ii. Asynchronous training sessions

As another alternative, you could record the judge-training session on video and post that video on the webpage for judges on your competition website. For instance, if you use your school's learning management system to create your website, you should be able to embed digital videos on that website.[102] This method of training will create flexibility for the judges because they will be able to view the session at their convenience.

Of course, you should restrict access to the video so that only competition administrators and judges may access it, perhaps by creating a password-protected page on your website. And if you intend to offer CLE credit to attendees, you should check your state's attorney-licensing

---

101. Zoom, https://zoom.us/ (last visited Feb. 8, 2023).

102. As an example, Indiana University Robert H. McKinney School of Law's learning management system, Canvas, integrates the digital video application Kaltura. Kaltura, https://corp.kaltura.com/ (last visited Feb. 8. 2023). With Kaltura, a user may record a video in digital format, edit that video, and post the video on Canvas.

rules to see whether those rules allow CLE credit to be given for asynchronous courses. If credit is allowed, you'll have to use a video application that allows you to monitor whether and when someone has viewed the video so that you may certify viewers to receive CLE credit.

iii. When to offer training sessions

For oral argument judges, you may offer training sessions as late as the day on which they are scheduled to judge, though you may certainly offer training sooner than this. However, training sessions for the brief judges must be held well before the oral argument rounds because you will need the competitors' brief scores before the oral rounds begin. You could, for example, hold your training for brief judges three weeks to a month before the oral rounds take place.

d. Addressing implicit bias in oral argument judging

i. The effects of implicit bias on competitors

The existence of implicit bias in oral argument judging is well documented. Research shows that judges generally prefer competitors who use oral argument styles that reflect masculine traits, particularly white male traits.[103] Thus, competitors who do not reflect these traits—women, people of color, and LGBTQ+ people, for instance—may be singled out for criticism by the judges.[104] For example, judges criticize women for using "vocal fry"[105] more often than they criticize men for using it.[106]

Of course, the stereotypes perpetuated by implicit bias may cause judges to give lower oral argument scores to competitors who don't conform to those stereotypes than to competitors who conform to them.[107] Moreover, the competitors' growth as advocates may be thwarted when

---

103. *See generally* Michael J. Higdon, *Oral Advocacy and Vocal Fry: The Unseemly, Sexist Side of Nonverbal Persuasion*, 13 LEGAL COMMC'N & RHETORIC 209 (2016); Susie Salmon, *Reconstructing the Voice of Authority*, 51 AKRON L. REV. 143 (2017).

104. *Id.*

105. "Vocal fry is the lowest register (tone) of your voice characterized by its deep, creaky, breathy sound." *What is Vocal Fry?*, JOHNS HOPKINS MED., https://www.hopkinsmedicine.org/health/conditions-and-diseases/is-vocal-fry-ruining-my-voice (last visited Feb. 8, 2023).

106. Higdon, *supra* note 103, at 212, 213.

107. *See, e.g.*, Lind-Martinez, *supra* note 21, at 126–27.

they receive feedback based on implicit bias.[108] And when that growth comes to a halt, they will lose further opportunities to develop their lawyering skills—the very skills that their future clients will rely upon them for.[109]

ii. Constructively addressing implicit bias

Given the harm that damaging stereotypes inflict upon competitors, adopting measures to reduce implicit bias among your competition's judges will be among the most important tasks that you should undertake in running your competition. To be sure, it will be a challenging task because you may struggle to find enough judges to volunteer in the first place. And those who do volunteer probably have long-held and deeply ingrained beliefs about what good oral advocacy is—beliefs that they may want to cling to.[110] And confronting implicit bias, which some judges will be completely unaware of unless they've explored their own implicit biases before, may even cause some judges to react defensively.

Despite this challenge, below are some constructive and concrete steps that you can take to prevent judges from indulging their implicit bias when they judge oral arguments. Fortunately, you may already have taken some of these steps to address other areas of concern in your competition. Thus, you may find that addressing implicit bias among your judges may be a little less challenging than you anticipated.

- *Recruit a diverse pool of judges.*

To the extent that you can, recruit a diverse pool of judges.[111] If there are diversity-oriented bar organizations in your area, ask them to help you in your recruitment drive. For instance, ask them to put out a call for judges in their newsletter or in postings on their email listserv.

- *Incorporate implicit bias training into your judge materials and judge-training sessions.*

---

108. *See* Salmon, *supra* note 103, at 163–74 (discussing the ways that implicit bias hinders competitors' growth as advocates).

109. *Id.*

110. *Id.* at 183.

111. Lind-Martinez, *supra* note 21, at 142.

If the judges are aware of their own implicit biases, they may avoid acting on them.[112] Thus, consider incorporating advice and resources on recognizing implicit bias into your judging materials and your judge-training sessions.[113]

- *Encourage the judges to focus their assessments on substance instead of style.*

Get the judges to focus their scoring and critiques on the substance of competitors' oral arguments rather than on the competitors' argument styles. Some methods of achieving this are the following:

  - Use weighted scoring in the scoring rubrics.

As recommended previously in this chapter, create scoring rubrics that give the most weight to the competitors' knowledge of the law, knowledge of the facts, and ability to give thorough substantive answers to the judges' questions.[114]

  - Include warnings in the judging materials.

Include express warnings in the judging materials, including the score sheets, that judges should not deduct points allotted to the substance of a competitor's argument simply because the competitor made minor style mistakes.[115] Likewise, include an express admonition that discourages judges from commenting on or unduly focusing on the competitors' attire or physical appearances during the arguments and the critiques.[116]

  - Encourage the judges to consider real-world consequences.

---

112. Salmon, *supra* note 103, at 186.

113. *Id.*; *see also* Lind-Martinez, *supra* note 21, at 141 ("To ensure anti-racist instruction, law schools should first provide training to make volunteer judges, instructors, and competitors in Moot Court competitions aware of their implicit biases.").

114. Salmon, *supra* note 103, at 184.

115. *Id.* at 186.

116. *Id.*

Remind the judges that their assessments of the competitors should be based on "how much the advocate's argument would assist a real court in arriving at a just decision."[117]

- Make it easy for the judges to grasp the problem's substance.

Create a problem with legal issues that the judges can easily understand.[118] Similarly, avoid creating a problem with a complex procedural posture or history.

B. Orienting the competitors

At the outset of an internal competition, the competitors will need to know what lies ahead of them. Thus, you should hold one or more orientation sessions to prepare the competitors for the competition. If the competition is integrated with another course, these sessions may be built into the class schedule.

The orientation should discuss the following topics:

- *The competition problem.* Give a basic overview of the competition problem, including a summary of the issues presented and a brief discussion of the case underlying the competition problem.
- *The competition rules.* Distribute the competition rules and provide a brief overview of the format, procedures, and scoring methodology for the competition.
- *The competition calendar.* Give the competitors the competition calendar so they will know any deadlines—such as the deadline to submit their briefs—and the oral argument schedule.
- *Future moot court opportunities.* Discuss future opportunities for moot court experiences, such as external competitions and moot-court-board service.

Competitor orientation is also an ideal time for you to answer questions that the competitors may have about the competition.

117. *Id.* at 185.

118. *Id.*

C. Administering the brief scoring

Your system for administering the brief-scoring portion of your competition should include the following components:

- the system that the competitors must use to submit their briefs to you for scoring;
- the system that you will use to distribute the briefs and the scoring materials to the brief judges;
- the possible assignment of some brief-scoring duties to the moot court board; and
- the system that the brief judges will use to submit brief scores to you.

1. BRIEF-SUBMISSION REQUIREMENTS FOR THE COMPETITORS

If your internal competition has a briefing requirement, the competition rules will set a brief-submission deadline. For your and the competitors' convenience, and to reflect modern law practice, you should require the competitors to submit their briefs online. The learning management systems discussed above in Part I usually have templates for creating secure online drop boxes that competitors may use to submit their briefs. Or, with an online file-sharing application, you may create secure online folders to which competitors may upload their briefs.

Your competition rules might also require the competitors to submit their briefs anonymously. This is usually done by having the competitors identify themselves in their briefs by a randomly assigned ID number. If your competition uses outside brief judges, you may require anonymous brief submissions to prevent bias that could arise should a brief judge learn a competitor's identity.[119]

119. *But see* Lind-Martinez, *supra* note 21, at 130–31 (arguing that anonymous brief-scoring in moot court may perpetuate the myth of a color-blind society by preventing judges from seeing competitor names that mark their racial or ethnic identity, thus depriving the legal community of an opportunity to confront and constructively address the myth and its deleterious effects on the legal system).

2. DISTRIBUTING BRIEFS AND SCORING MATERIALS TO BRIEF JUDGES

After the competitors have submitted their briefs, the briefs must be distributed to the brief judges. With the briefs, you should give the judges the scoring materials, such as scoring rubrics, that the judges did not receive during training sessions that you may have previously conducted.

a. Distribution to faculty judges

If the competition is integrated with another course and the faculty teaching that course are scoring the briefs, getting the briefs to those professors is easy. In this situation, the professors can use the learning management system that they're using for the course website to create drop boxes to which the competitors must submit their briefs. Then, the professors may download the briefs from the drop boxes.

b. Distribution to outside judges

If you are using outside judges to score the briefs, you may have to create a different system to disseminate the briefs to those judges. For example, you could email the briefs to the judges. Or you could use a cloud-based file-storage application to upload the briefs to secure online folders to which only the judges have access. From there, the judges could download the briefs.

c. Distribution timing

Distribute the briefs and scoring materials as soon as possible after the competitors have submitted their briefs. The time required for the brief scoring to be completed will depend on the number of briefs each judge has been given to score. For instance, if a single faculty member is scoring twenty-five briefs, that faculty member will probably need several weeks to complete the scoring, particularly if the professor must give detailed written feedback to each competitor. By contrast, an outside judge scoring five briefs may need only a week or two to complete their job.

3. ASSIGNING SCORING DUTIES TO THE MOOT COURT BOARD

Consider using moot court board members to score citations and technical portions of the briefs. These portions may include the brief's cover page, its tables of contents and authorities, and its formatting. By doing this, you will relieve some of the burden on the brief judges, who will need to focus only on substance and organization. Further, you will provide more consistency in the scoring process.

4. SUBMITTING THE BRIEF SCORES

If the competitors' brief scores will not be used to determine their advancement through the oral-argument stage of the competition, the brief judges will not need to submit their scores before the oral rounds begin. If, however, the brief scores will be factored into the oral rounds, the brief judges must submit those scores before the oral rounds begin. In this circumstance, require the judges to submit their scores at least a week to ten days before the oral arguments begin. This will provide you with a buffer period in which to call in standby judges to score briefs should any outside judges fail to timely submit their brief scores. It will also give you time to sort out mathematical errors that may have occurred during scoring and time to enter the brief scores into the tabulation spreadsheets that will be used during the oral arguments.

If you're working with outside brief judges, the most convenient method of score submission for them will be by email or by a secure file-sharing folder that you've made available to them online. Always check the brief-scoring rubrics upon submission to make sure that the judges have completed them correctly.

D. Conducting the oral arguments

Your system for administering your competition's oral arguments should include the following components:

- a system for reserving rooms for the oral arguments and for the administrative tasks that you will need to perform during the argument rounds;

- a system for scheduling the oral arguments, including accommodations for competitors and judges;
- a system for matching competitors against each other in each oral argument round;
- a system for running the rounds, including directing judges to their assigned rooms and tabulating the scores;
- a system for handling protests; and
- a plan for dealing with unexpected emergencies.

1. RESERVING ROOMS FOR ORAL ARGUMENTS AND ADMINISTRATIVE TASKS

Your school's building is probably a very busy place. Rooms are likely to be taken quickly for classes, student organization meetings, and other law school events.

Because you should create the best possible experience for the competitors and the judges, you must carefully consider the physical space that you'll need to conduct the competition's oral arguments.

Generally, you'll need rooms for two purposes:

- the oral arguments; and
- administrative tasks.

a. Reserving rooms for oral arguments

i. Reserve a sufficient number of rooms in your building.

To ensure that you'll have enough rooms for oral arguments, contact your building's facility manager several months before the oral argument rounds begin to reserve those rooms. Check in again a few weeks before the oral rounds to verify you still have those rooms reserved.

If room availability for the arguments is an issue, be creative. Unused offices, conference rooms, computer labs, classrooms, library study rooms, and seminar rooms can often be used for oral arguments.

Finally, if you don't plan to limit the number of competitors who are eligible to compete, set a deadline for competitors to register to participate in the competition. By doing so, you'll give yourself ample time to reserve additional rooms and dates for oral arguments in case the number of competitors exceeds your original expectations.

ii. Consider outside venues.

You might explore whether a local courthouse will let you use courtrooms for oral arguments. If you pursue this option, note that you probably won't have access to the courtrooms during the court's normal operating hours. Therefore, you'll have to schedule arguments for times when the courthouse is closed. Because of this, you may have to pay for the time of any court personnel necessary to oversee your use of the courthouse, such as security personnel.

iii. Reserve a special venue for the final elimination round.

In most competitions, the final elimination round is a ceremonious event to which many people are invited. If convenient, you might schedule the final round during a school day in a large classroom or in your school's courtroom to encourage students to attend. Or to inject some realism and ceremony into the occasion, you may schedule the final round at one of your jurisdiction's appellate courts, provided that your school is near the court and that the court is willing to accommodate your request to stage the final round there.

b. Reserving rooms for administrative tasks

You should also reserve a room for a judges' lounge where the judges may check in upon arrival at the building, have refreshments, and receive training before the arguments. If your building has a faculty lounge, this room probably will be ideal to serve as the judges' lounge.

If your moot court board doesn't already have its own office, reserve a room that the board may use as its competition headquarters. There, the board may perform administrative tasks such as tabulating scores and handling any protests that may arise.

2. SCHEDULING THE ORAL ARGUMENTS

When it comes time for you to schedule the oral arguments, you'll need to include the following considerations in your scheduling plan:

- allowing for scheduling accommodations for competitors and judges;
- possibly scheduling multiple rounds and heats during each day of the competition;

- handling cancellations and rescheduling;
- examining how much time each oral argument will take, including scoring and post-argument critiques; and
- including a buffer period between each oral argument round.

a. Accommodate the competitors' class schedules and personal schedules.

i. Consider the competitors' class schedules.

You should require competitors to tell you their class schedules so that you don't schedule them to give oral arguments when they must attend classes. For example, some schools have a part-time division that may offer most of its classes during evenings. To accommodate part-time students, you could schedule oral arguments for a single weekend or during several weekends. For instance, you could stage the preliminary rounds on a Friday, including the announcement of the teams advancing to the elimination stage. Then, the elimination rounds could be held on Saturday (and on Sunday if need be).

Alternatively, you could hold some rounds on weeknights after evening classes have concluded. Keep in mind, however, that some judges may be unwilling or unable to judge late-evening rounds.

ii. Consider the competitors' personal obligations.

When you set the oral argument schedule, you should consider the competitors' personal obligations, such as family responsibilities and religious observances. Permit competitors to ask that they not be scheduled for rounds during certain times or days because of unavoidable conflicts due to these obligations.

Require competitors who ask for scheduling accommodations to explain in detail the reason that they're asking for an accommodation. This may discourage competitors from making frivolous accommodation requests. For example, you may refuse a competitor's request for a scheduling accommodation because the competitor wants to attend a concert yet grant a competitor's request for an accommodation because the competitor has a scheduling conflict due to childcare obligations.

b. Accommodate the judges' professional and personal schedules.

To recruit an adequate number of judges, you'll need to consider their professional and personal schedules when you schedule oral arguments. For instance, some faculty may balk at having to judge arguments in the evenings after they've been in the building all day teaching class and attending to scholarly or administrative obligations. Or they may have unavoidable personal obligations in the evenings, just as some competitors may have. So to encourage faculty participation, you might schedule some rounds during the day, when faculty are more likely to be in the building.

Because of their professional obligations, members of the bench and bar may not be available to judge oral arguments during the day. Thus, you might consider scheduling some arguments in the evenings or on weekends to give local attorneys and judges an opportunity to participate.

c. Determine how you will handle cancellations and dropouts.

In internal competitions, the unexpected can occur and often does. Indeed, you can count on competitors becoming ill before they are due to argue. Some competitors might even drop out of the competition for personal reasons. Thus, you should decide how you will handle cancellations and dropouts.

If a competitor has to miss an argument for a bona fide reason, such as an illness, consider whether you'll allow the competitor to make up the argument by rescheduling it, or whether you will require the competitor to forfeit the round. Similarly, determine what you will do if a team makes it to an elimination round and one team member drops out. Your choices include allowing the remaining competitor to continue while arguing both issues or automatically eliminating a team if a team member drops out.

d. Consider scheduling multiple rounds or heats on each day of the competition.

If circumstances permit, consider scheduling multiple oral argument rounds during a single day or evening. For example, you may schedule the first preliminary-round arguments at 6:00 p.m. and the second at 8:00 p.m., thus completing the entire preliminary stage of the competition in one evening.

If the number of preliminary-round arguments exceeds the number of rooms available at one time, you might divide each round into two heats. Under this scheme, half of the competitors would argue in the first heat and the other half would argue in the second.

Scheduling all preliminary rounds and heats on one day also permits judges to judge multiple rounds or heats, which reduces the number of judges that you must recruit. If judges are used in multiple rounds or heats, you should try to ensure that no judge sees the same competitors more than once to promote fairness.

e. Consider each argument's duration, including the post-argument assessment period.

To set the oral argument schedule, you must also determine how long each oral argument round will last. Most competitions allot fifteen minutes of argument time per competitor. If the competition is team-based with two-person teams, each oral argument will last an hour. In an individual-based competition, where each argument is one competitor versus one competitor, each oral argument will last only thirty minutes.

In either situation, the judges will need time to complete the scoring rubrics and to give feedback after the argument. This post-argument process may take anywhere from fifteen to thirty minutes. Therefore, in a team-based competition, an entire round may last from seventy-five to ninety minutes, including the post-argument process; in an individual-based competition, an entire round may last from forty-five minutes to an hour.

Because your competition probably will be on a tight schedule, you should limit the time that the judges have to complete their scoring rubrics and post-argument critiques. For instance, you might plan to allot fifteen minutes for post-argument scoring and critique in an individual-based competition and thirty minutes in a team-based competition.

f. Include a buffer period between rounds.

Whatever time limit you impose for post-argument scoring and critique, include a buffer period between rounds to give yourself time to attend to logistical matters. These matters include having the competitors choose a side for the next argument (which will be discussed in more detail below), allowing the moot court board to tabulate the scores from the round, and giving the competitors and judges time to find the rooms for the next round of arguments. The buffer period should be at least fifteen minutes long, though you might need more time depending on the number of tasks that you need to accomplish between rounds.

3. DETERMINING THE ORAL ARGUMENT MATCHUPS

When setting the oral argument schedule, you must also determine the method that you'll use to match the competitors against one another for each round of the competition. For the purposes of the following discussion of different matching schemes, assume that the competition pits individual advocates against one another, though these schemes also will work if the competition pits two-person teams against one another.

You should consider the following principles when you determine oral argument matchups:

- how many times you should schedule each competitor to argue during the preliminary rounds;
- whether you should require each competitor to switch argument sides during the preliminary rounds;
- whether you should match competitors against each other more than once during the preliminary rounds;
- whether you will randomly match competitors during the preliminary rounds, or whether you will match them by "power protecting" some competitors;
- how many competitors you will choose to advance to the competition's elimination rounds;
- which competitors you will choose to advance to the elimination rounds;
- how you should match competitors when you have an odd number of competitors;
- how you will match competitors during the elimination rounds; and
- how you should break ties when a round requires a winner.

a. How many times should you schedule competitors to argue in the preliminary rounds?

As recommended in Part I of this chapter, you should schedule competitors to argue at least twice in the preliminary rounds. You may, however, schedule more than two preliminary rounds if that is logistically feasible for your school. For example, you may schedule three or four preliminary rounds. This is useful if you wish to increase the likelihood that the most-skilled competitors will advance to the elimination rounds by giving those competitors more opportunities to display their skills in the preliminary rounds.

b. Should you require the competitors to switch argument sides during the preliminary rounds?

As recommended in Part I of this chapter, you should schedule each competitor to argue each side of the case at least once in the preliminary rounds. If your competition has a briefing requirement, this may be accomplished by having all competitors argue on brief in the first preliminary round and off brief in the second preliminary round.

If you schedule further preliminary rounds beyond the second round, you may—

- continue to require competitors to argue a specific side (e.g., you may require them to argue on brief a second time);
- randomly determine argument sides; or
- assign sides according to a coin toss, with the higher-seeded competitor calling the toss, and the competitor winning the toss choosing which side they wish to argue.

c. Should you match competitors against each other more than once during the preliminary rounds?

If it is logistically feasible for your competition, you should match the competitors so that they do not argue against each other more than once in the preliminary rounds. Doing so promotes fairness because competitors aren't forced to face anyone to whom they've previously lost a round.

d. Should you use random matchups or "power-protected" matchups?

If your preliminary rounds require the suggested minimum of two arguments for each competitor, competitors may be matched against one another in each preliminary round using one of the following two methods:

i. Random matchups

Competitors may be randomly matched in each round. This approach is the easier of the two matchup methods and is best used if your competition doesn't include a briefing requirement, though some competitions use random matching even when the competition has a briefing requirement.

ii. Power-protected matchups

If your competition includes a briefing requirement, the competitors may be "power protected" in each round according to their brief scores. The term "power protecting" refers to the process of seeding each round so that competitors with high brief scores are matched against competitors with low brief scores, thus "protecting" the high-scoring competitors by increasing the likelihood that they will win the round.

For example, if your competition has a sixteen-competitor field and you use power-protected matchups, the first preliminary round would pit the competitor with the best petitioner brief (petitioner seed 1) against the competitor with the worst respondent brief (respondent seed 8), the competitor with the second-best petitioner brief (petitioner seed 2) against the competitor with the second-worst respondent brief (respondent seed 7), etc. On the whole, the first-round matchups, in which all competitors would be arguing on brief, would look like the following:[120]

120. In this and the remaining tables used to illustrate matchups, each competitor is labeled according to the side of the case the competitor briefed and the seed the competitor received through power protection. For instance, "P1" refers to the competitor who briefed the case for the petitioner and received the top seed for the petitioner. Similarly, "R8" refers to the competitor who briefed the case for the respondent and received the eighth seed for the respondent.

Preliminary Round 1		
Arguing as Petitioner		Arguing as Respondent
P1	v.	R8
P2	v.	R7
P3	v.	R6
P4	v.	R5
P5	v.	R4
P6	v.	R3
P7	v.	R2
P8	v.	R1

Keep in mind that the competitors may have to switch sides in the second preliminary round so that they're arguing off brief. In addition, ideally, competitors should not be scheduled to argue against the same competitor that they argued against in the first round. And to maintain power-protected matchups for the second preliminary round, you must continue to pit competitors with higher brief scores against those with lower brief scores. So using a sixteen-competitor field as an example again, power-protected matchups for the second round might look like this:

Preliminary Round 2		
Arguing as Petitioner		Arguing as Respondent
R1	v.	P7
R2	v.	P8
R3	v.	P5
R4	v.	P6
R5	v.	P3
R6	v.	P4
R7	v.	P1
R8	v.	P2

e. How should you determine the number of competitors that will advance to the elimination rounds?

Once you have organized the preliminary-round matchups, you must determine how many competitors will advance to the elimination rounds. The number of advancing competitors should be divisible by four. Thus, you may choose to advance four, eight, or sixteen competitors.

The number that you choose will depend largely on the number of competitors in the entire competition field. For example, if thirty-two students are competing, you may opt to advance eight or sixteen of them to the elimination rounds. By contrast, if only eight students are competing, you could choose to advance only four of them.

f. How should you determine which competitors will advance to the elimination rounds?

After you've determined how many competitors will advance to the elimination rounds, you must determine which competitors will advance to the elimination rounds. Whether a competitor advances to the elimination rounds is determined by ranking the competitors based on their performance in the preliminary rounds. This ranking may be achieved through two alternative methods:

- *Win-loss record.* A winner is declared for each preliminary-round argument, and the competitors with the best win-loss records in the preliminary rounds advance to the elimination rounds.
- *Highest scores.* A winner for each preliminary-round argument is not declared. Instead, the competitors with the highest total scores or highest average scores through the preliminary rounds advance to the elimination rounds.

i. Advancement based on win-loss record

Under the first matching scheme, the competitors' advancement from the preliminary rounds to the elimination rounds of the competition is based on win-loss record. So for example, if you have chosen to advance eight competitors from the preliminary rounds to the elimination rounds, the eight competitors with the best win-loss records advance.

- *How should you determine a round's winner?*

Who wins a round may be determined under one of two methods:

  - The competitor who received the higher aggregate oral argument score from the judges wins; or
  - The competitor who received the higher average oral argument score from the judges wins.[121]

If the competition has a briefing requirement, the competitors' brief scores ideally should be factored into their oral argument scores for each preliminary-round argument to reflect the importance that briefing holds in real appeals.

- *How should you determine which competitors advance to the elimination rounds based on win-loss record?*

In a scheme under which advancement to the elimination rounds is determined by win-loss record in the preliminary rounds, undefeated competitors usually advance. However, there may be more undefeated competitors than there are spots in the first elimination round. In that case, you'll need a system of ranking the undefeated competitors beyond their win-loss records to determine which of them to cut. This ranking may be achieved by cutting undefeated competitors with—

  - the lowest brief scores;
  - the lowest total points accrued in the preliminary rounds; or
  - the lowest cumulative point margins.

The term "cumulative point margin" refers to the total number of points by which a competitor has defeated their opponents in the preliminary rounds.

To illustrate this situation, assume that in a twenty-competitor competition in which the competitors compete in two preliminary rounds, the competitors finish the second round with the following records: nine 2-0, two 1-1, and nine 0-2. Assume further that eight competitors will

---

121. As discussed above, each judge panel should be composed of at least three judges. However, it's not unusual for a judge to cancel and a replacement for that judge not to be found. If no-shows mean that some rounds have only two judges, you might average the oral argument scores of the two judges to create a "ghost judge" score.

advance to the elimination rounds. In this situation, one of the nine 2-0 competitors will need to be cut from the field for the first elimination round. The 2-0 competitor with the lowest brief score, the lowest aggregate point total, or the lowest cumulative point margin from the preliminary rounds could be cut so that the first elimination-round field ends up at eight competitors.

You may also encounter the opposite issue: you may not have enough undefeated competitors to fill out the brackets for the first elimination round. In this case, you'll need some competitors with at least one loss to fill out the field. To determine which of these competitors to advance, you'll once again need a ranking system. More specifically, you may advance the mixed-record teams with—

- the highest brief scores;
- the highest total points accrued in the preliminary rounds; or
- the highest cumulative point margins.

To illustrate this situation, assume that in a sixteen-competitor competition in which the competitors compete in three preliminary rounds, the competitors finish the third round with the following records: three 3-0, four 2-1, seven 1-2, and two 0-3. Assume further that eight competitors will advance to the elimination rounds. In this situation, all 3-0 competitors and 2-1 competitors advance. This, however, leaves the eighth elimination-round slot available to one of the seven 1-2 competitors. The 1-2 competitor with the highest brief score, the highest aggregate point total, or the highest cumulative point margin from the preliminary rounds could be chosen to fill out the field.

ii. Advancement based on highest scores

Under an alternative scheme, you may decide not to use win-loss record from the preliminary rounds to determine which competitors advance to the elimination rounds. Rather, whether a competitor advances to the elimination rounds may be based on either—

- the total number of points that the competitor accrued during the preliminary rounds; or

- the average number of points that the competitor accrued during the preliminary rounds.[122]

For example, at the end of the preliminary rounds, the sixteen competitors who accrued the most points during the preliminary rounds could be chosen to advance to the elimination rounds.

This scheme has two advantages over a scheme that uses win-loss record to determine which competitors advance to the elimination rounds. First, competitors do not necessarily need to be power protected in the preliminary-round matchups because win-loss record is not considered in determining whether a competitor advances to the elimination rounds. Rather, matchups in each preliminary round may be done randomly, though you may still decide to power protect competitors based on brief score in each round if your competition has a briefing requirement. Second, competitors may be less likely to "check out" of the competition if they aren't faced with a loss or two in the preliminary rounds. Rather, they're more likely to be fully invested in each argument, which results in a better learning experience for the competitors.

This scheme, however, has a disadvantage: it may be more likely to lead to arbitrary results than a scheme that uses win-loss record to determine advancement to the elimination rounds. More specifically, whether a particular competitor advances to the elimination rounds may depend on the whims of the judges who judged that competitor in the preliminary rounds. If a competitor appears before preliminary-round judges who tend to give higher scores than other judges, that competitor is more likely to advance to the elimination rounds than a competitor whose judges were stricter with their scoring.

g. Should you schedule more than two preliminary rounds?

As noted above, you may decide to schedule more than two preliminary rounds. If you schedule at least three preliminary rounds, matchups in the first two rounds may be random or power protected according to brief score, as discussed above. But for the third preliminary round

---

122. Keep in mind that under a scheme of advancement based on highest scores, the competitors' brief scores may be factored into the determination of whether a competitor advances to the elimination phase (provided, of course, that the competition has a briefing requirement). Under this scheme, competitors with good brief scores increase their chances of advancing to the elimination phase.

and beyond, you may "power match" the competitors rather than randomly matching them or power protecting them.

i. The basics of power matching

The term "power matching" refers to the practice of pitting competitors with similar win-loss records against one another. Power matching in a third preliminary round is useful when scheduling only two preliminary rounds makes it difficult to ensure that the most skilled competitors will advance to the elimination rounds. It also gives competitors who have lost a round a chance to pull themselves back into contention to advance to the elimination rounds.

When competitors are power matched in the third round of a competition with three preliminary rounds, competitors with a 2-0 record are matched against each other, competitors with a 1-1 record are matched against each other, and competitors with a 0-2 record are matched against each other.

ii. Matching competitors within each win-loss category

To further determine matchups within each power-matched win-loss category, you may use one of three methods:

- *Random matchups.* You may randomly match the competitors within each win-loss category, which is the easiest method to use.
- *Power-protected matchups based on brief score.* You may power protect competitors within each win-loss category based on their brief scores. Under this scheme, the 2-0 competitor with the highest brief score would be pitted against the 2-0 competitor with the lowest brief score, the 2-0 competitor with the second-highest brief score would be pitted against the 2-0 competitor with the second-lowest brief score, etc.
- *Power-protected matchups based on cumulative point margins.* You may power protect competitors within each win-loss category based on their cumulative point margins from the first two preliminary rounds. Recall that the term "cumulative point margin" refers to the total number of points by which a competitor has defeated her opponents in

the previous preliminary rounds. A competitor's cumulative point margin will be a positive number if they are 2-0 after the first two rounds and a negative number if they are 0-2 after those rounds. The cumulative point margin may be either positive or negative for a competitor with a 1-1 record depending on how wide or narrow the margins were by which that competitor won and lost in the first two rounds. Thus, if competitors are matched within a win-loss category based on cumulative point margin, the 2-0 competitor with the highest cumulative point margin is pitted against the 2-0 competitor with the lowest cumulative point margin, the 2-0 competitor with the second-highest cumulative point margin is pitted against the 2-0 competitor with the second-lowest cumulative point margin, etc.

iii. Matching an odd number of competitors within a win-loss category

You must consider the possibility that you may end up with an odd number of competitors in a win-loss category after the first two preliminary rounds. If this occurs, you will have to match one competitor in that category against a competitor in the next win-loss category.

The competitors chosen from each win-loss category for this matchup may be selected under one of two methods:

- *Random matchup.* You may randomly choose one competitor from the win-loss category in which there was an odd number of competitors and one competitor from the next win-loss category. This is the easier matchup method to use to even out the bracket.
- *Power-protected matchup.* If you're power protecting competitors within each win-loss category, you may decide to match the lowest-seeded competitor in the odd-numbered win-loss category against the highest-seeded competitor in the next win-loss category.

To illustrate a power-protected matchup, assume that the competitors in a sixteen-competitor field have the following records after the first two preliminary rounds: five 2-0 competitors, six 1-1 competitors, and five 0-2 competitors. To power match the competitors, four of the five 2-0 competitors can be matched. But because there is an odd number of 2-0 competitors, one 2-0 competitor must be pitted against one of the six 1-1 competitors. This matchup in turn leaves five of the six 1-1 competitors to be matched. Four of these five 1-1 competitors can be matched. But again, because an odd number of 1-1 competitors is left after matching one of them against a 2-0 competitor, you must match one of the 1-1 competitors against a 0-2 competitor. After this matching is achieved, the four remaining 0-2 competitors can be matched.

Expressed in a table, these matchups would look like the following. The numbers in parentheses represent the seeds in each win-loss category if each win-loss category uses power-protected matchups rather than random matchups:

(1) 2-0	v.	(4) 2-0
(2) 2-0	v.	(3) 2-0
(5) 2-0	v.	(1) 1-1
(2) 1-1	v.	(5) 1-1
(3) 1-1	v.	(4) 1-1
(6) 1-1	v.	(1) 0-2
(2) 0-2	v.	(5) 0-2
(3) 0-2	v.	(4) 0-2

h. How should you match competitors in the preliminary rounds if you have an odd number of competitors?

An odd number of competitors may participate in your competition. This makes the administration of the preliminary rounds more difficult because, to ensure that each competitor argues the same number of times, one competitor will have to sit out each preliminary round and make up that argument at some point. Adding a special or "bye" round that occurs in addition to the "regular" rounds solves this problem.

The competitors chosen to argue in the special or "bye" round may be selected in two different ways:

- *Random selection.* The competitors may be chosen at random.
- *Brief scores.* If your competition includes a briefing requirement, the competitors with the highest and lowest brief scores may be chosen, which is probably the fairer method.

Remember that ideally, each competitor should argue once on brief and once off brief. Further, keep in mind that each competitor should face a different opponent in each round.

To illustrate the addition of a special round to account for an odd number of competitors, assume that a competition contains two preliminary rounds and nine competitors—five who briefed the case for petitioner and four who briefed the case for respondent. In this situation, the competitor with the highest brief score for respondent would sit out round one, and the competitor with the lowest brief score for petitioner would sit out round two. These two competitors would also meet in the special round so that they will have argued twice in the preliminary rounds like the other competitors.

The preliminary round schedule might look like this:

Special or "Bye" Preliminary Round		
Arguing as Petitioner		Arguing as Respondent
P5	v.	R1

Preliminary Round 1 (R1 sits out)		
P1	v.	P5
P2	v.	R4
P3	v.	R3
P4	v.	R2

Preliminary Round 2 (P5 sits out)		
R1	v.	P4
R2	v.	P3
R3	v.	P2
R4	v.	P1

i. How should you determine matchups in the elimination rounds?

You will also need a matching system for the elimination rounds. To determine the matching system that you will use, you should consider the following things:

- how you will seed and match the competitors in the first elimination round;
- how you will determine which side each competitor will argue in each round; and
- how you will determine the winner of each argument.

i. How will you seed and match competitors?

The competitors participating in the first elimination round should be seeded using established criteria. If advancement to the elimination rounds is based on win-loss record from the preliminary rounds, you might use this win-loss record as the first seeding criterion and one of the following as a second seeding criterion:

- cumulative point margins from the preliminary rounds;
- total preliminary-round points;
- average preliminary-round points; or
- brief scores.

If you're not using win-loss record to determine which competitors advance to the elimination rounds, you might use one of the following as your sole seeding criterion:

- total preliminary-round points;
- average preliminary-round points; or
- brief scores.

After you've seeded the competitors, they should be ranked in order and placed in a traditional elimination bracket. Elimination brackets are traditional power-protected brackets with the highest-ranked competitor competing against the lowest-ranked competitor, the second highest-ranked competitor competing against the second lowest-ranked competitor, etc.

ii. How will you determine which side each competitor will argue in each round?

To determine the side that each competitor will represent in each elimination round, you may use one of three alternative methods:

- *Coin toss.* You may have competitors toss a coin, with the winner of the coin-toss getting to choose the side that they wish to argue.
- *Higher seed chooses.* You may allow the higher-seeded competitor in each bracket to choose which side to argue.
- *Random assignments.* You may randomly assign sides.

iii. How will you determine the winner of each argument?

The competitors who win in each elimination-round argument advance to the next elimination round. To determine the winner of an elimination round, you may use one of two schemes:

- *High score.* The winner may be determined in the same way that the winner of a preliminary round argument is determined—the competitor with the highest aggregate score or the highest average score wins. If your competition includes a briefing requirement, you may or may not choose to factor the brief scores into the determination of whether a competitor wins an elimination round.
- *Majority vote of the panel.* The winner may be determined by a majority vote of the judging panel. In this case, you'll want to ensure that an odd number of judges sits on the panel. In some competitions, the winner of the final elimination round is always determined by panel vote.

j. How should you break ties?

For rounds in which a winner is required, you'll need to adopt a tie-breaking procedure in case opponents end up deadlocked in a round. Consider three alternatives for breaking ties:

- *Brief score.* If your competition has a briefing requirement, the tiebreaker could be determined by brief score, with the winner of the round being the competitor with the higher brief score.

- *Majority vote.* The winner could be chosen according to a majority vote of the judging panel.
- *Higher cumulative point margin or aggregate point total.* The winner could be the competitor with the higher cumulative point margin or aggregate point total from previous rounds.

4. RUNNING THE ORAL ROUNDS

Once you have set the oral argument matchups, you should be ready to run the oral rounds. During those rounds, you will have to do the following:

- Manage the judges;
- Set up your building for the arguments;
- Stay on schedule;
- Keep time during the arguments;
- Administer the judges' score sheets; and
- Tabulate the results for each round.

a. How should you manage the oral argument judges?

i. Contact the judges with pre-argument reminders and instructions.

Several days before the competition begins, call or email oral argument judges to remind them of their judging commitments. This is also a good time to tell outside judges where to park at the school. If your school charges for parking, offer to cover the judges' parking fees if your budget permits it.

Also, give the judges specific instructions on where to report. Ask them to arrive at least forty-five minutes before the round is scheduled to begin so the competition administrators have time for orientation and time to make last-minute adjustments for no-shows and late arrivals without inconveniencing the judges and competitors who arrived on time.

ii. Provide on-site hospitality to the judges.

Stock your judge check-in area with friendly board members, light refreshments, and a place for the judges to sit as they wait for orientation and room assignments. Have volunteers—perhaps the bailiffs who will keep time during the arguments—available to escort the judges to their assigned rooms. And if you are holding rounds during the evening, consider serving a light meal to your judges.

iii. Cover logistics and procedures with the judges.

During the judges' orientation, cover logistics of the round and special instructions for the competition. Instruct judges on conflict procedures: a judge who recognizes a participant should immediately notify the bailiff or a designated volunteer so that the judge can immediately be moved to a different room. In suburban communities or small towns, it may be especially helpful to show the judge at check-in the names of the students who will be arguing before the judge so the conflict can be resolved in a timely manner. Further, provide each judge with a judging packet containing the scoring rubrics, and blank paper and a pen for notes. And have extra copies of the competition problem and bench brief available.

b. How should you set up your building for oral arguments?

i. Set up rooms for the arguments.

On each competition day, make sure all rooms are unlocked and set up for oral argument. Specifically, each room should have a lectern for the competitors, an area where each competitor or team may sit when they're not arguing, and an area to serve as the bench for the judges. Arrange each room so that competitors are not standing or sitting so close to the judges that they can see the scoring rubrics or the judges' written comments during the argument. Set up lecterns that allow competitors sufficient room for their materials. Provide bottled water or pitchers of water and glasses for the judges and competitors.

ii. Identify for the competitors and judges the areas of the building that will be used for arguments and for other competition-related matters.

Post directional signs or moot court board members around your building to help judges find the check-in area and competitors to find the rooms where they're arguing. If the competition will take place during the school day, send an announcement to the faculty and student body reminding them that the competition is underway. Likewise, post notices on doors of the rooms where arguments are being held that arguments are underway.

iii. Identify who will be permitted to attend the arguments.

Decide ahead of time whether observers will be allowed to attend the oral arguments. Many competitions allow and encourage observers during the elimination rounds but limit observers during preliminary rounds. Regardless, no team member who is still active in the competition should be allowed to watch another team compete. If one purpose of your internal competition is to place competitors on external competition teams, external competition team coaches may want to attend at least the elimination rounds of the competition to scout potential team members.

c. How can you stay on schedule?

Make every effort to start rounds on time. To accomplish this goal, you should first remind the judges that the score sheets and the post-argument critiques need to be completed by a specific time. Second, make sure that judges and competitors know the rules so that abundant questions about procedure aren't necessary and thus will not slow down the arguments. Third, if possible, provide a bailiff for each room to keep time during the arguments. If your volunteer list makes that option impossible, require each competitor to furnish their own bailiff, or ask one judge in each room to keep time. Finally, before each round begins, competitors should tell the judges how each team's speaking time will be divided and how much time the petitioner/appellant is reserving for rebuttal.

d. How should time be kept during oral arguments?

Distribute a set of time cards in each room for the bailiffs. Typically, competitors are shown time cards when the speaker has five minutes, two minutes, and thirty seconds remaining, and a "stop" card when time has expired. If the bailiffs are responsible for calling the court to order when the argument begins, provide the bailiffs with a script that covers what they are to say to call the court to order.

e. How should you administer the judges' score sheets?

i. Have the bailiffs to pick up the score sheets after the judges have completed them.

When the judges receive the score sheets at check-in, politely remind them that they must complete the score sheets by a designated time. Furthermore, make sure that the bailiffs pick up the score sheets while the judges are giving critiques and then bring them to the competition scorekeeper for tabulation.

ii. Have the bailiffs verify the score sheets before the judges depart.

Judges sometimes make mistakes when completing the score sheets, such as incorrectly adding the subcategory scores in a score sheet. Likewise, a judge may create ambiguities in the score sheets after completing them. For instance, a judge's handwriting may be difficult to read. A judge may have completed the sheet "backwards" by filling in a final score before filling in the scores for the subcategories, making it unclear whether the judge intended the final score in the sheet to be the true final score. Or a judge may have inadvertently failed to complete portions of the score sheet.

After the bailiffs have picked up the score sheets, they should never try to interpret what a judge who made a math error or left an ambiguity in the sheet actually "intended" in the sheet. Thus, you should require the bailiffs to check the sheets before the judges leave the building.

Specifically, this check should require the bailiffs to examine—

- whether the sheet's subcategory scores correctly add up to the final score;
- whether any ambiguities exist in the sheet;

- whether the sheet is signed by the judge, provided that your competition's rules require the judges to sign the score sheets; and
- whether the judges' ballots clearly indicate the round's winner, provided that the competition's rules require the judges to determine the winner by a majority vote instead of by scores.

If a bailiff detects any error or ambiguity in the sheet, the bailiff *must* notify the judge about it before the judge leaves the building and ask the judge to correct the error or eliminate the ambiguity. Only then should the bailiff submit the sheet to the competition's scorekeeper for tabulation.

iii. Instruct the bailiffs to pick up any judging materials left behind after the arguments.

Instruct bailiffs to scan the rooms where the oral arguments have taken place after each round for left-behind materials, such as bench briefs or scoring rubrics. This suggestion may seem overly cautious, but one of the most serious allegations of cheating can involve a competitor gaining access to the bench brief.

f. How should you tabulate the results for each round?

Create a tabulation sheet to use as the score sheets arrive. A simple Excel spreadsheet works well. Transfer the scores from the individual score sheets to the tabulation sheet. This should be done by two people working together to avoid errors in transferring. If time permits, have another person check to make sure that the tabulation sheet entries are correct. Use the master tabulation sheet to identify the rankings for the elimination rounds.

5. HANDLING PROTESTS

Though you may not encounter protests from the competitors during the competition, you should be prepared to deal with them. Specifically, you must—

- determine who will handle protests;
- determine whether the alleged misconduct or mistake harmed the protesting competitor;
- set a deadline for lodging protests; and
- resolve protests promptly.

a. Determine who will handle protests.

An administrator who can decide the outcome of a protest should be on-site during every round of the competition. Although this administrator can be a member of the moot court board if the competition is completely student-run, it is more appropriate for a faculty advisor, competitions director, or some other member of the law school faculty to decide protests. If the protest involves two competitors, placing the decision in the hands of another student can be untenable. If the protest involves judging, a member of the law school faculty or staff can best handle the dispute to prevent its escalation.

b. Determine whether the alleged misconduct or mistake harmed the protesting competitor.

To resolve a protest, you must determine whether actual harm occurred to the protesting competitor. If a score was miscalculated but the same competitor would have prevailed regardless, then no matter what the mistake was, no harm occurred. If, however, the results of a round would have been different had a mistaken score been calculated correctly, then the administrator must figure out the fairest way to correct the mistake. For instance, if the mistake resulted in one competitor being erroneously eliminated from the competition, an extra "play-in" round may be scheduled to allow the competitor a chance to come back into the competition.

On the other hand, if one competitor accuses another competitor of violating a competition rule, an administrator will need to speak to the judges and the competitors to determine what happened and whether the act violated the rules before deciding how to resolve the situation. If a rule violation occurred and harmed the competitor who lodged the protest, you could have the competitors argue again. Or, if the violation is egregious enough—for example, the offending competitor read the bench brief before the argument—you could eject that competitor from the competition and declare the complaining competitor the winner of the round.

c. Set a deadline for lodging protests.

Set a deadline for filing protests. For instance, if a protest involves competitor or judge behavior, you could require the protest to be brought to the administrators' attention within ten minutes after the round has ended. But if the protest involves a scoring error, it may not be discovered until much later. Unfortunately, in that circumstance, it may not be possible to create a remedy for the protesting competitor.

d. Resolve protests promptly.

Try to resolve protests promptly. Prompt resolution is possible only if you have anticipated conflicts and established procedures ahead of time for resolving them. Thus, before the competition begins, work through hypothetical protest scenarios so that you may create clear procedures for handling them. The more clearly that these procedures are spelled out to the competitors, the less likely it will be that they will have incentive to lodge petty or frivolous protests.

6. HANDLING UNEXPECTED EMERGENCIES

An unexpected emergency, such as a public-health emergency like the COVID-19 pandemic, can create significant challenges for competition administrators. If an emergency like this occurs while you're running an internal competition, you may need to decide whether to continue the competition in person, whether to move it online, or whether to cancel it.

Depending on the emergency, moving the competition online may be a feasible option. In fact, your university's policies for dealing with the emergency may leave you with no choice but to move the competition online if you wish to continue it. Chapter Six of this book discusses how to administer a virtual competition. If you want move your competition online, you should consult that chapter for advice.

If, however, your university's policies do not require the strictest measures for handling the emergency, you may be able to continue running the competition in person, but with some measures designed to mitigate the emergency (for example, in the case of a pandemic, requiring masking or social distancing). If you decide to continue in person, you must still pay close attention to your university's policies for navigating the emergency so that your competition implements those policies.

Under the worst-case scenario, you may have to cancel the competition because the emergency is too severe to continue the competition, or because moving the competition online is logistically infeasible—for instance, you don't have the personnel to handle the move online. If this occurs, you might consider whether you may still award the competitors some credit based on work that they've already done in the competition. For instance, if they've completed their briefs, you ought to explore whether you may at least declare a winner of the competition based on the competitors' performance on the briefs. You might also give awards to the competitors who wrote briefs that were in the top five percent or top ten percent of all competitors.

E. Announcements and awards

1. ANNOUNCEMENTS

At various stages of the competition, you will need to make announcements to the competitors, such as which competitors have won a round and which side the competitors will argue for the next round. Before the oral rounds begin, inform the competitors when and where the announcements are to be made for various phases of the competition.

a. Announcements about side choice

Because competitors who have advanced to the elimination rounds may need to decide which side they will argue in each elimination round, side-choice announcements may need to be made live. Recall that side choice for each elimination round may be determined by coin toss or by giving the choice to the higher-seeded competitor in the round. Consider requiring the competitors to be present when the side-choice announcements are made so the choice and the brackets may be completed immediately. You might also emphasize that any competitor who fails to attend will default to the other competitor's choice of sides. If neither competitor attends, the competition rules should state how the sides will be chosen—perhaps the lower-seeded competitor will by default argue for the petitioner.

If it is not possible due to a round's timing to make a live announcement, announce the winning competitors online or by email. In this situation, you may have to establish a predetermined method for deciding which competitors argue which side.

b. Announcements about competition awards

Announcements about competition awards, such as best oralist and best brief, may be made at the final elimination round. Because most final rounds do not include the brief scores as a component and the round's winner usually is determined by the panel's vote, the judges should be able to confer in chambers for a few minutes, take a vote, and quickly reconvene to announce the competition's winner. Because top oralist awards are often based on the preliminary rounds and can be calculated well before the final round, those awards can be announced at the same time. You may also choose to announce competition awards at a reception or banquet that immediately follows the final round.

2. CASH AWARDS AND SCHOLARSHIPS

If your school is fortunate, you may have a sponsor for your competition. While sponsors may choose to underwrite only the direct costs of the competition, it may be worth asking donors or sponsors to underwrite cash awards or scholarships to—

- the competition finalists;
- the competition winners;
- the competitors who wrote the best briefs; and
- the top oralists,

in exchange for naming rights to the competition. Chapter Two includes a more extensive discussion of getting funding for your moot court program, including funding for an internal competition.

Before the competition, inform the competitors of any cash awards or scholarships that will be given. Try to anticipate extenuating circumstances; while you can ensure through the judges' deliberation process that there will be a clear winner in an oral argument, it is possible to have a tie for the top oralist or best brief award. Be clear about what will happen in such a situation—whether the award or scholarship will be divided in case of a tie, or whether there is a mechanism for breaking the tie.

3. AWARDS AND RECOGNITION

Standard awards for an internal competition include recognition of—

- the winning competitor or team;
- the top oralists; and
- the best briefs.

a. Special considerations when determining oralist awards

In most competitions, oralist awards are based only on performance in the preliminary rounds. This method of determining oralist awards allows superior oralists to be recognized regardless of how well their team performed in the competition.

Oralist awards may be determined by—

- considering the competitors' total or average oral argument scores during the preliminary rounds; or
- adding oralist ranking points.

To use oralist ranking points, add a line to the oral argument score sheet that asks the judges to rank the competitors in each round; in a team-based competition, the rankings would be from 1 to 4, with 1 being the best oralist and 4 being the worst during each round. If each round has three judges, then at the end of three preliminary rounds, the best total oralist ranking score would be a 9, and the worst would be a 36. Use individual total scores or average total scores across all preliminary rounds to break ties.[123]

b. Memorializing the awards with mementos and events

If your program does not have funds available for awards and scholarships, it costs very little to print certificates for competitors who win the competition and who finish among the top oralists and brief writers. If your school has an awards day where scholarship recipients are recognized, ask that the winners of the internal competition be recognized. As discussed in Chapter Two, consider seeking funds for a moot court luncheon or banquet to be held at the end of the school year so competitors

---

123. For example, if after the end of the preliminary rounds, two oralists are tied for fifth place with a total of 18 oralist ranking points, examine the total argument scores for each oralist. If oralist A has a total oral argument score of 850 and oralist B has a total oral argument score of 840, then oralist A beats oralist B.

in both internal and external competitions can be recognized at this event.

Another option for recognizing winners is to purchase a plaque or trophy for display in the law school that provides space for engraving the names of winners from multiple years. Although such a plaque or trophy may initially be more expensive than award certificates, the year-round recognition of both the competition and the winners can be worth the added expense. And once you purchase the plaque or trophy, the year-to-year engraving expenses will be minimal—at least until you've filled up an existing plaque or trophy and must purchase another.

c. Publicizing the competitors' achievements

After the competition, use your school's resources to applaud the achievements of your moot court board and the competitors in your internal competition. Post results on your school's website and on any social media accounts maintained by your school or by your moot court board. If your school publishes an alumni magazine, provide information about your competition for inclusion in the next issue. Photos always make an article more interesting. Indeed, you may want to assign a board member, a faculty member, or a staff member to take photographs during the final elimination round. In the optimal situation, see if you can arrange to have a professional photographer—perhaps someone on staff with your university—to take photos to ensure that the photos are of good quality.

d. Thanking the judges

You should also send a thank-you note or email to each judge. Consider dividing the writing of thank-you notes among board members before the competition. As judges arrive, hand them their packets along with a handwritten thank-you note on top. The judges immediately feel appreciated, and you have ensured that the notes were written and delivered.

III. Conclusion

An internal moot court competition can serve several key purposes. It can bring recognition to your school, your moot court board, and the competitors. It can give your moot court board an opportunity to build leadership and collaboration skills. And it can give your students a way to polish their lawyering skills—a winning combination for all involved.

CHAPTER 4

Advising External Competition Teams

THIS CHAPTER WILL HELP YOU TO:

- **Choose your law school's external competition roster;**
- **Select the students for each team;**
- **Manage competition preparation through planning, timing, and fostering communication;**
- **Navigate the competition arena itself;**
- **Use a competition to teach students about brief writing, oral advocacy, and professionalism; and**
- **Exploit teachable moments at a competition and debrief students after the competition.**

One hallmark of a successful moot court program is the strength of the external moot court teams that compete across the country. Some of these competitions have multiple regional rounds leading to a final national competition. Others are specialty competitions that focus on a particular subject. Participating on an external competition team is a competitive endeavor, and your goal as a moot court advisor is to facilitate your teams' success. This chapter discusses how to promote that success, from choosing competitions and teams, to planning the practices, teaching brief writing and oral advocacy, and mentoring the team during and after the competition. At each step in the process, you will foster a team's investment in a competition. You should also balance the goal of winning competitions with the goal of creating a fruitful learning experience for your students.

I. Choosing a Roster of Competitions

One of the more difficult decisions you'll need to make as a moot court advisor is how to choose the external-competition roster. At one time, schools could choose from only a handful of external competitions, such as the National Moot Court Competition, sponsored by the New York City Bar Association, or the Philip C. Jessup International Moot Court Competition, sponsored by the International Law Students Association. But now, you must balance multiple factors when choosing the competitions your students will attend each year.

Indeed, now students can travel the world and compete at smaller moot court competitions in specialty subject areas as diverse as animal law, security law, and entertainment law. So, on the one hand, students who are chosen for moot court teams may scour the web and ask to attend competitions that involve cutting-edge subject areas and take place in exciting cities. Those students may want to go to as many competitions in a year as they possibly can. On the other hand, a moot court advisor needs to think about not only the limited financial resources available at their school, but also the limited "personnel" resources necessary to ensure a meaningful educational experience for the students. Ultimately, your goal should be to maximize the number of opportunities for the students, but to do so in a responsible manner so that the students receive valuable guidance from faculty, practitioners, and experienced student competitors at the school.

Advisors should consider several factors when making these choices:

- How important is it to attend the well-established, larger, and potentially more "elite" competitions?
- What are the benefits and disadvantages of attending competitions that have a subject-specific focus?
- Who is going to coach the team?

Of course, these questions overlap and asking these questions will lead to similar conversations. But what follows below should help facilitate the conversations among moot court advisor, students, faculty, and the law school administrators who ultimately control the purse strings.

A. Choosing among the three major competitions

The three largest competitions, based on number of schools or teams participating, are the National Moot Court Competition ("NMCC"), sponsored by the New York City Bar Association and the American College of Trial Lawyers;[1] the National Appellate Advocacy Competition ("NAAC"), sponsored by the American Bar Association;[2] and the Philip C. Jessup International Law Moot Court Competition ("Jessup"), sponsored by the International Law Students Association.[3] These competitions are also among the oldest in the country: the NMCC was established in 1950, the NAAC was established in 1977, and Jessup was established in 1959. All three of these competitions begin with regional rounds typically held in large cities. Teams in the NMCC and NAAC who win their respective regional rounds advance to a national round, and in Jessup, they advance to an international round.

In planning their competition slate, many law schools first consider whether to field a team for one or more of these larger, multi-level competitions. The larger competitions are generally considered the most prestigious, so doing well at them brings greater visibility to a law school and its students. The competitions are also well run and address general topics of wide interest to students. Students often consider it the highest honor to be chosen to compete in the NAAC, Jessup, or the NMCC, because law schools place some of their best advocates on these three teams. Advocates may want to know how they place against the best advocates from other law schools.

In developing your moot court program, you may want your teams to attend these competitions so that your students can learn from other strong teams. You can get to know the advisors and coaches at other schools and pick up new techniques, even as you build your teams to attend other, smaller competitions. Schools also tend to send more established coaches—coaches who are more intertwined in their pro-

---

1. *National Moot Court Competition*, N.Y.C. B. Ass'n, http://www.nycbar.org/law-students/national-moot-court (last visited Feb. 13, 2023) (noting that over 120 law schools participate in the competition).

2. *National Appellate Advocacy Competition*, Am. B. Ass'n, http://www.americanbar.org/groups/law_students/events_competitions/practical_skills_competitions/naac.html (last visited Feb. 13, 2023).

3. *Philip C. Jessup International Law Moot Court Competition*, Int'l L. Students Ass'n, https://www.ilsa.org/jessup-competitors/jessup-faq/ (last visited Feb. 13, 2023) (noting the Jessup is the world's largest moot court competition).

grams—to these competitions, which gives the coaches great networking and learning opportunities.

Another reason to include a large national competition like the NAAC or NMCC on your roster is that the University of Houston Law Center sponsors the Hunton Andrews Kurth Moot Court National Championship, which is an invitational competition for law schools that have demonstrated a capacity to win at other moot court competitions.[4] The Championship invites sixteen schools to participate based on points accrued for success at other moot court competitions throughout the year.[5] To determine which schools to invite, the Championship has created a tier-based scoring system to rank student performance at other moot court competitions. Other than the Championship itself, the NAAC and NMCC stand alone in tier one.[6] The other moot court competitions fall into three other tiers based on their size and prestige.[7] Law schools may self-report success to earn participation points for the Championship.

However, law schools may see drawbacks to attending the larger competitions based on cost and distance. Sending a team to any of the larger competitions can be expensive. For example, the 2022–23 NAAC had a registration fee of $700 for the first team and $650 for a school's second team.[8] Most law schools that attend this competition send two teams of three students, so registration alone is $1,350.

Moreover, the large competitions may be held far from your law school, increasing travel expenses and time. You should keep these travel-budgeting considerations in mind when deciding whether to register a team for a competition. The NAAC regional rounds are usually held in larger cities such as San Francisco, New York, and Boston. Although those cities allow for easy air travel to major airports, hotels in those

4. *Hunton Andrews Kurth Moot Court National Championship*, U. Hou. L. Ctr., https://law.uh.edu/blakely/mcnc/homepage.asp (last visited Feb. 13, 2023).

5. *Rankings*, U. Hou. L. Ctr., https://law.uh.edu/blakely/mcnc/2022/competitors.asp (last visited Feb. 13, 2023).

6. *Hunton Andrews Kurth Moot Court National Championship Scoring Methodology*, U. Hou. L. Ctr., http://www.law.uh.edu/blakely/mcnc/scoring.asp (last visited Feb. 13, 2023).

7. *Id.*

8. *2022–23 NAAC Regionals*, Am. B. Ass'n, https://abaforlawstudents.com/event/naac-regionals/ (last visited Feb. 13, 2023).

cities can be expensive when compared to hotels in the cities where some smaller specialty competitions are held. The costs of the NMCC regional rounds vary depending on the regional host law school's location. If you and your team decide to switch the location where the team enters the regional competition from one year to the next, you will also need to anticipate the cost difference in your budget. Finally, be sure to consider the potential cost of sending a team to the national round.[9]

Another possible drawback to the larger competitions is they are hard to win. Accordingly, your teams may need time to learn how to succeed through trial and error. So, if you are looking to grow a moot court program and would like to bring some awards back to the school, these competitions might not be the place to expand initially.

Jessup is organized differently from the NMCC, the NAAC, and other competitions. Like some other competitions, Jessup spans two semesters, and it starts earlier in the fall. In addition, Jessup is both a large international competition and a specialty competition, making it a unique and challenging competition with which to become familiar.

On balance, you should strongly consider fielding a team for at least one, if not more, of the three major competitions. The rigor and strong organization of the competitions, as well as the level of advocacy your students will experience, are worth it.

B. Choosing subject-specific competitions

Now law students can compete in moot court competitions in just about any subject area, including space law, sports law, environmental law, products liability law, and corporate law, to name a few. A subject-specific competition may provide several advantages. Students may have significant interest in the subject area, and faculty members at your law school may specialize in that subject and be particularly excited about coaching a moot court team. Your school may also save some money if a competition is hosted in a smaller city, especially if it is within driving distance. Finally, a smaller competition may bring a

9. National rounds are held in New York City for the NMCC, Chicago for the NAAC, and Washington, D.C. for Jessup. *National Moot Court Competition*, N.Y.C. B. Ass'n, *supra* note 1; *National Appellate Advocacy Competition*, Am. B. Ass'n, *supra* note 2; *Philip C. Jessup International Law Moot Court Competition*, Int'l L. Students Ass'n, *supra* note 3.

greater likelihood of success, which almost always is a boost for your moot court program.

Student interest is an important factor in selecting competitions. If you solicit student input in choosing competitions, students will inevitably search for competitions with subject areas that intrigue them. For example, students may suggest competitions like the Tulane Mardi Gras Sports Law Invitational[10] in New Orleans or the Cardozo/BMI Entertainment and Communications Law Moot Court Competition[11] in New York. Generating excitement among the competing students is obviously important to any moot court program. Moot court advisors do not want to be in a position where they have difficulty finding students to field a team in a competition their school has already entered.

You may want to consider fielding teams in specialty competitions that correspond to any subject areas of expertise at your law school. This provides another avenue where your law school can showcase its talented students and successful program. Specialty competitions help students learn the subject because they apply substantive law in the practical setting of an appellate argument, rather than merely applying the law in an end-of-the-semester exam. You can promote the competition to students who are studying in that subject area or who are involved in an affiliated student organization. You may even find that the competition fosters connections among faculty, students, and alumni who are practicing in the field. Forging those connections can help students find jobs and help the law school stay connected with its alumni.

Perhaps the more challenging effort lies in finding and recruiting faculty or practitioner coaches who are the right fit for subject-specific competitions. For example, if your law school is lucky enough to have an amazing and energetic tax law professor, you might want to consider approaching that professor to coach a team at one of the two national moot court competitions dedicated to tax law.[12] Enthusiastic professors

---

10. *Tulane Mardi Gras Sports Law Invitational*, TUL. U. L. SCH., https://law.tulane.edu/students/moot-court/mardi-gras-invitational (last visited Feb. 13, 2023).

11. *Cardozo/BMI Entertainment and Communications Law Moot Court Competition*, BENJAMIN N. CARDOZO SCH. L., https://sites.google.com/site/cardozobmimootcourtcompetition/home (last visited Feb. 13, 2023).

12. *See, e.g., Albert R. Mugel National Tax Moot Court Competition*, SUNY BUFF. L. SCH., https://www.law.buffalo.edu/beyond/competitions/mugel.html (last visited Feb. 13, 2023).

with an expertise in an area typically have more success at the competitions than ones whom you have to beg to coach. So, for instance, though students may be genuinely interested in competing in the Judge John R. Brown Admiralty Law Moot Court Competition, they are much less likely to be successful at the competition if no admiralty-law professor or practitioner is willing to coach. Further, the students would likely find it difficult to have a quality educational experience.[13]

Once you have identified specialty competitions that match student, faculty, and coaching interest at your school, you should consider how the competitions align with your travel budget. You can save costs if the teams drive to the competitions. Be flexible about what you consider driving distance. Although many students initially balk at the idea of an eight-hour drive, they typically appreciate the opportunity once you explain that the school can possibly go to one or two more competitions per year if the teams drive to some of them. Also, look for competitions that are held in smaller cities. For example, a hotel in St. Petersburg, Florida, or Wilmington, Delaware, may be less expensive than one in New York City or San Francisco. Once you calculate the cost difference of multiple hotel rooms for multiple team members for multiple nights, you might see more opportunities for student participation.

Finally, subject-specific competitions often provide the best opportunity to do well at a moot court competition. Of course, there is no science to knowing exactly how rigorous each moot court competition is, but the smaller size of most specialty competitions is something to consider strategically. Yet bear in mind that specialty competitions are not always small. For example, the Robert F. Wagner National Labor and Employment Law Moot Court Competition,[14] held at New York Law School, typically draws close to 50 teams, and the Jeffrey G. Miller National Environmental Law Moot Court Competition at Pace Law School has approximately 54 teams.[15]

---

13. *Judge John R. Brown Admiralty Moot Court Competition*, Sch. L. U. Tex. Austin, https://law.utexas.edu/advocacy/admiralty-competition/ (last visited Feb. 13, 2023).

14. *Robert F. Wagner National Labor and Employment Law Moot Court Competition*, N.Y. L. Sch., https://www.nyls.edu/academics/specialty-areas/competition-teams/moot-court-association/annual-robert-f-wagner-national-labor-and-employment-law-moot-court-competition/ (last visited Feb. 13, 2023).

15. *The Jeffrey G. Miller Pace National Environmental Law Moot Court Competition*, Pace L., https://law.pace.edu/nelmcc (last visited Feb. 13, 2023).

However, many specialty competitions have fewer than 25 or so teams,[16] so the chance of a law school team returning with some award increases when compared to larger competitions. Specialty competitions may also give less experienced students a better opportunity to advance because the level of advocacy may not be as high as the level of advocacy at the larger competitions, to which schools usually send their more experienced teams. That's not always the case, though. You should plan to send top advocates to specialty competitions, and you can expect to see a high level of competition among the top teams, at the very least. Student interest at some schools may be especially high for a certain subject, again raising the bar of advocacy.

C. Choosing competitions based on coaching availability

Typically, a moot court advisor cannot coach and travel with every moot court team the school fields, so, before registering for a competition, you need to find someone to coach each team, if the competition permits coaching. Schools may find coaches in the following groups:

- law students who have previously competed on an external competition team;
- local practitioners;
- faculty; and
- a combination of these people.

All of these models can work, and each has its advantages and disadvantages. Student coaches participate in an external competition before they coach, so they have first-hand knowledge of the competition's workings. Student coaches also are regularly on campus, potentially making scheduling practices easier. And student coaches are not as likely to need to balance an active professional life with their coaching, as practitioner coaches usually must. However, student coaches must be adept at mentoring their teams and must be professional in leading the team. Therefore, student coaches require faculty training and supervision.

---

16. *See, e.g.*, *National Tax Moot Court Competition*, Tax Sec. Fla. B., https://floridataxlawyers.org/new-tax-lawyers/students/national-moot-court-competition/ (last visited Feb. 13, 2023) (limiting the competition to 16 teams).

Practitioner coaches are a good choice because they have wisdom coming from their work in the field. Alumni may be looking for a way to connect with their law school alma mater, and practitioners in general may be eager to work with law students as they enter the profession. Coaching is a good way to do that. Some coaches become highly invested in the team from year to year. However, practitioner coaches can find scheduling practice times to be difficult, or they may get called away with deadlines or work travel.

Faculty are well suited to coach external competition teams because of their expertise in teaching and mentoring students. And like the practitioner coaches, faculty coaches are experts in their respective substantive fields. But faculty coaches must balance their coaching with other teaching and scholarship obligations. At some schools, faculty coaches may receive stipends, particularly if faculty members need incentives to coach and will be required to spend a substantial amount of time mentoring the team.

Time is the most important resource that a coach brings to a team. As a moot court advisor, you must explain to anyone who volunteers to coach that the time commitment is huge. The coach must organize practice sessions, attend practice sessions, and understand the law and facts of each problem.

In addition to the ability to devote time to the team, the coach should be someone who has expertise in the subject matter of the problem, someone who has expertise in appellate advocacy, or both. Rarely will a moot court advisor find one coach who is an expert in both, so consider pairing two professionals as co-coaches. Such an ideal pairing might be a professor with appellate advocacy expertise and a professor or practitioner with substantive expertise. A doctrinal faculty member with no moot court experience and little or no practice experience will have more trouble preparing a team to succeed because they will not know the formalities and conventions of oral argument or of moot court competitions. The faculty member does not necessarily need a full partner but should identify at least one person with moot court experience to attend at least one practice and teach the students the conventions of moot court and critique their presentations for style.

Regardless of the person or persons chosen to coach the team, remember that participation in moot court is an educational experience that leads to academic credit at many law schools and is governed by

ABA Standard 305.[17] Therefore, before choosing to send a team to a competition, you must designate full- or part-time faculty to supervise team preparation. A faculty member needs to supervise the number of hours the students accrue in participating on the team. Team members should use a system to record their time. A faculty member also needs to oversee the quality of the educational experience, including the team's research and brief writing, and the number and quality of oral argument practices and instruction. Students should receive a syllabus with expected learning outcomes. And even if the students' participation on a team will not result in academic credit, the moot court advisor should do everything to ensure a quality educational experience—and good coaching from someone with time and expertise is necessary for that.

It is of primary importance that in selecting coaches, you pick coaches who will demonstrate professionalism in working with your students and representing your institution when they travel with your team. Whenever possible, vet the coach with others in the legal community who will give you an unbiased assessment of the person's maturity and level of commitment. This includes such important matters as a commitment to diversity and inclusion and an ability to communicate effectively with others. A coach must be a person you can trust around your students. That person needs to be trusted to provide helpful feedback to students without hurting their feelings or marring their professional or personal identity. The coach must also be someone safe who can be trusted to handle travel with students. It would be beneficial to formalize your expectations of professionalism when bringing a coach on board your program. Students also need to understand these expectations. Include training on cultural competency and implicit bias as part of your expectations and training for everyone involved with the moot court program.[18] These are important matters of professional identify forma-

---

17. *ABA Standards*, AM. B. ASS'N, http://www.americanbar.org/groups/legal_education/resources/standards.html (last visited Feb. 13, 2023) (linking to the Standards and Rules of Procedure for Approval of Law Schools). Standard 305(a) provides that a law school may grant credit for moot court. Standard 303(a)(2) states that a law school shall offer a curriculum that includes at least one writing experience in the first year and one upper-level requirement supervised by faculty. A moot court experience, under Interpretation 305-1 qualifies as a writing experience if it meets the requirements of Standard 303(a)(2).

18. Marcus Lind-Martinez, *Latinidad, White Supremacy, & Reforming First-Year Moot Court Competitions to Confront Racial & Ethnic Bias*, 23 HARVARD LATINX L. REV. 125, 138 (2020).

tion and reinforcement, and the joint work of your students, coaches, faculty advisors, and judges can do much to teach and foster empathy within the profession.[19]

Maximizing quality opportunities for students should be your goal in all aspects of choosing to send teams to competitions. One of the more controversial questions that arises when fielding moot court teams is how much emphasis to place on "winning." Usually, if you carefully consider and discuss the competition and coaching selections with the students, faculty, and administration involved, the "winning" will take care of itself. In other words, if you, as the moot court advisor, balance attending some of the larger competitions with some smaller competitions and mix in energetic, quality students with excellent faculty coaching, you will have a winning combination.

II. Scouting and Selecting Team Members

Assembling the right team is an exciting process for both a faculty advisor and the new teams. There are several ways to approach this process. Scouting is about recruiting and building momentum and interest in team participation. In selecting students for teams, you'll want to consider the timing and method of selection and how you inform the new teams and their coaches.

A. Scouting new team members

Law school goes by quickly for students, and students have many different activities to try. Thus, you'll need to reach out actively to each class, especially the first-year students, to build enthusiasm for moot court. Reaching out means first and foremost informing the students. Students need to be educated about what moot court is and how moot court is different from trial advocacy or other skills competitions. First-year students often don't know the difference between trial and appellate advocacy. The various competitions may all sound the same. Tell the students how they can learn more about moot court. If your law school offers an organization fair for incoming first-year students, be sure your

19. *Id.*

board participates. Come prepared with flyers about moot court and the selection process. Make sure the first-year students know what steps they need to take to get on a team. Neither you nor they want to find out after the fact that they missed the entry point for the selection process or some key prerequisite.

If you have a link on the law school's website, make sure it's regularly updated with competition information and contacts. If your school uses social media, consider using it to update the students. Be sure to check with your administration before creating or using social media. Instagram, Snapchat, and Twitter can be good ways to inform students about your moot court program and to keep interest alive in the national competitions. Be sure to include a roster of competitions that include affinity competitions. Actively reach out to affinity groups at your school to make sure students are aware of affinity moot court competitions that might be of interest to them.

You'll then need to carry through the line of communication, so students know about information sessions and key dates for selecting new team members. Consider holding information sessions about the selection process. Your moot court board can run these sessions and generate a positive atmosphere. Students should understand why moot court is beneficial to their skill development and long-term job development. You likely will have some teams entered in specialty competitions, and at least some of those teams will likely link to student organizations devoted to the study of that area of law. Reach out to those organizations to let students know how beneficial participating in moot court can be to their career and job placement. You can also promote moot court through your 1L legal writing or legal skills classes or upper-level advocacy courses.

You may be lucky enough to run a program at a school that recognizes the value of moot court. If so, generating student interest in moot court is usually not a concern; many students recognize that competing in an external competition will develop their lawyering skills and set them apart from other students at their law school. In other institutions, different activities are elevated in prestige or support. For example, some schools prohibit students from participating in both moot court and law review. If your school allows participation in both, it's helpful to communicate with the law reviews at your school about working together to facilitate the schedules of students who are doing both moot court and law review, especially in their busy second year of law school. That communication can go a long way to making participating students' lives easier and developing rapport.

B. Selecting students for a team

How you choose to select students for a team depends on when you want the students to start participating on a team and whether students will be eligible for one team or more than one team over the course of their law school careers.

1. SELECTING STUDENTS FROM THE FIRST-YEAR CLASS

You may choose to put students on teams starting in the fall of their second year. To do so you'll need to select among the first-year students. If your first-year legal writing curriculum includes an appellate brief-writing and oral advocacy exercise, you can use the students' performance on that exercise to find the students with the most potential.

Alternatively, you could conduct a short internal competition at the end of the 1L year to assess the students. Talk to your administration about the timing of this sort of competition. Students should demonstrate both their writing and oral argument abilities. Before the competition, you may want to provide a short tutorial about appellate advocacy with the help of your moot court board or coaches. You'll want to consider whether to select teams all on your own or to seek input from the moot court board, faculty advisors, and coaches. Selecting the teams all on your own may be time consuming, but you'll have an excellent sense of the competitors' strengths and weaknesses. Enlisting your moot court board's help will reduce the time the process takes, and the moot court board members may have insights into which students would work well together.

The advantage of having students start competing in the fall of their second year is that you can place the top-performing students on another team as 3Ls, and the team will benefit from their experience. Or they can compete in the fall and spring of their second year and participate as coaches in their third year. Either way, your most experienced and dedicated students are on your top teams. Consider that these students are committing a significant portion of their law-school careers to moot court, and you need to manage expectations about that. You'll also end up with a small group of highly competitive students who get to participate on select teams. That may not be the best option if your goal is to provide educational opportunities to a larger group of law students. After all, the purpose of moot court at its core is to teach skills. Be sure to weigh these considerations carefully to fit with your moot court program's objectives.

2. SELECTING STUDENTS FROM THE SECOND-YEAR CLASS

Another option is to hold a moot court class for 2Ls as a prerequisite to competing. In such a system, students take the moot court class in the fall of the second year, which then makes them eligible to be selected for a team. Students should apply for teams before they complete the fall course. The moot court board then interviews the students with your help. Because the students have gone through the class, you'll have a more accurate sense of their capabilities than you would by evaluating their performance in their first year. Students can start to compete in the spring of their second year or in either semester during their third year.[20]

You may hold an internal competition as part of a class. Or you may separate the class from the internal competition. In the latter case, you may invite the best students from the class to participate in an honors competition, or you may simply require the class for general participation in the internal competition. The students' success in the internal competition, whether as part of a class or separate from it, will give you good data on how the students compete under pressure.

3. ASSIGNING AND INFORMING THE TEAMS

Once the students have applied for a team and passed through what is essentially an audition or tryout, you'll need to assign the students to teams.

---

20. *See, e.g., Robert F. Wagner National Labor and Employment Law Moot Court Competition*, N.Y. L. Sch., *supra* note 14 (competition fully contained in the spring semester).

First, consider logistics. Check each competition's rules carefully to make sure you assign the right number of students to each team. Some competitions provide for two-person teams, three-person teams, or even more. Some limit student coaching. Also make sure you know whether your school is likely to get into a competition or if the competition administrators regularly admit fewer teams than those who applied to compete. If that's the case, be sure to tell the potential competitors if you think you might need to find an alternate competition. Determine whether the prospective team would be comfortable switching the semester in which they compete.

Assess which students are interested in participating on a given team. While you could assign students without regard to their personal interests in a competition or who their teammates will be, students often do better when they are working with teammates they like and respect. If you have identified prerequisites for team participation, such as coursework, be sure that the students have fulfilled those prerequisites.

Second, if you have faculty coaches, or even practitioner coaches, consult with them as you are assigning the teams. Faculty may prefer to have certain students on their team. Practitioner coaches may know students from internships or from having scouted them at an internal competition at your law school. For each team, you want to find the right fit of personalities and team dynamics, in addition to the students' talent and academic background. You could even allow the faculty or practitioner coaches to interview prospective candidates for their team. The more invested the team members and coaches are, the more likely the team is to succeed.

Third, consider any needs the students may have regarding the timing of the competition. If a student has a particularly tight schedule, an internship, or an impending family event such as a wedding, take that timing into account. A student who is especially busy one semester, or during part of a semester, may simply be too overloaded. Sometimes a student may have religious observances or holidays to consider; be sure to schedule around those dates. If students are observant on certain days of the week, they may prefer to participate on the team only as brief writers if the competition oral arguments conflict with the students' availability for those arguments. Also discuss any accessibility needs a student might have in traveling to or participating in a competition to make sure your institution and the host of the competition are fully engaged in supporting the student. Competitions are very willing to accommodate students' needs if you communicate about an accommodation request.

Once you have compiled the necessary information, you can slate the teams. Don't be surprised if it takes a couple of weeks to do the slating. Set a deadline for when you will inform the teams and how. You could email the team members individually, along with their coaches, or you could post the news on TWEN or on a law-school news-distribution system. Whichever way you choose, tell the teams at the same time. In fairness to everyone, don't let information about some teams leak too early. If some people did not make the cut, let them know first individually to avoid embarrassment. Be ready to explain your decisions. For most of those students, you can explain that they were not the right fit for a team. If you anticipate cutting some students in the selection process, explain this before the team selections go out so that students are not surprised when they find out they did not make a team.

Connect students and coaches as soon as possible. Provide an email address where they can reach each other. Also explain when they can expect the competition to start and how to register for their competition credits.

III. Preparing Your Team for the Competition

Most competitions provide that once the problem set is released, students must research, draft, and submit the brief without assistance. Oral argument preparation should commence right after a team submits its brief, so the team has time to practice. That means you need to prepare your teams before the problem is released to allow the teams to hit the ground running when their competitions start.

A. First steps before the competition starts

When the competitors get the good news that they have made it onto a team, they should receive information about how to register for any credit hours, as well as how many credits they will receive. Provide your administration with a list of the competitions, competitors, and credit information at the same time. Time the release of the team selections so students have plenty of time to register. Your competitors and law-school administration may find it helpful to have a chart detailing the ways students can get credit for moot court, which you or your board can prepare. If students are receiving credit, they should also get a syllabus with learning outcomes and clearly defined expectations. Even if they are not receiving credit, it's good to send them a contract or similar document setting forth clear expectations for student conduct on competition teams and obligations for participating on moot court. This information should also be provided in the student moot court handbook and shared with faculty advisors and coaches.

Your facilities staff will be thankful if you develop an efficient way to reserve practice rooms and register guest judges. An online form like Survey Monkey, Google Forms, or Qualtrics can work well for this purpose. Provide a link to the form with instructions on how and when to reserve rooms and register judges. Remind students not to move podiums out of classrooms or change the layout of a classroom. Another helpful online form is a timekeeping spreadsheet for student hours that you and your board may access. Students should plan to submit their hours regularly—once a week or every two weeks—so you can quickly see if a team is keeping up with its hours. Remind students of the hours they need to accrue to receive credit.

If you have any practice expectations or other requirements students must fulfill to receive credit, give those requirements to them in writing. Similarly, provide the team coaches with a checklist of tasks they should do in supervising their teams.

B. Assigning team responsibilities

Once you have selected a team, you'll need to think about whether to assign individual responsibilities for brief writing and oral argument, or whether you will allow the team members to select their own roles. The answer depends partially on the dynamics between the team members and the number of students on the team. You'll also want to consider whether to assign responsibilities immediately or closer to the date of the competition. But most importantly, you should rely on your own assessment of the individual team members' strengths and weaknesses to assign roles.

If you have a two-person team, it's fairly easy to divide the responsibilities because most moot court briefs present two issues for argument. Each student researches and writes about an issue, and the students divide the remaining sections of the briefs. Each student argues the issue they briefed.

Some competitions assign the side the students will brief, but if you field two teams for a competition, the teams may be able to choose a side. In the rare instance when students cannot negotiate the side they will brief without hard feelings, it is most fair (and avoids bad feelings) if the teams flip a coin to determine their sides.[21]

Assuming a three (or more) person team, things get a bit trickier. Here it's especially important to understand the individual strengths of the competitors, as well as team dynamics. If one person is an especially good brief writer, and the other two students are better oralists, you may want to assign one student to the role of brief writer. However, the two students responsible for the oral arguments need to research their issue individually and provide feedback to the brief writer during the writing process.[22] Otherwise, the oralists may not sufficiently engage with the material in time to fully develop their understanding of the arguments. Similarly, the brief writer may get overloaded writing the brief on their own. The oralists should plan to assist with finalizing the brief: proofreading, creating the tables and formatting, and perhaps helping to draft the statement of facts or statement of the case. The brief writer should also help to coach the team by attending practices and acting as a practice judge or bailiff.

Some schools purposefully select a strong writer (who may not be the best oral advocate) with the idea that he or she will take primary responsibility for drafting and revising the brief. Other advisors do not favor this approach.[23] For one, dividing responsibility this way may not mimic the way attorneys divide a case in practice. Students learn to argue by

---

21. Mary Beth Beazley, A Practical Guide to Appellate Advocacy § 14.3, at 315 (4th ed. 2014).

22. *Id.* § 14.4.1, at 316.

23. *Id.* § 14.4, at 315.

researching and writing the argument and then preparing and delivering their oral argument.

Alternatively, the team members can write the brief together and share the oral arguments. This approach works well when all three students are talented writers and oralists. Two students divide an issue so one is responsible for the on-brief oral argument and the other is responsible for the off-brief oral argument.[24] Those two students research and write the argument for that issue.[25] Try to pick the issue that's more complicated for the two students to work on together.[26] The third student is responsible for researching, writing, and arguing the second issue.[27] The three students divide the other sections of the brief and the editing process. There are other ways to do this, too. For instance, one student can write each issue and make the on-brief oral argument for each issue. Another student on the team can be the overall "brief editor," and then two students divide the on-brief and off-brief oral arguments for one of the issues. Whatever approach you take, aim to play to each team member's strengths.

The personalities and dynamics of the team may affect how you construct the team. It's worthwhile to meet with a team of three to discuss the alternatives and ask the students to help you decide the best approach after discussing the pros and cons of each option. Reserve the right to make the final decision but ask the students to discuss it. This meeting is a good opportunity to discuss teamwork and good communication.[28] Setting the right tone with the team from the beginning can reap big dividends.

C. The initial meeting

Whether you have a team of two or three, you should schedule an initial meeting with your team to discuss the competition. At the initial meeting, calendar deadlines for researching and brief writing, reserving time for the editing process and last-minute contingencies. Review the

24. *Id.* § 14.4.1, at 316.
25. *Id.*
26. *Id.*
27. *Id.*
28. *Id.* § 14.4.2, at 317.

competition rules and the brief-submission process with the team.[29] Make sure the team knows how to submit the brief—online or by mail, for instance—and the required digital format for the brief (e.g., PDF or Microsoft Word) if the brief is to be submitted online. A team will lose a lot of points if they don't properly submit their brief.

Another point to discuss with the team is who is responsible for travel arrangements. Most moot court boards facilitate travel and hotel arrangements but having one team member be the point person for communicating about those arrangements makes things easier. Discuss with the team the date by which they should make their travel and hotel arrangements. Establishing a date helps to avoid last-minute hassles and additional cost. Consider whether students can share a room to save costs. Review what hotel the competition hosts recommend. Some competitions reserve rooms at pricey hotels. Check to see if less expensive hotels are nearby. Some schools will only reimburse for the designated competition hotel, even if the alternative is less expensive, so make sure you check those rules first.

At the meeting, each team member should receive a competition binder or access to an online platform to share resources among team members such as TWEN, Canvas, SharePoint, or Google Docs. The binder or online platform should include the following items:

- the competition rules, scoring rubrics, and a calendar of important dates;
- the law school policies and instructions on travel, reimbursement, and academic credit;
- a printed log for keeping track of hours for credit and a room reservation form or instructions for accessing these forms online; and
- the "white-glove inspection checklist" provided in the online appendix.

Address room reservations and guest access at your meeting to make sure the students understand the logistics and the importance of following school facilities management policies. Team coaches should also share with the teams the oral argument practice schedule and a list of

29. *Id.* § 14.1, at 313.

practitioners and judges who have been recruited to participate in those practices.

Finally, around the time of the initial meeting, and typically at the beginning of each semester, offer brief-writing and oral advocacy training workshops that the teams can attend before their competition begins. Remind students to attend those trainings. You may wish to bring in a guest speaker who is an expert on appellate practice to offer tips for success. You may also choose to record the trainings and make them available online with the other competition materials, which has the benefit that the training needs to be created only once. In addition, remind students to review their class notes from their first-year legal writing courses or their appellate advocacy course (if your law school requires the course as a prerequisite to participation).

IV. Promoting Effective Brief Writing

In many competitions, the brief score is weighed heavily, so a team seals its fate with the quality of its brief.[30] A challenge for you as the faculty advisor or coach is to encourage a quality brief while at the same time not breaking any competition rules, which almost always prohibit aid during the brief-writing process. All of the help you can give to your team must be before the team receives its problem set, and you'll want to keep that date in mind so you can do any training before then. To give the team all the time it needs, be sure to forward the competition record the minute you receive it. Even a few days wasted without the record can hurt a team's chances.

A. Building the foundations for good brief writing

As the faculty advisor or coach, you may or may not have taught or previously worked with students who are participating on a moot court team. Accordingly, you may or may not know the exact strengths and weaknesses of the team's brief-writing capabilities. You may have a student who has previous experience writing a brief in a competition or for an internship or clerkship in an appellate practice setting. Or you

30. *Id.*

may have team members who have never written an appellate brief at all. With that in mind, you need to prepare the students for the type of writing that they are expected to produce.[31]

1. NO ASSISTANCE POLICIES

The very first thing you need to keep in mind in preparing your students is that virtually all moot court competitions prohibit the team from obtaining any assistance in writing the brief.[32] At most, a competition may allow students to discuss the issues with non-team members.[33] If two teams are going to the same competition, they cannot work together on their briefs. You'll want to make the team aware of these rules. Some competitions even require the team to certify that they did not receive assistance on the brief.[34] The question then for you becomes how to elicit a good brief while complying with the usual no-assistance policies.

2. DEVELOPING A TEAM OF STRONG BRIEF WRITERS

There's no "I" in moot court. Moot court is a team activity. As a team, the students should discuss the steps in the research and writing process with you. The early steps are research, outlining, and drafting. The later steps are reviewing, revising, polishing, and finalizing the brief for sub-

---

31. For an in-depth discussion on writing an appellate brief consult Beazley, *supra* note 21, chs. 2–12, at 13–286. Other helpful resources on writing appellate briefs include Ruggero J. Aldisert, Winning on Appeal: Better Briefs and Oral Argument (2d ed. 2013); Linda L. Berger and Kathryn M. Stanchi, Legal Persuasion: A Rhetorical Approach to the Science (2018); Linda H. Edwards, Readings in Persuasion: Briefs that Changed the World (2012); Ross Guberman, Point Made: How to Write Like the Nation's Top Advocates (2d ed. 2014); Antonin Scalia and Bryan A. Garner, Making Your Case: The Art of Persuading Judges (2008).

32. *See, e.g., National Moot Court Competition Rules*, N.Y.C. B. Ass'n, http://www.nycbar.org/law-students/national-moot-court/competition-rules (link to PDF Rules and Comments) (last visited Feb. 13, 2023) (Rule 9 prohibits assistance, and the Comment to Rule 9 provides that each team member "must certify their brief is their sole collective work product"); *see also* Beazley, *supra* note 21, § 14.1, at 313.

33. *See, e.g., National Appellate Advocacy Competition Rules*, Am. B. Ass'n, http://www.americanbar.org/groups/law_students/events_competitions/practical_skills_competitions/naac.html (last visited Feb. 13, 2023).

34. *See, e.g., National Moot Court Competition Rules*, N.Y.C. B. Ass'n, *supra* note 32.

mission. Walk the students through deadlines for each. In addition, discuss with the students how they plan to divide writing the sections of the brief other than the Argument and who will oversee the final stages of submitting the brief. The students should know how to contact the competition if they have questions about the rules or requirements while they are writing the brief because the rules may forbid them from asking you.[35] Soon after the team is established and well before the problem is released, meet with the students and establish deadlines for each step in the brief-writing process. The students should agree about these deadlines and how to divide responsibility. If the students are receiving academic credit, meeting these deadlines should be part of the criteria for receiving a passing grade in the class.

Ask the team members if they have written something with a partner before. Use this question as a starting point for discussing peer editing, collaborative drafting, and communicating with team members.[36] You may want to talk about conflict resolution and professionalism.[37] Don't forget to address ethics and plagiarism. It's always helpful to remind the students that they are representing the law school throughout the competition.

You can and should train students on brief writing before the competition begins. This training can be informal, or you can conduct a short series of workshops, training videos, or podcasts that can be posted on the team's online platform. Even if students have already taken a course on appellate advocacy or have some working knowledge from an internship or other work experience, you should still review good brief-writing concepts with them. Consider asking the students on the team to provide you with samples of their writing that you can use as a starting point for discussion. If the competition provides sample scoring sheets, they can be a good tool for identifying items for a final review checklist. If the students have written an appellate brief before, consider providing additional feedback on it or designing peer-review exercises that allow teammates to evaluate the brief for adherence to best practices you have identified in workshops. Past winning briefs from the competition, or

---

35. *See* Beazley, *supra* note 21, § 14.1, at 313.

36. *Id.* § 14.4.2, at 317–18.

37. *See id.* § 14.4.2, at 317 (discussing professionalism when students critique others' work).

strong briefs from past teams fielded by your law school, provide excellent models and teaching tools.

B. A primer on good brief writing

Writing briefs for moot court competitions is not as daunting a task as it may initially seem, so long as students use a process and stick to it. Before a competition begins, a faculty member or alumni coach should review the brief-writing process and the principles of good writing with the team. The basic steps involve (in order)

- identifying the issues;
- researching the law;
- outlining the arguments;[38]
- drafting the argument section;
- crafting the other portions of the brief;
- reviewing and revising the brief; and
- polishing the final product.

Each of these steps can be accomplished most effectively by following a basic approach. And, happily, for several of them, the case file for the competition often reduces the amount of work required. You can share these materials, including the team-editing checklist and "white-glove" checklist, with your team, or you can use these materials to prepare your own handouts and presentation on brief writing.

1. IDENTIFYING THE ISSUES

Unlike appellate practice in the real world, identifying the issues to be argued in moot court competitions is relatively easy. You can point out to the team that a typical case file consists of lower court opinions that clearly identify the issues for review. And, since most moot court arguments are often set in the United States Supreme Court, the issues are more definitively identified in the order granting certiorari, which is normally the last page of the case file.[39]

---

38. *Id.* §§ 4.1.4–4.1.5, at 76–78 (describing how to use reverse roadmaps and working outlines).

39. *Id.* § 14.2, at 314.

Students often get into trouble by failing to brief the issues certified. Sometimes those issues are stated in such a way as to reduce the complexity of the case; sometimes they are stated in a way to suggest a different substantive direction than the lower court opinions seemed to indicate. No matter: you should advise students to stick to the specific issues stated in the orders certifying the issues for review.

In rare instances, the appeal is to a lower court, or in international moot court competitions, the issues for appeal may be less clearly identified. In these instances, students should still fall back to the lower court opinions to identify the issues that need to be argued. They should be careful not to get too creative here. The issues the students may find interesting may not be the ones the problem targets, and many a team has lost before even giving an oral argument by briefing issues that don't appear in the brief graders' bench memo.

As the students read through the issues, they should bear in mind the way most moot court issues are framed. The issues presented for review generally fall into one of two types.

The first type of issue normally encountered in a moot court competition is an issue that flows from a split of authority. Here, the problem asks a student to argue which of two previously held positions is correct and why that line of reasoning is correct. This kind of issue can range from the very simple (a split in the circuits on exactly the problem set's facts) to the more complicated (divergent views on similar facts in previous opinions, but where the facts are sufficiently different from each as to make neither view clearly controlling). To argue a circuit split effectively, students must understand and use the reasoning the various circuits employed in adopting a position. Then, they must use that reasoning to advocate for that position in a new jurisdiction.

The second type of issue is the "next case" scenario. Here, the problem is asking a student to argue where the law should go since the facts require an extension or modification of existing law. This kind of issue can be intellectually more demanding than the first type because the advocates are being asked to be creative in arguing what the result should be for this "next case." Next-case issues require strict use of the basic paradigm all lawyers use—applying law to facts—but these issues allow advocates more latitude to make policy arguments because the issues are not clearly answered by existing law.

Both types of issues afford students an opportunity to argue policy, sometimes for the first time in their law-school careers. Discuss with students the sources of policy arguments—secondary sources, both legal and non-legal, as well as sources of legislative history (which may address the underlying policy rationale for a statute), and even a court's discussion of its rationale supporting its decision.

2. RESEARCHING THE LAW

Research is always an important part of any appellate brief, but in moot court, again, the task is usually less difficult than it can be in the real world. Most competitions follow a standard format for presenting the issues to be briefed, and, in so doing, they provide much of the potentially controlling authority on those issues.

So, before beginning an extensive and exhaustive research process (perhaps beginning with law review articles that provide background on the law), students should be advised to look to the lower court opinions in the case file. If, as with most competitions, the problem is laid out with a district court opinion, followed by a court of appeals opinion (perhaps including a concurring or dissenting opinion), the basic legal authorities relevant to the students' ultimate arguments are probably contained in those opinions. Some competitions provide just a few starting sources, while others are more generous with the number of sources provided.

A good law review article or a section of a treatise on point may still provide students with a good overview of the issues to be addressed, but they should not ignore the work that has already been done in the lower court opinions to identify relevant authority for the arguments to be made.

On the other hand, tell students not to assume that the entire universe of potential cases and other authorities has been identified in the lower court opinions in the case file. Indeed, one trick some competitions use is to refer to a less relevant or well-considered case for a point where a better one should be used. So, the team should use the cases in the lower court opinion as a starting point. Using those starting sources and updating them, the team will find others that may be more helpful in crafting the strongest possible arguments.

Also, the team should not assume that the characterizations of the cases in the lower court opinions are either correct or binding on the arguments the team will need to make. This is another trick the drafters of moot court problems sometimes employ (using a case for a proposition, but not using it as precisely as a careful reading of the case would require). Thus, that critical step in all legal research—reading the actual authority—is equally important in moot court. Students may be tempted to use artificial intelligence resources on the Internet and should be cautioned about the reliability of those tools for legal research, as well as the fact that competition rules may prohibit their use for research or drafting purposes.

3. OUTLINING THE ARGUMENTS

Remind the team that all good writers, and especially all good legal writers, outline what they intend to say before they actually compose the text of their document.[40] In drafting legal documents, all of the heavy lifting (i.e., the analysis of the issues and the structure of the arguments) should take place during this part of the students' work.

The team's goal is to create an outline for each main argument that is complete and detailed enough to provide a template from which the actual Argument section of the brief can be written. In other words, in the outline, the students should note not just the substantive points they are going to make, but the actual authorities they will be using and how they will show their relevance and persuasiveness. The students should also keep in mind counterarguments and how to respond to those arguments.

A complete outline accordingly includes everything the students need to write the actual arguments contained in it. Students should be able to type out the argument from the outline as essentially a mechanical process, with only their personal writing style needed to convert the outline to persuasive prose. You can tell the team, however, that some advocates prefer mapping—a visual technique for linking case authorities[41]—and that approach is fine too. Still other advocates use informal

---

40. *See generally id.* ch. 4, at 67–85 (on pre-drafting and early drafts).

41. Programs such as Thinker Analytix are available online to assist with argument mapping. *Methods & Research: Argument Mapping & Mastery Learning*, THINKER ANALYTIX, https://thinkeranalytix.org/methods/ (last visited on Feb. 13, 2023). Bryan Garner's nonlinear way of outlining (the "whirligig" method) is helpful for students who find it difficult to use linear outlines. *Conquering Writer's Block with Whirligigs and Mad-*

outlines and go back and forth between their outline and rough draft. Discuss with students what their personal pre-drafting approach is and how they can improve on it.

4. DRAFTING THE ARGUMENT SECTION

If the team's outline is a complete and detailed summary of their actual arguments, finishing the Argument section should now be relatively easy. The team simply needs to convert the outlines for each of their arguments into persuasive prose, applying law to facts to show why their view of the issue is the correct one.[42]

Just as with trial-level brief writing, students should use a consistent CREAC (syllogistic) format throughout the Argument and emphasize their conclusions up front. Headings should be used to highlight the main points. Under the headings, the students should include an introductory paragraph, sometimes called a roadmap, where they summarize their argument for that section of the brief. Using roadmap paragraphs helps a reader to understand rapidly what the argument is about, allowing the reader to better digest the supporting law and arguments below.

One of the main shifts from trial to appellate brief writing is that an advocate must address the standard of review and weave the standard of review throughout the argument.[43] Another shift is that an advocate must argue what the substantive law should be. In other words, an advocate is not merely applying well-settled law to the facts but must argue the state of the law and convince a reader to agree to apply the more favorable law to the facts of the case. A good argument emphasizes this form of advocacy, while at the same time being mindful of the facts of the record.

Finally, students writing a moot court brief should be prepared to use public policy to support their argument. As noted above, tell students

---

men, NCAJ, https://www.ncaj.com/news/conquering-writers-block-with-whirligigs-and-madmen (last visited on Feb. 13, 2023).

42. *See generally* Beazley, *supra* note 21, ch. 5, at 87–115 (on drafting the rules and using structure).

43. Gerald Lebovits, Drew Gewuerz, and Christopher Hunker, *Winning the Moot Court Oral Argument: A Guide for Intramural & Intermural Moot Court Competitors*, 41 Capital U. L. Rev. 888, 904 (2013) (discussing the importance of accounting for the standard of review in an appellate argument).

before they receive the problem that they may use secondary sources, both legal and non-legal, to make their policy arguments. They may form a public policy argument by looking to legislative history, or perhaps they may find support for a policy argument in a court's rationale. Other sources of policy arguments include newspaper editorials, the websites of advocacy organizations, and amicus briefs. Students should be aware that sometimes a policy argument is based in common sense and that they may not find a citation to support their policy argument.

5. CRAFTING THE OTHER PORTIONS OF THE BRIEF

The rest of the brief flows from the Argument section. The "ancillary" parts of the brief (in particular, the Issues Presented, the Statement of the Facts, the Summary of the Argument, and the Conclusion) should be drafted to support and reflect accurately what the team set out in the Argument section.[44]

The Issues Presented (sometimes called the Questions Presented or Statement of the Issues) should represent the team's best effort to convert the presumably neutral statement of the issues contained in the problem to persuasive issue statements that suggest how the issues should be decided. And remind students to include in these formulations those key facts that give rise to (and resolve) the issues, as well as to write the issues in parallel form. The traditional form of an issue statement is one sentence beginning with either a question word (and ending with a question mark) or whether (and ending with a period). The issue statement should provide the legal question and a relevant factual basis for the question—the pivotal fact.[45] Bryan Garner has identified another approach: the deep issue format, where an advocate lays out the foundation for the issue by stating the procedural history and factual basis leading up to the legal question in a series of sentences.[46] All of these approaches are recognized and acceptable ways of framing the issue.

The Statement of the Facts can be organized chronologically or topically, depending on which best suits the factual and legal issues pre-

---

44. *See* BEAZLEY, *supra* note 21, ch. 9, at 189–226 (on drafting other parts of the brief).

45. *Id.* § 9.1, at 190–99.

46. SCALIA AND GARNER, *supra* note 31, at 85 (citing BRYAN A. GARNER, THE WINNING BRIEF, 53–97 (2d ed. 2004)).

sented by the problem. In either event, however, the cardinal rule for this section is to include all facts that are referred to in the Argument section. The reader should never learn of a fact for the first time in the Argument section of the brief. The facts must be stated neutrally without argument, but they should be presented in a compelling narrative using good storytelling techniques to maintain interest and highlight key facts.

Some competitions require a Statement of the Case as a separate section of the brief. That section relates the case's procedural history. Other competitions combine the Statement of the Facts with the Statement of the Case. The team should check the rules and review the winning briefs from past years to confirm how the competition organizers want this part of the brief to be presented. The procedural history should include information about the pleadings and motions, as well as dates, relevant to the appeal, as well as a brief summary of key arguments and the lower courts' decisions and rationale.

The Summary of the Argument should provide an overview of the specific arguments contained in the Argument section. Here, the team should give a reader enough detail so they understand the points the team will argue and an idea of how the team will argue those points. Caution students not to get too deep in the weeds on the details of their arguments. If they are citing heavily to cases in this section of their brief, they are probably too deep in the weeds, and they should aim not to cite to authorities.

The Conclusion is a final and important opportunity to persuade, but it should be brief. The Conclusion provides a reader with a summary of what the team argued as to each issue. An easy way to provide that summary is for the team to restate the headings for each argument. The team can then revise that restatement into a cohesive final argument. The Conclusion should be limited to one paragraph (not a sentence more) for each of the main arguments. The last sentence is the "prayer" for the court's disposition.

The other ancillary portions of the brief (a jurisdictional statement, an oral argument statement), if they are required for the competition, should not be substantively difficult to draft. The team should keep these portions simple and short. In most instances, the team only loses points on these portions for sloppiness or improper formatting. The same is true for the cover page. Citation form is key in the Table of Authorities. Again, the team should carefully review the winning brief from the previous year's competition and the competition rules (such as whether the competition is following the Supreme Court Rules) for guidance.

6. REVIEWING AND REVISING THE FIRST DRAFT

On a team, students receive feedback from their team members.[47] Collaborative brief writing is an important skill to learn, as many times in real-life legal practice, attorneys work together on briefs. The peer-editing process is a great way for students to learn about their own writing in a dynamic environment. It's also a great way for students to learn to be better supervising attorneys in the future.

To facilitate that editing, students should set a date for exchanging their drafts. It may be helpful for students to know that the first draft doesn't need to be perfect. In reviewing a team member's draft, a student should start with the larger-scale concepts first, examining the content and overall structure of the argument. As a reviewer, a student should ask whether they can understand the flow of the argument. Does the argument make sense? Is the theme of the argument evident, and does that theme match the other sections of the argument? Does each section lead with the strongest arguments but also address any counterarguments?

After the first edit, the team members should plan to do a second review examining whether the arguments are cohesive, whether the headings flow well from one section to the next, and whether the arguments have a good balance of legal and factual arguments: arguments grounded in the law and arguments grounded in the facts of the record. See the online appendix for a team editing exercise to facilitate this process.

7. POLISHING THE FINAL DRAFT

Even if a team has put a lot of work into the document they consider to be the final draft, the team is probably still at risk of losing a sizeable chunk of points on their brief score. Points are lost, notwithstanding the solid research the team conducted and the creative arguments the

---

47. Beazley, *supra* note 21, § 14.4.2, at 318.

advocates crafted, when a brief just doesn't read well.[48] It may be strewn with all kinds of errors or may just be difficult to read, or both.[49] For this reason, the polishing of an appellate brief—the process that results in a completely error-free and reader-friendly document—is the critical last step to ensure a quality brief that will be rewarded with a top score.[50] Neuroscience research shows that editors are more likely to pick up errors in their own writing if they put it aside for a while and then come back to it.[51] Using a five-day period will really help.

The team should give itself as many as five days to subject the brief to a "white-glove inspection." The term derives from military "boot camp" training, when the company inspector would enter the barracks of the new recruits wearing a white glove to conduct the inspection of the barracks. A thorough white-glove inspection of an appellate brief includes these ten steps, each of which should be conducted with a break (some other activity, so as to be fresh when conducting the step) before and after it is attempted. The team should use the following "white-glove inspection" checklist over the course of those five days and redraft or edit as necessary:

- Review the logical consistency and organizational flow of the entire document. Focus particularly on the Argument section. Locate gaps in logic and confusion in organization.
- Consider whether paragraphs are too long or contain more than one thesis. Break overly long paragraphs into shorter ones; add or edit thesis sentences.
- Examine whether each sentence follows logically from the one that precedes it and leads logically to the one that follows it. Add transition words and phrases.
- Consider whether each sentence is worded as carefully, accurately, and succinctly as possible.

---

48. *Id.* § 14.4.3, at 319.

49. *Id.*

50. *Id.* Chapter 12 of BEAZLEY provides comprehensive advice on polishing. *See id.* ch. 12, at 279–86.

51. *See* Nick Stockton, *What's Up With That: Why It's So Hard to Catch Your Own Typos*, WIRED (Aug. 12, 2014, 11:21 AM EDT), https://www.wired.com/2014/08/wu-wt-typos/ (suggesting that it's easier for writers to find typos in their own writing when they adopt proofreading strategies designed to "trick [their] brain into pretending that it's reading [the writing] for the first time").

- Check each sentence for correct grammar and punctuation. Look for comma splices, run-on sentences, and incomplete sentences.
- Check all citations for accuracy and case names for correct spelling.
- Check for typos and hidden mistakes (e.g., "statue" instead of "statute," "lead" instead of "led") in both words and citations. Review any tables to make sure pincites are correct.[52]
- Use spell check and grammar check.
- Read the draft yet one more time. This time read it for "pleasure," taking pride in your final product, but looking for hidden glitches.
- Print out the final copy of your draft for submission. Check for print quality, pagination, proper margins, and any formatting required by the competition. Make adjustments and reprint as necessary.

Each of these "white-glove" steps must be conducted independently of the others. A brief writer can't try to combine these steps to save time. Accordingly, a committed moot court team will devote five days to the perfecting of the final brief. With two or three team members fully engaged in all ten steps, the final result should be a completely error-free document that is written in reader-friendly prose. The team should receive a copy of the "white-glove inspection" checklist, which is included in the online appendix.

And another good white-glove inspection practice is for the brief writers to "clean as they go." In other words, a good brief writer anticipates the work required in these ten steps by eliminating as many errors as they can while drafting the brief.

Writing a strong appellate brief for a moot court competition is far more important than the sometimes-minimal weight it is given compared to the oral arguments. Because many oral argument scores are closely bunched, the score a brief receives, even if it only counts for a third of the final ranking for a team, can be critical.

---

52. *Id.*

Using a structured approach, such as presented here, to complete the brief-writing task will result in stronger briefs that students and coaches can be proud of and that will help a team bring back awards for its school.

V. Practicing Oral Arguments

Once the team submits its brief, its members must then turn to oral argument. Like any skill, a good oral argument takes practice. The good news is that practice does significantly improve the quality of a competitor's oral argument at competition.

A. Oral argument basics

Most oral arguments at a moot court competition are fifteen minutes per advocate, with both advocates for the appellant or petitioner's team going first, followed by both advocates for the appellee or respondent's team.[53] The competition's rules, however, may provide a different sequence and may allot a longer or shorter time period for the oral arguments. Accordingly, read the rules carefully to see how the oral arguments are structured. If the rules don't provide that information, then call the competition chair to learn more.

Each advocate presents their argument in three parts: the opening, the body of the argument, and the closing. Further, one advocate from the petitioner team will have a fourth part to their argument: the rebuttal. [54]

1. THE OPENING STATEMENT

Judges often allow students to get through their opening statement before asking questions, but students should practice being interrupted. The opening statement should be approximately one minute long or less.[55] Students should weave in a theme word or phrase and their theory of the case to hook the judges' attention and center their argument on a

53. *See id.* § 13.2, at 289. Chapter 13 of Beazley provides a comprehensive guide to oral argument. *See id.* ch. 13, at 287–310.

54. *Id.* § 13.5, at 295.

55. *Id.* § 13.5.1, at 295.

focal point.[56] This theory should be encapsulated in a sentence or two. They should also highlight the three most important points they plan to cover using one sentence per point and numbering each point.[57] These three points are referred to as a roadmap. Finally, during the opening, the first student arguing for the petitioner or appellant should mention that their team has reserved a certain number of minutes on rebuttal.[58] Before the argument, counsel for the petitioner or appellant should discuss the rebuttal time with the bailiff so the bailiff can adjust the amount of time on the clock. Two minutes is a standard rebuttal time. See the online appendix for a sample fill-in-the-blank opening statement.

Memorizing the opening statement helps students to gain confidence at the competition and to pace their speech. An advocate should speak a bit more slowly during the opening statement so the judges can pay attention to what the student is saying and can jot down the points the student plans to argue.[59] This advice is especially good for your speediest talkers—if an advocate starts the argument by speaking more slowly than is comfortable for that advocate, they may naturally speed up, but will tend to maintain a slower pace than would normally be the case. Be sure to record your team on video and play the recording back. This helps an advocate realize that their pace is too fast and helps the advocate slow down at the next practice.

2. THE BODY OF THE ARGUMENT

The body of the argument is devoted to setting forth the arguments in favor of the rule of law the student is asking the court to adopt[60] (for most competitions are set up to require students to argue for the adoption of a new rule or the modification of an existing rule). Students should also prepare to address their opponent's counterarguments. While the advocates should begin with and emphasize the arguments in their favor, they should weave in responses to their opponent's counter-

---

56. *Id.*; *see also* David C. Frederick, The Art of Oral Advocacy § 5.3, at 92 (2d ed. 2011) (discussing how to develop a mantra).

57. Beazley, *supra* note 21, § 13.3.1, at 290; § 14.5.1, at 321.

58. *See id.* § 13.5.1, at 296.

59. *See id.* § 13.5.1, at 298 (discussing how an advocate should pause after articulating the thesis).

60. *Id.* § 13.3.2, at 292.

arguments as they go along.[61] Incorporating those responses may draw out a dialogue with the judges, especially if the bench is cold. To create cohesion, students should aim to connect every point they make, including their answers, to their main theme and the bottom-line argument they are making.[62]

Sometimes, a team can tell if the judges are following their arguments by how many questions the judges are asking. A lively and engaged bench often is a sign that the advocate is doing a good job of connecting the dots for the judges. But sometimes a bench is just cold, particularly in the early rounds of competition, and a student shouldn't feel bad about it. In real life, sometimes benches are cold, and there may be multiple reasons for that. Sometimes judges want to hear more of the argument before jumping in and asking questions. Judges who are more used to trial practice may be particularly prone to wait to ask questions. You can prepare a team for the possibility of a cold bench by holding cold-bench practices where the judges ask few or no questions.[63] Students should prepare two outlines for oral argument: one for a cold bench (with more upfront detail of cases, arguments, and counterarguments) and one for a hot bench (relying more on bringing in authority and arguments through questions).[64]

Because a moot court competition is a fictional argument setting, students don't have the benefit of reading the opposing side's brief before "going to court." However, a number of competitions post the briefs online, and your team should read through those briefs carefully to assess the strongest arguments on the other side. As noted above, the team will find it helpful to outline the other side's arguments and the responses to those arguments. As soon as your students find out which teams they will face in the competition, they should review those opposing teams' briefs (if provided) to make sure they have thought about good responses to the other side's arguments. Often a team's argument will evolve significantly between briefing and oral argument.

---

61. *See id.* § 14.5.2a., at 322 (noting that an advocate should keep in mind the "tough questions" that favor the other side and address those as the advocate moves through their argument).

62. Richard E. Finneran, *Wherefore Moot Court?*, 53 Wash. U. J.L. & Pol'y 121, 130 (2017).

63. Beazley, *supra* note 21, § 14.5.2a., at 322.

64. Lebovits, Gewuerz, and Hunker, *supra* note 43, at 910.

The team going first should bring up anticipatory responses to the second team's argument. The team going second in the round should practice weaving in specific responses to the other side's argument. Brainstorming the other side's arguments also is a good way to prepare to argue off-brief.

3. THE CLOSING STATEMENT

The closing statement should be no more than a minute long, summarizing the key points and emphasizing any special thematic points of significance.[65] Students should practice launching their closing statements when they see the one-minute marker.[66] If a student has been allowed to go beyond the allotted time, the student should be prepared to ask the bench for permission to give a brief conclusion.[67] Alternatively, the student may just end by saying "thank you."[68] Students should prepare three conclusions:

- The "kitchen sink" conclusion, where they have a full minute to hammer home their points;
- The "usual" conclusion, where they hit indispensable points and their request for relief; and
- The "quick-and-dirty" conclusion where they tag a quick conclusion and prayer for relief onto the end of the answer to a question.

4. THE REBUTTAL

After the second team has argued, one of the students from the first team should provide a short rebuttal covering one to two arguments.[69] Students should avoid the temptation to be overambitious and skim over a larger number of arguments. The student arguing the rebuttal should be someone especially comfortable with extemporaneous speech and should have a strong sense of the drama associated with a polished re-

---

65. BEAZLEY, *supra* note 21, § 13.5.3, at 301; § 14.5.3, at 325.
66. *Id.* § 14.5.3, at 325.
67. *Id.* § 13.5.3, at 301; § 14.5.3, at 325.
68. *Id.* § 14.5.3, at 325.
69. *See id.* § 13.7, at 305–07.

buttal. Most moot court judges appreciate a short, to-the-point rebuttal that homes in on the key problems with the other side's argument.[70] That means the students on the first team need to take careful notes during the second team's argument.[71] The best rebuttal is one that directly addresses the weaknesses in the appellee's or respondent's arguments, and students offering rebuttal should practice this type of extemporaneous response. Students should therefore anticipate the weaknesses in the other side's argument and practice speaking about those issues, so they are ready for this extemporaneous performance.

B. Fielding questions

Students should prepare for questions from the bench. Ideally, the team members will have already studied the usual types of appellate oral argument questions in a law school class. If they haven't, they should review books such as *A Practical Guide to Appellate Advocacy*[72] and *The Art of Oral Advocacy*,[73] which cover the different forms of questions in detail. Briefly, students can expect questions about a number of concepts:

- the record;[74]
- the current state of the law—including circuit splits;[75]
- what the law should be and why;[76]
- why the other side's argument is wrong and why theirs is correct;[77]
- public policy;[78] and
- hypothetical factual or legal scenarios.[79]

---

70. *Id.* § 13.7, at 306.

71. *See id.*

72. *Id.* § 13.6, at 302–05.

73. Frederick, *supra* note 56, chs. 3–4, at 37–79 (on answering questions).

74. *Id.* § 3.1d, at 43–44.

75. Beazley, *supra* note 21, § 13.3.2, at 292; Frederick, *supra* note 55, § 3.2a-d, at 46–52 (questions about precedent, case law distinctions, statutes, and legislative history).

76. Beazley, *supra* note 21, § 13.3.2, at 292; Frederick, *supra* note 55, §§ 4.1-4.2, at 56–75.

77. Frederick, *supra* note 56, §§ 4.1-4.2, at 56–75.

78. *Id.* § 3.2e, at 52–55.

79. *Id.* § 4.2a, at 65–70.

Students need to be prepared for interruptions and resistance from the judges,[80] as well as how to deal with questions that are confusing or for which the student does not know the answer.[81] Students should be prepared to speak about topics that may arise, but they will be awarded more points if they can accurately pick out the other side's unique weaknesses in oral argument and respond to those areas of concern. Students can use the following five steps to answer questions fully and properly:

1. Listen to the question and make sure they understand it;
2. Take a moment to think about the question and how to answer it (and breathe);
3. Provide a direct answer, echoing back phrasing from the question, if possible;
4. Explain the rationale of the answer; and
5. Connect the answer to how it supports and furthers the argument in the case at hand.[82]

In addition to preparing to answer accurately, directly, and succinctly, students need to practice eloquence and poise and how to develop a rapport with the judges. Developing a rapport with the judges means listening actively and answering the questions the judges have asked.[83] Students should aim to engage the judges in a conversation and to build momentum as their argument progresses.[84] The team should videotape at least one practice and watch with their coach or advisor. Doing so helps the team to see and hear what they are doing successfully, and to catch mistakes in their body language, volume, and other potentially annoying habits.[85] A team should also watch old competition videos when available. Watching past videos early in the practice process will

---

80. Beazley, *supra* note 21, § 13.6, at 302.

81. *Id.* § 13.6, at 303.

82. James D. Dimitri, *Stepping Up to the Podium with Confidence: A Primer for Law Students on Preparing and Delivering an Appellate Oral Argument*, 38 Stetson L. Rev. 75, 95 (2008) (citing experienced appellate attorney Jon Laramore for these five steps); *see also* Michael Vitiello, *Teaching Effective Oral Argument Skills: Forget About the Drama Coach*, 75 Miss. L.J. 869, 888 (2006) (stressing the importance of a student's ability to answer questions thoroughly).

83. Beazley, *supra* note 21, § 13.6, at 302.

84. *Id.* § 13.6, at 302–04.

85. Ronald J. Rychlak, *Effective Appellate Advocacy: Tips from the Teams*, 66 Miss. L.J. 528, 533–34 (1997).

show the team early on what they can generally anticipate at the competition and what winning teams do.

Learn as much about the culture of the competition as possible so that you can mimic the types of questions and competition environment in your practices. For instance, some competitions are known for judges who ask abstract, theoretical questions, while others tend to ask fact-oriented questions and hypotheticals. While the team should be prepared for all types of questions, they should especially practice answers to the questions that are most similar to what they can expect at competition. Ask this year's competitors to write down their observations about the competition for next year's competitors and ask the old and new teams to meet to discuss, among other things, the competition culture. This is also a good reason to ask past competitors to come back as practice judges. Be aware that there are regional differences in judges' stylistic preferences for oral argument. You may wish to take note of those differences and share them with students.

C. Proper etiquette at counsel's table

The custom of the side where the appellant or petitioner's team sits varies from jurisdiction to jurisdiction and even by competition. While a student is arguing, the other students, regardless of which team is arguing, should remain still with a neutral expression. The advocates should not stare at the judges or at the student who is arguing. Similarly, the advocates should not fidget in their seats. The seated advocates should take notes, either to prepare comments on response or rebuttal, or simply to record some of the questions being asked, especially if they are good questions. When the advocates stand up to walk to the podium, they should push in their chairs. They generally may drink water while seated and may bring water up to the podium when arguing. However, some competitions do not allow food or water in the courtroom, especially when the competition is held at an actual courthouse. Some competitions also do not allow competitors to move anything around in the courtroom.

D. Practicing the oral argument

"Practice makes perfect." Both the frequency and the quality of practices contribute to a student's successful oral argument preparation.

1. PLANNING THE PRACTICES

The first step in a successful oral argument is to plan the practices. Planning should start before the competition begins. Before the problem is released, students and their coach or advisor should meet to discuss their schedules and map out times each week when the students are available to practice. The team should read the competition rules carefully before the problem is released to find out when the competition permits teams to begin practicing. Some competitions allow practices before the brief is submitted, and some require practices to commence after the brief is turned in.

If you are fielding two teams, review the rules about the teams practicing together. Some competitions, such as the National Moot Court Competition, limit the number of times teams from the same school can practice together.[86] These joint practices can be valuable for both teams. The joint practices should be spaced carefully to ensure that each one provides the maximum benefit to both teams. Spacing the practices helps the teams to have time to fix problems before the next joint practice.

Ideally, students should speak to their teammates about their class and work schedules as they are signing up for courses concurrent with their competition. They should plan to practice at least three times a week when they all can commit to practice times. Doing so makes scheduling significantly easier and ensures that practices will be a priority for students. Write down dates and times for practices on a calendar accessible to all team members. If you have regular coaches assisting the students with their practices, scheduling dates and times for practices in advance will help the coaches, who are likely busy attorneys, free time in their schedules. If students participate in a moot court competition for credit, you may require that they practice a certain number of times a week to earn credit. Having a set schedule also helps you to schedule

---

86. *See, e.g., National Moot Court Competition Rules*, N.Y.C. B. Ass'n, *supra* note 32 (Rule 9.2).

practice round judges. It's often helpful to have at least one evening practice per week to make sure practitioners can attend. If you also schedule some midday practices, especially early on, faculty who are subject matter experts are more likely to be able to attend one or more practices.

Planning ahead helps to avoid the temptation to forgo practicing right after students submit their brief. After handing in their brief, students are usually tired and want to take a break before practicing. That's understandable, but you can emphasize that the students don't want to waste a valuable chance to capitalize on the momentum of their brief writing and intense study of the case. You could give students a breather for a few days after they submit their brief, then have the team meet for a roundtable/planning session during which you and the team knock around ideas and strategies for the oral arguments.[87] After that, begin practicing in earnest.

Planning helps everyone on the team to visualize the competition timeline. Many competitions allow for about a month between the brief deadline and the competition weekend, but some have a slightly shorter period for practicing the oral arguments, and some are slightly longer. Visualizing the competition timeline helps to ensure that students truly appreciate how much (or how little) time they have to practice.

When you plan ahead, you can address details such as reserving a room for the practices at the law school and registering practice judges and coaches to enter your law school building. Speak to your facilities coordinator about what is the most efficient way to reserve a room and register guests. An online registration form is a streamlined method for reserving rooms and registering guests. Talk to the team about who is responsible for these technical details: the team learns good lessons about responsibility and professionalism by handling such things independently.

2. THE FREQUENCY OF PRACTICES

An advisor cannot overemphasize the importance of frequent and regular practices. Over the years, teams that repeatedly win competitions credit the number of practices they conduct each week. That number may be up to five or more practices per week. As noted above, you

87. *See* BEAZLEY, *supra* note 21, § 14.5, at 320.

may want to have students who sign up to participate in a competition agree to a minimum number of practices each week. Talk to students about the importance of regular and frequent practice to their success. Set expectations by saying that to obtain credit, students need to do at least three practices per week, but that to advance in the competition, they may need to practice even more. Describe the competitive advantage you've seen in teams that practice regularly and frequently.

Some coaches say it's nearly impossible to advance in some of the more prestigious competitions without more than three practices per week. Others say that too many practices burn out a team. You'll need to determine the frequency of practices based in part on your instincts—does the team have the drive for more practices and the time, do they need additional time to get up to speed, and do their schedules permit additional practices? Does the team benefit from time between formal practices to conduct shorter, more focused practices on especially challenging issues or questions? You may want to require students to keep a practice log that they submit to you to certify that they have complied with your practice requirements.

3. THE QUALITY OF PRACTICES

The quality of practices is equally important. You and the team can guarantee quality practices by considering the team's and the coaches' roles at the practices. From the very first practice, the team should treat each practice as if it were the competition. That means practicing not only the content but also the form of the argument. Simulate competition conditions as much as possible in terms of timing, questioning, and formality. While it's convenient to practice virtually, if a competition is being held in person, students should practice at least some of their arguments in person to simulate the competition environment and receive feedback on their live performance strategies.

Team members who are not arguing should record the questions being asked. The team should compile these questions in a master index that they can study at home. While studying the questions, the team can discuss their answers and even write out a few sentences. Engaging with the material orally and in writing, formally and informally, helps the students to be more proficient in creating a conversation with judges during the competition arguments. Recording the questions also helps a team to consider points they may have missed in the briefing, so they can do additional research. Students should not count on simply remembering the questions that they were asked in practice.

4. PRACTICE JUDGES

Keep a list of practice judges to call upon for each competition. Good sources of practice judges include past participants in the same competition, local attorneys who practice in the subject area, your faculty who have expertise in the area, your advocacy and writing faculty, and moot court board members. You can stage practices at the law offices of attorneys who have volunteered to serve as practice judges, or at the law school. Aim to have at least two or three people judging each practice round so the students have a panel experience each time. As with the coaches, invite practice judges well before the practices begin so they can make time in their schedules.

If you can find one or two regular practice judges—practice judges who come to one practice per week or more—your team will benefit greatly from the consistency in feedback. The team and regular practice judges often create strong bonds where the practice judges encourage the team and comment on how the students are progressing from one week to another. Newer attorneys are good people to ask to serve as practice judges, preferably recent graduates of your moot court program who participated in the same competition. Similarly, retired attorneys may be delighted to invest time in serving as practice judges. 3L moot court veterans also make good practice judges. On the other hand, having a variety of practice judges can be good, too, as students get a wider variety of questions and see different styles and approaches to questioning.

Having practice judges—whether 3Ls or recent grads—who participated in the same competition creates institutional knowledge about the competition. They can speak firsthand to the competition's ins and outs. Being a practice judge gives new attorneys an opportunity to get involved in the legal community with some community service. The practice judges too benefit by learning about good oral argument through teaching. It's wonderful to see students move up through a moot court program and then continue to participate as coaches. The coaches provide continuity from one year to the next as they often return for more than one year of coaching and take pride in their teams' successes.

You should give the practice judges the problem as soon as it's available so they can begin to study the case (without conferring with the team during the brief-writing process). As soon as the brief is turned in, the team should provide the practice judges with their brief, along with a short summary or outline of the arguments prepared by the team members or the coach. Giving this condensed version of the arguments to the coaches and practice judges, along with some sample questions for each issue and side, can be invaluable to anyone assisting a team practice.

All practice judges need to be trained on cultural competency and implicit bias.[88] You may wish to consider working with your law school or university to ascertain whether it has training modules to assist you with this process. For instance, practice judges should take care that gendered or racialized biases about what a "good advocate" looks or sounds like don't manifest through comments about clothing or jewelry choices, hairstyle, voice (vocal fry), or facial expressions ("smile more").[89] In addition to avoiding feedback that stems from implicit bias, coaches and practice judges should practice positive feedback that emphasizes a growth mindset.[90] According to mindset theory, oral advocacy is not a fixed skill—it is malleable.[91] Coaches and practice judges therefore need to reinforce to students that they can improve in their brief writing and oral argument skills with practice.

Moreover, you can create positive role models by finding a group of coaches and practice judges who represent a diversity of individuals in the legal community. Having a variety of voices creates multiple perspectives, which is beneficial to feedback and will help to eliminate stereotype threat.[92] Stereotype threat arises when a member of a traditionally underrepresented group is placed in a situation where they feel

---

88. Lind-Martinez, *supra* note 18, at 144.

89. Mairi Morrison, *May It Please Whose Court: How Moot Court Perpetuates Gender Bias In the "Real World" of Practice*, 6 UCLA Women's L.J. 49, 74 (1995); Susie Salmon, *Reconstructing the Voice of Authority*, 51 Akron L. Rev. 143, 155–62 (2017).

90. Salmon, *supra* note 89, at 167–68.

91. *Id.* at 168–71.

92. *Id.* at 171.

pressured to favorably represent their community.[93] That pressure can reduce working memory, thereby affecting a student's performance.[94] Your work to create an educational environment that is safe, supportive, and positive for both students and their coaches and practice judges will prevent potential emotional injury or even Title IX investigations and lawsuits. Just as importantly, when you foster a safe space for communication and train all the stakeholders in how to identify and respond to implicit bias, you will create a space where students can learn.

After the competition, the team should send a thank-you note to their coaches and practice judges. One of the benefits to the students in working with coaches and practice judges is they may form potential networking connections. Third-year law students may impress a coach or judge enough to be asked for their resumes or referred for jobs. At the competition, consider taking a photo of the team. A good place for a team photo is at the courthouse or law school where the competition is being held. You can make the photo into a thank you card to send to practice judges. These personalized notes are much appreciated.

5. PRACTICING AT HOME

Besides their work during the formal oral argument practices, the team members should practice individually at home. Practicing before a mirror is a surprisingly difficult exercise and helps students to learn to concentrate and to deal with the initial awkwardness of public speaking.

Students should write short summaries—a paragraph—about the facts, holding, and reasoning of the precedent cases.[95] They should also write out questions they anticipate getting from the judges and their answers to those questions. Writing the answers helps the students to create multiple mental connections that will allow them to focus during their oral arguments when being asked to consider their argument from different angles. Some students make flash cards and study the cards while traveling to the competition.

Students should be encouraged to speak informally with their friends and family about their argument so they can learn to distill their argu-

93. *Id.*

94. *Id.*

95. Beazley, *supra* note 21, § 13.3.2, at 292.

ments into short but precise discussions of the case. These discussions can help students to see practical implications of their arguments—the real-world application of the rule of law they are advocating.

6. TROUBLESHOOTING

The team should prepare for different things that could go wrong during the oral arguments. Besides the possibility of a cold bench, students should consider how to handle a judge who seems to dislike them or can't accept the position the advocate must take to win. Another problem is when a judge doesn't understand the facts of the record or misread a case's holding. What if the other side makes a false assertion about the law or the facts of the record?[96] Some judges are strong trial attorneys or judges but do not routinely practice in appellate courts. Those judges may ask questions that are more properly considered in a trial court.

Judges sometimes may ask questions about a partner's issue. To address that possibility, students should have some general familiarity with their partner's issue so when they are asked questions about that issue, they can give a basic substantive response and then tell the court that their partner is prepared to speak about the issue in more depth.

Anticipating and preparing to deal with these problems as a team will help an advocate to stay calm and confident when something inevitably goes off course during the competition. Judges ultimately score advocates on how the advocates react to problems and how composed the advocate stays, so practicing these responses will help your team to score points.

7. NOTES OR NO NOTES

Students likely will want to begin their practices with a long outline and notes. That's okay. By a couple of weeks into the practices, however, students should have revised their outlines and shortened them considerably. If a student feels comfortable not taking notes to the podium, then they may strive for that, as no notes can help a student concentrate

96. *Id.* § 14.5.2a–b, at 322–34.

on extemporaneous conversation[97] during the oral argument. Otherwise, an advocate should plan for a one- or two-page outline[98] that they can staple into a manila folder.[99]

Advisors are of different minds about whether students should use notes. Some advisors and judges do not like the no-notes approach because it's almost never effectively done in real life, and it may strike the judges as "show-offy." Others are quite impressed by it. If you have advocates who want to go without notes warn them that it can backfire. On the other hand, at some competitions, a courtroom may lack a podium, and students who are prepared to go without notes may have an advantage.

8. DELIVERING EFFECTIVE FEEDBACK

Providing effective feedback is a balancing act—a coach should give both positive feedback and constructive criticism. You may wish to discuss the kind of feedback that students will receive and even give each other at the outset of practices. It is helpful to tell students that they will receive a point of positive feedback followed by a point of constructive criticism. Encourage them to use that same methodology. It's also valuable to motivate them earlier in the weeks of practice by being a little harder on them in the beginning. As they wrap up their weeks of practice, build them up, especially right before the competition. No good purpose is served by crushing a student's confidence in the last practice before a competition.

9. WINNING STYLE

This leads to the final points of advice: students need to be coached on dramatic flair, cadence and rhythm of their speech, and style.[100] These concepts will elevate their oral arguments. Moot court competitions are, to some extent, forensics competitions where style matters in getting points.[101] Some students seem to come by this naturally. Other students need to learn to speak slowly, punctuate words or vary the volume of

97. *Id.* § 13.4, at 294.
98. *Id.* § 13.4, at 293.
99. *Id.* § 13.4, at 294.
100. *Id.* § 13.9, at 308–10.
101. *Id.* § 14.2, at 314.

their speech, and give off an air of polished sophistication.[102] Drama coaches—perhaps students from a university theater program—can demonstrate theater exercises to the students to help them practice their polish. It helps to watch videos or listen to audio recordings of accomplished oralists in action. Ultimately, you want to help each advocate find their own style. Advocates need not strive to present cookie-cutter duplicates of some arbitrary style, and that won't work anyway for many advocates.[103]

VI. On-Site: The Oral Argument Rounds

Your team has submitted its brief, each competitor has spent hours practicing oral argument, and now it's time for the face-to-face portion of the competition. You've provided your team with critical support at various stages of preparation for the oral argument rounds. But at no point is your support more vital than perhaps at the competition itself.

A. Whom to send

While it is possible for students to travel alone, doing so is not advisable. Teams should be accompanied by one or more attorney-coaches, faculty advisors, student coaches, or a combination of these. Whenever possible, the best approach is to send, at a minimum, a faculty advisor. Sending coaches to the oral argument portion of the competition serves at least three important objectives:

- it helps ensure that your team is properly checked-in at the competition and arrives at the arguments on time;
- it allows students to focus on their arguments rather than logistics; and
- it aids the student competitors before, during, and after each competition round.

Law schools generally send between one and three coaches to any particular competition. The number of coaches traveling with the stu-

102. *Id.* § 13.9, at 308.

103. *See id.* § 14.2, at 314.

dent competitors may vary depending on the number of teams representing your law school at the competition as well as the number of team members on each team. Send too few coaches, and they will not be able to fulfill their intended functions. Send too many, and it will be unnecessarily costly and potentially counterproductive. Sending one coach per team is generally a good rule of thumb.

No specific criteria exist for determining which coach or coaches should travel with a particular team. It is generally best, however, to pick those who have helped coach the team since the beginning. Doing so allows the coaches and students to develop a rapport with one another, and it ensures that the coach is knowledgeable about the details of the competition problem. It is also beneficial to send a coach who is familiar with the competition and knows what is generally rewarded there.

A common and potentially effective pairing is to send one attorney-coach and one faculty-coach.[104] This pairing provides the students with both academic and practical perspectives.

Another related decision is whether to send non-competing students to the competition. Some moot court programs increasingly involve non-competing students in the competition process to prepare those students to compete in future competitions. As any former competitor will tell you, being comfortable with the competition setting can be just as important as being comfortable with a particular argument. Providing students with first-hand opportunities to experience the administration of a competition can greatly increase their comfort level in subsequent competitions. For example, the NAAC requires that each team provide a bailiff responsible for keeping time during competition rounds. A law school could choose to send a non-competing student to serve as bailiff in an effort to prepare that student for future participation at the NAAC or another moot court competition.[105]

Of course, you should consider the expense of travel, lodging, and food when determining whether to allow non-competing students to travel to competitions. Consider framing your request for funds to send a non-competing student to a competition as an investment to ensure

---

104. Chris Lund, *Law Professors and Moot Court Competition Teams*, PRAWFSBLAWG (March 13, 2009, 1:24 PM), http://prawfsblawg.blogs.com/prawfsblawg/2009/03/law-professors-and-moot-court-competition-teams.html (last visited Feb. 13, 2023).

105. *See, e.g., National Appellate Advocacy Competition Rules*, AM. B. ASS'N, *supra* note 33.

continuity of team success. Also, remember to check the competition rules before sending a non-competing student because some competitions allow only coaches to observe the rounds, and others may limit the total number of observers in each round. Sometimes competitions send pairings and round schedules by email in the days before the competition. Make sure to share that information with the team and review the pairings, including briefs written by the other side.

B. On arrival

The team can set itself up for success by taking steps on arrival to prepare for the competition.

1. ARRIVAL AND PRACTICE

Even if competition rules do not require you to arrive the day before the competition begins, it is usually best to do so. Not only will allotting a day for travel give you and your team flexibility and alternatives in the event of travel delays, but it will also give you an opportunity to do a final practice round in the host city. A word about checking luggage: consider whether to pack a carry-on instead of checking a suitcase. Even if the students check a bag, they should have at least one suit and required accessories in a carry-on because lost luggage happens.

Students need to practice professionalism when traveling.[106] Setting clear expectations about professionalism, including written policies in a handbook or bylaws, is essential. Remind your team that they are representing themselves and their law school. Competitions are a great place for students to learn that they need each other to succeed.

After spending hours traveling, students may not want to spend even more time polishing the same arguments they've been practicing for weeks now, but coaches should consider whether to encourage them to run through the arguments once or twice. Students usually are more effective advocates if they are well rested for the competition, rather than if they practice until the wee hours of the morning of the competition. It's best to rest and relax the night before the competition, but you can consider doing a quick warm-up run through the morning of the competition. If practicing in a hotel room, an ironing board may serve as a

106. Beazley, *supra* note 21, § 14.6, at 326–27 (on professionalism).

substitute for a lectern. Try to visit the competition site the day before the competition so the team knows precisely how to get to that site and won't risk arriving at the site late for the competition. The team may also benefit from seeing the types of rooms in which they will be arguing if your travel arrangements permit you to get to the site the day before.

2. COACHES MEETING /CHECK-IN

Many competitions have a meeting for participants and coaches shortly before the competition begins. At this meeting, teams are usually informed about the competition schedule, the scoring process, and other relevant matters. Coaches may use this opportunity to seek clarification of competition rules or ask questions not covered by the rules. How will teams be scored when they have only two-judge panels rather than three-judge panels? When will the teams receive oral argument and brief scores? Will each team receive copies of all teams' scores or only their own? Sometimes a combined coaches and competitors meeting may be where you get brief scores. It's not unheard of for competition staff to miscalculate brief scores, so always check the math.

C. The competition

Coaches serve a vital role at the competition itself. From the team's arrival until the competition ends, coaches should actively assist their student competitors and provide feedback to them after they argue.

1. BEFORE THE ROUND

Just before the round, students can control their nerves by setting up in the courtroom and hearing a positive pre-game pep talk.

a. Getting set up

A lot of things may distract or stress students at the outset of the competition. Students may forget such things as socks, ties, belts, and undershirts, and they will scramble for ways to improvise the morning of the competition. But even if everything runs smoothly pre-competition, students will undoubtedly be nervous as they review their arguments one final time. Here is where coaches step in. Coaches should ensure that students get from the hotel to the competition site, check-in, and get to the correct room. A coach may want to bring some items that can help in a pinch like a small first-aid kit, a sewing kit, a stain-removal pen or similar item to help with the inevitable spills and other disasters, and a couple of extra pens and pads of paper.

b. Pre-game pep talk

Another key role a coach can fulfill is one of a motivator and encourager. Students will naturally feel insecure or nervous before a round begins. As Alan L. Dworsky noted in his book *The Little Book on Oral Argument*, "When you stop being nervous, start worrying. You've either stopped caring or stopped breathing."[107] If the competition rules allow, coaches should give students a final pep talk minutes before the round begins. Students have spent countless hours over the past several weeks writing their brief and preparing for oral argument. The reality is that they know the issues and the record better than many of the competition judges. A good coach will remind the students of this fact. Confidence is a key to excelling at oral argument; coaches can help instill that confidence. Some might say confidence is 90 percent of winning.

Oral argument can be an incredibly stressful experience for both students and practitioners.[108] One of the benefits of participation on moot court is that students practice how to overcome nerves during oral argument. To assist students in learning to relax in a public speaking setting, remind students to control their nerves by breathing.[109] They should take a breath before and after every question, for instance. Their nervous feeling—the fight or flight response—comes from the amygdala in the brain, which sends hormones through the body. Breathing slowly and deeply can assist in regulating the amygdala and preventing it from overreacting.

Remind students of their professionalism during the competition, including at the end of the round. They should maintain a calm face while being questioned and during the other competitors' arguments. Sometimes a judge will ask an off-the-wall question, and students should

---

107. Alan L. Dworsky, The Little Book on Oral Argument 4 (1991).

108. Larry Cunningham, *Using Principles from Cognitive Behavioral Therapy to Reduce Nervousness in Oral Argument or Moot Court*, 15 Nev. L.J. 586, 592 (2015) (discussing how stressful oral arguments can be for students and how to use cognitive behavioral therapy to manage the stress of oral argument).

109. *See* Robert Zeglovitch, *The Mindful Lawyer*, 70 Tex. B.J. 234, 237 (2007).

not act surprised. Some judges purposefully ask random questions to see how students think on their feet, and the student who appears calm and confident, or rolls with the questions, will score better than one who seems surprised or unsure. At the end of the round, they may receive feedback that is surprising or even unfair. If so, they should not retort. Each judge's feedback presents a datapoint about their advocacy. They should try to see trends in feedback, which is one of the reasons it's good to participate in these competitions before graduating and practicing in a real courtroom. Students should thank the judges at the end of the round and shake their hands.

2. DURING THE ROUND

During the round, coaches can assist the team by taking notes and looking up the judges in the courtroom, if the competition rules permit that practice.

a. Taking notes

During the competition round, coaches should take copious notes if the competition rules permit.[110] Notes can be taken on anything relevant. But at a minimum, they should cover three broad topics: (1) arguments or counterarguments that were particularly effective or ineffective; (2) the judges' questions; and (3) new arguments, legal authority, or concerns that were raised during the round. Many times, questions from the bench give you insights into what the bench brief says. The purpose of these coach's notes is to help students improve both stylistically and substantively in later rounds. Noting questions also can help future teams prepare more effectively.

b. Google judges' names

Aside from style and substance, coaches should write down the names of each judge. If cell phones, tablets, or computers with Internet access are allowed in the room, you may wish to search those names online. Knowing the judges' professional backgrounds will give context to their ques-

110. Most competitions allow coaches to take notes during the competition rounds, but most competitions prohibit scouting. *E.g.*, *National Moot Court Competition Rules*, N.Y.C. B. Ass'n, *supra* note 32 (Rule 10).

tions and comments. It will also help determine how much weight to give to their comments. For example, it is not uncommon for a judge to resist certain arguments because of their past case experiences.

3. AFTER THE ROUND

a. Debriefing

Immediately following the oral arguments, competitors and everyone in the audience will usually be asked to step outside while the judges complete their score sheets. Check competition rules, but coaches are generally allowed to speak with competitors at this point. If so, students should meet with you to debrief the round.

Debriefing includes identifying the successes the students realized during the round as well as noting the mistakes they made. Use the notes that you took during the round to provide students with specific feedback that will allow them to make improvements before the next round. Often this debriefing takes place in a hallway outside a courtroom. Be sensitive to privacy concerns and to the opposing team. Encourage your students to maintain a professional demeanor outside the courtroom as well as inside.

The debriefing period allows you to talk with the students about the strengths and weaknesses of opposing counsels' arguments. The students may argue on behalf of the opposing side in a future round. Students should use the time between rounds to refine their arguments.

No matter how poorly the round went, be sure to give some positive feedback to each competitor. Otherwise, you risk completely crushing the team's spirits as well as their chances of succeeding in subsequent rounds. You may wish to limit critical feedback to the team significantly during competition. Urge students to resist tailoring their arguments too much to address one bench's comments. Changing the argument on the fly at the competition almost never results in improvement. If the teams are well prepared, then a competition judge shouldn't find too much to say that could warrant making significant changes during competition. That said, one exception might be for the intransigent student who only internalizes a critique coming from someone other than their coach.

b. Advocating on the students' behalf

Another potential matter a coach may need to address immediately following a round is how to raise protests or other administrative issues. Coaches should be familiar with competition rules before arriving at the competition and should keep a hard copy of the rules with them at all times. Coaches should ensure that their competitors comply with the competition rules and take advantage of the rules to earn the maximum score. In particular, the competitors should understand the way scoring affects seeding and changes from the preliminary rounds to the elimination rounds.

If the competition was not administered correctly or if a team violated a rule, a coach must be ready to act quickly. For example, the rules for the NMCC require competitors to argue the issues in order (first issue then second issue).[111] If opposing counsel were to address the second certified issue first, that would technically constitute a rule violation. Then the question becomes whether a complaint should be filed.

Determining whether to file a complaint requires professional judgment. There may be instances when technically a minor violation of the rules has occurred, but the violation did not impact the outcome of the round. In that case, it may not be worth filing a complaint and running the risk of your school developing a reputation as a "chronic complainer." On the other hand, nothing is more heartbreaking to a student than to lose a round they would have won had the rules been followed. This scenario happens only rarely, however. Most competition rules don't have provisions in place to protect teams from the true heartbreak of losing to a team that is dead wrong on substance but gets away with it because the judges aren't sufficiently prepared and are wowed by superficial style. Avoid gamifying the process: it sets a bad example for the students and is unprofessional. A moot court program can get a bad reputation within a competition for this sort of behavior, just as lawyers can get a bad reputation within a courthouse for such antics. The more likely and constructive role for a coach is to protect students against other teams who assert spurious challenges. Sometimes the coach needs to protect a team; more often, the coach's presence deters gamesmanship by unscrupulous competitors or coaches.

---

111. *Id.* (Rule 6.1).

Every competition is different, but usually there is a very short window—perhaps only minutes—after a round ends to raise an issue or lodge a complaint. If a team fails to act timely, its complaint will likely be waived even if it is valid.

c. Networking

Many competitions conclude with a banquet or other social event where students can network with the attorneys and judges involved in the competition. These networking opportunities can help students with possible job opportunities or references. Remember, though, that the entire event is a networking opportunity. You should encourage students to be cordial to everyone in the building and nearby—you never know who is a judge, future colleague, or client (a great professionalism lesson they should carry into real life). Students may eventually appear in court before these very judges, or they may eventually work with an attorney on the panel if they are competing in the location where they will practice law upon graduation. They should view the competition as they would an internship: an opportunity to practice professionalism and integrity.

Good sportsmanship is key. Being a good competitor does not mean being rude to (or even just aloof from) the other team. The team may also find opportunities to socialize a bit with each other and with the other teams after the rounds are done. Within reason, socializing offers the students an additional chance to practice networking.

D. Staying positive

The final function a coach should serve is to maintain a positive attitude. A competition can yield only one ultimate winner. While your team may reach other milestones such as "making the break" (i.e., being selected to compete in the elimination rounds of the competition), someone on your team will probably go home disappointed unless you win it all.

It is natural to feel disappointed after losing a competition.[112] Despite putting hours of preparation into the competition, students will not be able to list "champion" on their resumes or return to your school a com-

112. Beazley, *supra* note 21, § 14.6, at 327.

petition "rock star." Though disappointed, sometimes students will know that they were simply bested by better competitors. At other times, your students may have been the better team and objectively should have won the round. But that is the nature of the beast. Moot court has long been criticized for its occasional episodes of "substandard" and "even atrocious" judging.[113] As a coach, you cannot do anything about that. But you can keep the students' spirits up by letting them know that you appreciate their hard work and reminding them that, especially in moot court, learning is more important than winning. Encourage students to be good sports and attend awards ceremonies and other events hosted by the competition even if they have already been eliminated. Their presence will be appreciated, and they will learn valuable lessons in professionalism.

VII. Arbitrary and Capricious: Teachable Moments at the Competition

As with real-life cases, things don't always go perfectly at a competition. These moments provide students with realistic experience in handling tough courtroom situations and dealing with problems as a team. Problems during a competition offer a coach an opportunity to maximize the students' learning experience. A coach traveling with a team—in debriefing the arguments with the students—can take a negative experience and turn it into a positive teachable moment.

One common problem you might see during an oral argument is a panel of ill-prepared judges. You may see the judges scrambling through the record or staring blankly at the students as they present their arguments. One way lack of preparation manifests itself is in a cold bench. Students can prepare for this challenge by practicing arguments before a cold bench.[114] They should also know that some judges warm up with their questions, so the very first advocate will likely have the fewest questions, and the last student arguing will likely have a hot bench. Or it may work the other way around, where the judges' energy wanes over

---

113. Barbara Kritchevsky, *Judging: The Missing Piece of the Moot Court Puzzle*, 37 U. Mem. L. Rev. 45, 47 (2006).

114. Beazley, *supra* note 21, § 14.5.2a., at 322.

the course of the argument. After the round, talk to the team about how they were able to fill the time and keep their momentum going, despite the dearth of questions. If you saw the team drawing out questions from the judges, compliment them and discuss what worked in eliciting questions.

Another problem you may see is a judge who does not fully understand the facts of the record. Students should respectfully correct a judge's perception of the facts. Providing record cites can help to build credibility with judges who are not sufficiently well versed with the facts. Citing the record might seem overwhelming, but usually the key facts are found on a limited number of pages, so it's not as difficult as it may seem. And if your team offered a rebuttal, discuss how the rebuttal was used or could have been used to correct problems with the judges' knowledge of the record.

Similarly, you might observe a judge who does not fully understand the legal arguments, either because the judge doesn't understand the law or doesn't understand how the law applies to the facts of the case. Or you may find that the judging panel is populated by trial attorneys who are asking questions geared toward a trial-level argument. If the judge didn't adequately understand the law, discuss with your advocate how they walked the judge through the law. Did the student advocate turn into a teacher, and did they patiently explain the law? The key is not to make the judge feel inadequate and to keep the judge engaged in how the law fits into the argument.

When a judge asks questions that appear more geared toward a trial-level argument, look for whether the student advocate answered the question to the judge's satisfaction. Discuss whether the student connected the point to the broader picture. Transitions become especially important in pulling the argument together.

You may observe that judges sometimes give terrible advice in the critique after the oral argument. This is one of the most important reasons for a coach to be with the team: to listen to the feedback and tell the students if the advice was wrong. For instance, a judge may get the standard of review wrong, and students need to be ready to explain why the standard of review they are using is correct. A student should also explain the standard without making the judge feel incompetent.

If a judge gave bad advice in their post-argument critique, your team must be careful not to incorporate that bad advice into their next argument. If the team doesn't have an advisor or coach traveling with them, the students should review any questionable advice with their coach over the phone. The coach should be prepared to field questions with the team via email or phone during the competition.

Knowing the rules well is essential for a team to challenge any irregularities during a round. Some competitions allow a team to review the scoring for each round, and a team should always take advantage of that. The competition coordinators want to be known for running a fair competition, so approach the coordinators with confidence and respect, not an argumentative tone, if a problem arises. You can model good sportsmanship for your team by addressing concerns in a mature, calm way. Remind your team not to bad mouth another team, even if that team behaved poorly during the competition.[115] Moot court offers students an excellent opportunity to learn to abide by the rules, and your team will see that the teams that behave professionally and above board rise to the top.

VIII. Post-Competition: Evaluating Your Team's Experience and Performance

After the team comes home, you and the team members should sit down to evaluate their time at the competition. This evaluation helps to solidify the students' experience and allows you to capture important information about the competition so you can make next year's team even more successful.

Immediately when the team returns, gather the team members for a meeting to discuss how things went. For one, the team may be advancing from the regionals to the national competition in the NAAC or the NMCC. That means you'll need to schedule new practices and review the rules for the next round of competition. In addition, the team may need to resubmit its brief. So, the planning and implementing process starts all over. To prepare for the next round, the team should discuss what they did well and what they can improve. This is a good opportu-

115. *Id.* § 14.6, at 326.

nity to discuss the kinds of questions the students fielded and how they answered the questions. Consider compiling a list of the best questions to use in preparing for the next round of argument.

If the team participated in a specialty competition or the team is not advancing from a regional round, the team will still benefit from discussing the strengths and weaknesses of their performance. Self-assessment and reflection always improve the educational experience.[116] Debriefing also allows the students to think critically about things they learned from other teams or the judges. Participants should write a reflection on their experience based on a list of questions like the following:

- What did you learn about the research process in this area of law?
- Did you work with new research sources?
- What three brief writing skills did you most advance in writing this brief?
- What are three brief writing skills that you would like to continue to hone after writing this brief?
- What did you learn about writing collaboratively during the brief writing process?
- What are your three areas of greatest strength in oral advocacy?
- What would you like to continue to improve upon in your oral advocacy?
- Is there anything about the competition format or logistics you'd like to share with next year's team?
- Would you like to be contacted about coaching this team in the future?

If you didn't attend the competition in person, a debriefing meeting gives you a chance to learn more about what happened at the competition. Take notes so you have an advantage the following year in tailoring your advice to the unique aspects of that competition. Or you may find that after learning more about the way the competition was run, you

116. *See* Pam Jenoff, *The Self-Assessed Writer: Harnessing Fiction-Writing Processes to Understand Ourselves as Legal Writers & Maximize Legal Writing Productivity*, 10 Legal Comm. & Rhetoric, 187, 192 (2013) (discussing how self-assessment improves a writer's confidence and self-understanding).

may choose not to go back to the competition. Either way, the information is invaluable for you as the advisor.

At the debriefing, you can find out about the team's interest in participating in moot court in the future. Perhaps your program is set up to permit students to do more than one competition. Debriefing gives you the chance to discuss new opportunities—to assess student interest in participating in another competition. Or perhaps your program focuses on 3L competitors. In that case, get information about where the student plans to be after graduation and if they would like to help coach the team or be a practice judge. Your alumni are your most valuable resource in building up a volunteer base for your program. Consider an exit interview, either in hard copy or online through email or an online poll (using a service like Survey Monkey). Be sure to get permanent contact information such as a cell phone number and personal email address, as well as a work email, if possible.

Also introduce the current team to next year's team. That direct advice from one competitor to another is invaluable. Students pay attention to words of wisdom they receive from competitors. The current team's success stories can inspire the new team, especially when the current team discusses how their hard work paid off.

Finally, be sure to have the team thank everyone involved in helping them practice and prepare for the competition. A simple handwritten thank-you note sent to all who assisted works quite well for this purpose.

IX. Unique Issues with International Competitions

In addition to the previous sections of this chapter, there are a few more issues to consider if you advise a team that will compete in one of the three well-known international moot court competitions, Jessup,[117] the Willem C. Vis International Commercial Arbitration Moot ("Vis"),[118]

117. *Philip C. Jessup International Law Moot Court Competition*, INT'L L. STUDENTS ASS'N, *supra* note 3.

118. *The Annual Willem C. Vis International Commercial Arbitration Moot*, ORG. & PROMOTION WILLEM C. VIS INT'L COMMERCIAL ARBITRATION MOOT (THE VEREIN), https://law.pace.edu/willem-c-vis-international-commercial-arbitration-moot (last visited Feb. 13, 2023).

and the Price Media Law Moot Court Programme ("Price").[119] These competitions are all conducted in English, but they actively recruit students from schools all over the world to expose the competitors to a variety of diverse legal perspectives. This part of the chapter will touch on some of the general issues to be aware of for these international competitions.

Regardless of which international competition your team participates in, you and the team will be well served by reading the website and rules of the competition carefully. More so than a typical American moot court competition, the Jessup, Vis, and Price websites contain resources for students and coaches who have little or no experience with international-law research or moot court competitions. In turn, the rules of each competition make clear the scheduling and other expectations, some of which are quite different from American competitions.

Jessup has students participate in a dispute between countries before the International Court of Justice. The international rounds are held in Washington, D.C., though American teams may only participate in these rounds by excelling in a Jessup regional round. Teams from other countries may have different qualification requirements.

Vis has students resolve a dispute through arbitration with respect to a transaction covered by the United Nations Convention on Contracts for the International Sale of Goods. Vis is held in Vienna, Austria. Any team can register to compete in Vienna, though it is common for teams to participate in "pre-moot" competitions to practice their oral arguments before the official competition. The Willem C. Vis (East) International Commercial Arbitration Moot is a sister competition held in Hong Kong.[120] It uses the same problem but requires a separate registration and has separate award winners.

Price has students participate in a dispute between private parties and a country over the Freedom of Expression and other freedoms described in the United Nations Universal Declaration of Human Rights before a fictional Universal Court of Human Rights. The international rounds are

---

119. *Monroe E. Price Media Law Moot Court Competition*, U. Oxford, https://www.law.ox.ac.uk/monroe-e-price-media-law-moot-court-competition (last visited Feb. 13, 2023).

120. *The Willem C. Vis (East) International Commercial Arbitration Moot*, Chartered Institute of Arbitrators (East Asia Branch), https://cisgmoot.org/ (last visited Feb. 13, 2023).

held in Oxford, United Kingdom. Depending on your team's country, you may need to qualify for the international round based on your performance in a regional round.

Two major differences exist between these three competitions and most American competitions. First, the international competitions require teams to analyze a minimum of four distinct legal issues and write two briefs, one on behalf of the petitioner and one on behalf of the respondent, without a significant change in the page or word limits seen in many American competitions.[121] For this reason, they allow teams to contain six or, depending on the competition, more students, while not necessarily requiring all team members to participate in oral argument rounds. Another difference is the competitions' argument style and formality. That difference makes it crucial to enlist a coach and other faculty advisors who are experienced with the competition. Consider reaching out to the competition to see if they can recommend instructional materials to familiarize your team with the competition's unique style and formality.

Not surprisingly, the second difference is that the three competitions involve the analysis of international treaties and other international law materials in arguments made to an international court (Jessup and Price) or a panel of arbitrators (Vis). Students may have limited or no experience with the relevant legal materials. In addition, the nature of international law means that the mock tribunal to which students present their arguments is not bound by precedent or constrained to a rigid hierarchy of authority in the same way as the mock courts in most American moot court competitions. This more amorphous legal framework can make initial work on researching and analyzing a problem very challenging for students.

With respect to selecting team members, you will likely want to inquire about students' previous course or work experience with international legal materials to select students who need less of a learning curve with the use and research of those materials. The greater number of students allowed on a team opens the possibility to include interested, but

121. The terms "brief," "petitioner," and "respondent" are not the appropriate terms to describe the parties and the written filings for all three of these competitions, but they are used here for the sake of consistency with the other parts of this chapter. This is just one example of why a team needs to read the website and rules of a competition carefully.

less experienced, students in research assistance and editing roles. This approach has the added benefit of training new competitors to be full participants and leaders on future teams. At some schools, Jessup and Vis also involve a substantial classroom component.

Another concern for team selection is that the time frame for participation in these competitions is significantly longer than for most American competitions; students essentially must make a year-long commitment. Jessup and Price typically release their problems in the middle of September and require both briefs to be submitted sometime in early- or mid-January. The Vis problem is released in the first week of October and requires the petitioner's brief to be submitted in early December. Teams are then given another team's petitioner brief and are expected to respond directly to that team's arguments as well as include additional arguments in a respondent's brief due sometime in late January or early February. All of these competitions typically hold their international rounds sometime in early- or mid-April, though qualifying and practice rounds usually take place in February or March. Therefore, as an advisor, you probably want to select the core members of the team in the spring of the previous year. This will allow participants to familiarize themselves with the treaties that Price and Vis always use, or, for Jessup, to research the general topic, which is usually released sometime in May. These competitions demand extensive writing over a longer period of time, making it particularly important to select multiple strong writers for your team.

When dividing team responsibilities and setting up a schedule for your team, you should consider building in some research training time. If some or all of your students are unfamiliar with international legal materials, they will likely need some explicit training on the subject or additional time to familiarize themselves with the appropriate materials. You also should keep in mind that the format and citation requirements for the briefs are different from those requirements for American moot court competitions. For this reason, it likely will take longer than you might expect to confirm that the briefs conform to the competition rules. Viewing the winning briefs from past competitions is particularly helpful for this task, and you will want to build extra time into the team's schedule for cite-checking and reviewing past briefs.

Advocating to an international tribunal raises two unique concerns to keep in mind. First, it is common for some or all of the legal issues in each competition to require multiple arguments in the alternative. In some way, each competition delves into the nature of national sovereignty. Not only should teams discuss relevant precedents, but the judges will expect some exploration of why a decision in your favor is the best way to govern the community of nations that inhabits our world.[122] Because teams need to analyze four issues and respond to the opposing side's expected arguments, some of the advocacy will need to be very short and direct.

Second, teams are expected to use multiple scholarly writings in their written briefs. The courts and arbitration panels simulated for these competitions routinely look to the writings of leading legal scholars from all over the world when making their decisions. For that reason, teams need to identify which scholars are respected authorities on the various legal issues of the competition and make sure to use those writings as primary support for their legal arguments, not just as support added on to the end of an argument. Depending on who the individual is, saying that Scholar X interprets a treaty a particular way may be your most powerful argument, especially if that person helped draft the treaty. Official commentaries on treaties are critical resources to find and use in your arguments. Identifying official commentaries and leading scholars are tasks that can begin before the release of the competition problem. A team should know before the release of the competition problem if its law library has access to various print and electronic treatises or journals. You can also work with the library to have them create a library guide of international materials to get the team started.

Oral argument practice does not need to differ from the preparation required for other moot court competitions. For all three competitions, students need to prepare focused arguments supported by precedents and facts and be prepared to answer questions. Given the number of legal issues to master, teams commonly begin oral argument practice

122. For instance, a legal issue could break down as follows: Doctrine A should be adopted over Doctrine B for reason X because reason X is consistent with this Court's past decisions, and reason X best balances national autonomy with international safety. If this Court rejects reason X, Doctrine A should still be adopted for reason Y. If this Court applies Doctrine B, the Claimant prevails because of reason T. In addition, a ruling for the Claimant best interprets the purpose the United Nations' adoption of Declaration M.

before their briefs are due. The minor differences between the competitions can be quickly mastered with practice. For instance, there are terminology differences, such as "Your Excellency" (Jessup and Price) or "Madam Chief Arbitrator" (Vis) instead of "Your Honor," while "Compromis" is used instead of "Record" (Jessup and Price). All of the competitions allow the potential for sur-rebuttal, which is not typical in American competitions, and international competitions favor an even more formal and deferential style.

At Vis, competitors sit at their counsel table when they speak instead of standing at a podium during an oral argument round. Because Vis simulates arbitration proceedings, teams typically meet before their oral argument round and agree upon the order of the issues they will present to the arbitrators. If an agreement cannot be reached, the teams argue to the arbitrators about why their proposed order is better. Videos of rounds from these competitions are readily available from the competitions' websites or by searching online.

A final word to advisors who are working with students who know some English but are not in an exclusive English-language-degree program: all three competitions solicit teams from such schools as a way to increase education on the legal principles the competitions hope to advance. These teams' participation also greatly enhances the experience of all competitors because students are exposed to a more diverse set of viewpoints. If this is your situation, do not hesitate to reach out to the organizers of the three competitions and ask for guidance in how to make the experience as successful as possible for your students. Depending on the competition and its resources, you may receive some assistance with issue formulation, oral argument training, or contact information for other teams or experienced coaches with whom you can speak. If you already know of other people who have participated in past competitions or coach a current team, you should feel confident to reach out to them and ask for assistance. A real fellowship develops between the people who routinely participate in these global competitions, and you will find that the vast majority of people will be happy to share general ideas and their experiences with you.

If you are teaching a legal analysis course at the school, ask the competition if you can use its problem as the basis for coursework your students will complete during the semester. This will give you the opportunity to guide a group of students through the legal materials in a more organized fashion than you could as a typical extracurricular coach. No matter which of these competitions you choose, all three want your students to have a meaningful educational experience with the legal materials at issue. Use that as a guideline as you work with your students to prepare for the competition.

X. Conclusion

External moot court competitions offer students a chance to test their skills in a fairly independent environment.[123] When you provide a moot court team with sufficient scaffolding, you give the team a competitive advantage and the best opportunity to learn advocacy skills. By participating in an external competition, a team can learn about time management, professionalism, ethics, and integrity, modeled by you and the team coaches and practice judges.

---

123. Darby Dickerson, *In re Moot Court*, 29 STETSON L. REV. 1217, 1217–18 (2000) (citing three benefits of moot court: 1) skill building in research, written advocacy, and oral argument; 2) development of teamwork; and 3) practice of time management).

CHAPTER 5

Developing and Managing (or Hosting) an External Moot Court Competition

THIS CHAPTER WILL HELP YOU TO:

- **Realistically assess whether your program can and should host an external moot court competition;**
- **Navigate the logistics of administering an external moot court competition.**

Most law schools participate in at least one interscholastic, "external" moot court competition. As discussed in Chapter Four, these competitions give students the opportunity to develop their research, writing, and oral advocacy skills while representing their schools and interacting with other law students and professionals on the national or even international stage.

Someone creates and hosts these competitions. Sometimes it is a local or national bar association; for example, the American Bar Association puts on the National Appellate Advocacy Competition each year, and the New York City Bar Association has run the National Moot Court Competition since 1950. Sometimes, a national or international organization runs the competition, like the Native American Law Students' Association's annual Moot Court Competition. Often, however, a law school or an academic department or club within a law school creates and administers the competition.

Although tis chapter focuses primarily on issues related to creating, administering, and hosting a new competition, many of the same considerations and logistics apply to schools that simply serve as host locations for competitions administered by other entities.

I. Initial Inquiries: Why Start (or Host) an External Moot Court Competition?

Although simply hosting—much less creating and administering—an external moot court competition demands a tremendous amount of work, it can also bring a tremendous amount of prestige, recognition, and favorable publicity to the host school and its moot court programs or subject-matter specialties. In fact, schools often compete fiercely to host certain competitions, spending months making the case for their facilities and their locations to a selection committee. For a school seeking to make a name for itself in a particular area of the law or for its advocacy programs, hosting or founding an external moot court competition can be an invaluable opportunity to showcase the school's facilities, its faculty, its students, its local legal community, and its expertise, all on a national or international stage.

Creating or hosting an external moot court competition can also garner recognition for your advocacy programs or department within your school and for your school within your local legal community. This recognition can translate into stronger relationships with alumni, stronger ties between the local bench and bar and your school (which may be particularly important if your school is located in a city with multiple law schools), and increased enthusiasm among your own students. For current students, attending an external moot court competition is a great opportunity to observe their peers delivering high-quality arguments live and in person, which is especially good for 1Ls whose own first oral arguments loom.

Sometimes, schools that send teams to a particular competition must serve as host, either permanently or on a rotating basis. Other competitions move from site to site each year, and schools apply to host. Even competitions hosted by bar associations or other organizations unaffiliated with any law school may ask participating schools to host preliminary rounds. In those cases, it might be less intimidating to consider hosting, particularly if you can do so once or on a periodic basis, which is in most ways far less burdensome than hosting every year.

Even with all the potential benefits, however, creating or hosting a moot court competition is not always the right decision for every school at every time. In determining whether to undertake this endeavor, you and your school's administration must consider several variables, including the timing of the competition, available facilities, location, and costs.

First, though, you must ensure that you have your administration's full support for hosting or creating the competition. A mere rubber stamp from your dean will not suffice; you need a firm and unequivocal commitment that your school's administration will support this endeavor with dollars, people, facilities, and time. Running a competition is difficult enough without worrying about being pulled in multiple directions or having assistance diverted to other projects at the last minute. Ideally, you should submit a detailed proposal (including a tentative budget) to your administration in writing—and get it approved in writing—before taking any further steps towards hosting or creating the competition. Preparing that proposal, however, requires that you investigate some threshold issues to determine whether hosting or creating the competition is feasible for your school now.

A. Timing

In determining whether to host or create a competition, you must consider whether the timing of the competition works. Most existing external competitions have set timeframes. Some traditionally occur in the fall and others in the spring. Some span two semesters, with regional rounds in the fall and then national or international finals carrying over into the spring. The competition may have some flexibility—you may have a choice of three or four weekends over which to host oral arguments, for example—but you will need to make sure the general timing works well for your law school.

You will also need to rule out any date conflicts, both inside and outside your law school. First, avoid all major religious holidays. Second, all law schools run a variety of programs throughout the year, and the timing of the competition must not conflict with any other major events. Before agreeing to host, consult the law school's calendars for dates of fixed academic programs, internal competitions, on-campus interviews, court visits, homecoming, and exam periods. Be in touch with the alumni relations, events, facilities, and development staff to inquire about any significant institutional events that might impact your ability to host, such as major speakers, colloquia, conferences, construction, facilities renovations, or other events that might impact access to law school or courthouse buildings. In particular, be aware of other competitions your law school or university may be hosting during the same academic year, including undergraduate mock trial or moot court competitions. Human, physical, and financial resources are chronically limited, and you want to be sure not to overtax them.

Of course, you also want to be aware of major events in your community; a large festival, race, trade show, or convention could severely impair the availability of hotel rooms, public transportation, and other necessities for your competition attendees. Finally, if your law school shares a legal community with one or more other law schools, investigate whether those schools are hosting competitions or other events that may draw significant numbers of lawyers and judges. It can be difficult enough to find volunteers to judge briefs and oral arguments without competing for resources with another local competition.

If you are creating your own competition, you still need to consider the same timing issues, as well as the timing of other popular external moot court competitions or competitions in the same subject-matter area. You may be able to draw additional interest, for example, if you schedule your new competition at a time when not as many other competitions occur. Many competitions share a similar timeline: the problem is released in the fall, briefs are due right after winter break, and oral argument rounds begin in late February.[1] If you avoid that time frame, you may be able to attract competitors who wish to engage in more than one competition, or you may garner interest from schools on unconventional schedules for which competitions in the fall or later in the spring might be more convenient.[2]

---

1. Competitions sharing this timeline include Jessup, the ABA's National Appellate Advocacy Competition, the Pace Environmental Law Moot Court Competition, the Native American Law Students Association's Moot Court Competition, and others.

2. A growing number of law schools deviates from the semester system with their second- and third-year classes. Some divide the spring semester into two quarters. Still others have the second- and third-year courses on a quarter system for the full year, with a winter quarter that straddles the winter break. And some law schools take advantage of that schedule to place upper-level students in full-semester externships, which may affect

Finally, you need to determine how long the on-site oral argument rounds will take. Some competitions conduct all oral argument rounds in one day, from morning to evening. Others stretch the competition over two or three days. Much of this timing will depend on when your facilities are available. If you are using a courthouse, for example, you may only be able to use it evenings and weekends, which may mean that your oral argument rounds extend over several days. The size of the competition also affects your analysis: if you have many teams and few rooms, you may need to conduct multiple heats per round during the preliminary rounds, and this structure will require significantly more time.

B. Facilities

You also must estimate the number of competitors who will attend and make sure that you can provide the necessary facilities, either at your law school, at your university, or elsewhere in the vicinity. Some of these logistics are covered in more detail in Chapter Three, but basic facilities requirements include:

- Sufficient courtroom or classroom space to conduct all oral argument rounds;
- Common areas where competitors, bailiffs, coaches, and judges can check in and receive information;
- An office area for on-site competition administration and scoring;
- A large space for an orientation meeting of competitors, bailiffs, and coaches, and for briefing judges as a group;
- Meeting space for teams and judges to use before and after rounds;
- Library, Wi-Fi, and computer access, particularly for participants traveling from out of town; and
- Access to refreshments or dining facilities.

---

their ability to participate in external moot court competitions. Finally, Arizona permits its law schools to certify some third-year law students to take the bar exam in February of their third year, and a growing number of states is considering that option as well, which could also impact the competitions with February or March oral-argument rounds.

You will also need parking or other convenient means of access for participants and volunteers.

Before agreeing to host, check the proposed competition dates with your facilities management or calendaring staff and reserve the necessary rooms immediately to avoid unanticipated conflicts. Again, this is a good reason to make sure your law school's administration is on board before you commit to host the competition; if the administration backs the competition, you are less likely to face turf battles with other departments when it comes to space and timing.

As Chapter Three also notes, if your law school or university does not have adequate facilities, or even if it does, it may be possible and desirable to use space at a local courthouse. Student advocates generally enjoy the opportunity to argue in real courtrooms; logistically, however, arranging access on evenings and weekends can be complicated and potentially costly, particularly if court officers and security must be paid for working overtime.[3] Think creatively: bar associations, continuing legal education centers, and even local law firms may have facilities that they will open to law students, and they may also be willing to supply judges, refreshments, and sponsorship or financial support. You may consider hosting preliminary rounds in classrooms and moot court rooms at your law school and semifinal and final rounds somewhere more glamorous. For example, you might be able to host the semifinal and final rounds in the "showcase" courtroom in your local state or federal courthouse, at a tribal courthouse, or even in a theater or auditorium if you expect a significant number of observers.

C. Location

In addition to adequate facilities for the competition itself, host schools need to consider the features of their geographic location, including the balance of cost and convenience. Proximity to major airports with plentiful direct flights, the availability of public transporta-

---

3. If you choose to use courtrooms in a state or federal courthouse, be aware that most courthouses have strict security protocols. Not only might you need to pay security guards overtime, you likely also need to provide in advance the names of all competitors, judges, and observers. You also will need to inform competitors, judges, and observers of any special security issues. Often a courthouse will require identification for entry. Many courthouses ban certain electronic devices, particularly cameras.

tion, and the existence of a broad array of lodging and dining options can favor schools located in larger cities. At the same time, many of these services—aside from airfares—tend to be more expensive in larger cities, and most (if not all) participants will have limited budgets. Then again, the prospect of a two-hour drive from the airport to your school in wintry conditions may be a deal breaker for many schools and participants. Your school's admissions office or business office will have materials about area resources available to visiting students and professionals; those materials may help you to evaluate how accessible your location may be for traveling participants (and you can provide those materials to the participants if you do decide to host). If your school is part of a larger university that has a conference-services office, you may wish to talk through some of your logistical questions with staff there.

Finally, you may need to consider the weather. Weather not only can cause travel delays, safety concerns, and other inconveniences, it also can make a location more or less attractive to competitors. A destination that is delightful in October or April may be significantly less so in January, and it may deter competitors from selecting your competition (or a competition administrator from selecting your school to host).

D. Costs

In addition to personnel time and effort, schools incur significant costs in hosting a competition. You must ensure at the outset that your budget can cover these costs. Host schools incur many of the same costs that they would for an internal competition (as discussed at greater length in Chapter Two), such as printing, copying, mailing, technology, and parking and transportation for judges and other volunteers. Catering alone can increase your budget significantly, especially if you are providing full meals for some or all competitors.[4] Although some com-

4. For example, the total cost of hosting 45 teams at a 2-day regional round of the 2018–19 Native American Law Students Association competition at University of Arizona Law was approximately $25,000, over $20,000 of which was for catering costs (breakfast, lunch, and beverages for the participants and volunteers). The competition covered approximately half the costs through registration fees, approximately $2000 contributed by the host school, and the remainder through donations. The total budget for hosting 28 teams at the 2-day National Veterans Law Moot Court Competition at The George Washington University Law School was $14,000, which covered food and parking

petitions limit food to morning pastries and coffee, most provide full meals to at least some competitors (such as those advancing to a semi-final or final round, or those attending an awards ceremony), and many competitions feed judges and other volunteers.[5]

The school also needs to plan for personnel costs and incidental expenses that you might not anticipate, such as renting, repairing, or dry-cleaning robes for the volunteer judges. Will an administrative assistant need to incur overtime? What will the school's photographer charge for taking photos of a weekend event? Think carefully about everything you will need to maximize the value of this experience for the participants, volunteers, your department, and your school, and make sure you plan for any costs that those efforts will entail.

On the other hand, not all costs need to be borne solely by the host school. If competition rules permit, host schools may be able to charge participants a registration fee designed to spread competition costs among all participants each year. As discussed below, you will also want to explore sponsorship possibilities to offset your costs. Ultimately, the key is to understand the rules and expectations of each competition to minimize the costs and burdens to your school.

II. Founding Your Own National Moot Court Competition

With proper planning and resources, founding your own external moot court competition can bring positive recognition to your school, its programs, and your local community.

---

for judges, an off-site reception for judges and competitors, awards, administrative costs, an endowment for future advocacy competition, and incidental expenses.

5. Increasingly—likely because of the cost—competitions provide less food for competitors and instead build time into the schedule for competitors to find food in the area on their own.

A. First steps: Key decisions

Many of the same considerations that go into determining whether to host an existing competition—timing, facilities, location, and costs—will also influence whether your school should found its own national moot court competition. If you do decide to create your own competition, however, you can make some additional decisions that not only will impact the success of your competition, but also can be opportunities for creativity.

1. SUBJECT MATTER AND FOCUS OF THE COMPETITION

To draw interest and participation (and to help identify obvious avenues for marketing and participant recruitment), it is probably best to focus on a niche area of law rather than try to be a "general interest" competition like the National Moot Court Competition or the National Appellate Advocacy Competition. Do your research online: is there an area of law in which your school has some expertise, but for which there are few—if any—competition opportunities for law students? If there are competitions in a more general area of law—say, criminal law—is there a niche area on which your competition can focus? As always, do not hesitate to collaborate: consult faculty members in areas where your school has certificates or other programs and make sure to keep them in the loop, particularly if you decide that the competition will focus on their area of expertise. For example, if your school has a business law program, the head of that program and other faculty members who teach in that area may help you brainstorm not only a focus for your competition but also topics for problems, potential semifinal- and final-round judges who are prominent in that field, opportunities for participant recruitment, marketing, exciting locations for semifinal or final rounds, and even funding opportunities.

2. FEES

You also will be able to decide whether to charge a fee to competitors to offset your costs, and how much that fee should be. Ideally, the registration fee would cover your expenses but would not be so high as to deter all but the most cash-flush schools from sending students. As of

2022, most of the smaller to mid-sized competitions charge somewhere between $500 and $700 per team, so most schools will find a fee somewhere in that range to be reasonable.[6] When you sit down to determine your budget for the competition, you should also run the numbers for your anticipated number of participants to see how much of a registration fee you need to charge to offset costs. In evaluating how much to charge for registration, consider implementing a multi-tiered registration system that encourages teams to register early, which will facilitate your planning. Some competitions, for example, offer a discount of up to 15% for registering before a particular date, after which registrants must pay full price. Still other competitions add further tiers, offering successively lower discounts for registering eight months before the competition, six months before the competition, and so on.

B. Marketing your new competition

To ensure the success of a brand-new moot court competition, you need to spend significant time, effort, and resources marketing the competition. Although much of that marketing can take place online, you may want to consider doing some old-fashioned hard-copy advertising as well.

In planning your marketing efforts, you will want to work closely with your school's marketing and public relations department. Not only are the staff in that department experts in the area, they also know any rules or conventions that your school or university may require you to follow. Most schools have expensive, professionally designed branding schemes that include everything from logos and mascots to colors, fonts, and backgrounds. Some even have specifications regarding paper quality, email signatures, and layout. These rules may seem nitpicky and arbitrary, but people may have spent a great deal of time and money ensuring that your school has an instantly recognizable and indelible visual signature. You will want to take advantage of—and not undermine—those efforts. The marketing staff can also connect you with

6. As noted in Chapter Four, however, some of the larger and more-established competitions, like the ABA's National Appellate Advocacy Competition and the Jessup International Law Competition, charge more. Registration fees for the ABA competition are up to $700 per team for the first team (a school sending two teams pays a discounted rate of $650 for the second team), and those for Jessup now exceed $900 per team.

approved vendors who may have all the font and logo information on record, which can streamline your ordering process. The marketing staff usually also works closely with photographers, graphic designers, and the school's webmaster, all of whom will be crucial to your efforts.

Probably the first piece of marketing you will want to create is a website for your competition. This website will serve multiple functions over the course of the competition, from marketing, to information hosting, to conveying competition rules and updates, to serving as a time-stamped "drop box" for competitor brief submissions. Again, you will want to work closely with your marketing department and webmaster, and you will want to incorporate any school- or university-mandated branding to make sure that your competition is associated with your school visually as well as by name. Make sure you keep the website accurate and up-to-date, prominently listing registration fees and deadlines, competition location and dates, problem release dates, brief deadlines, and other key information on the main page. You probably want to have sub-pages with information about lodging locations, reservation deadlines, and rates; the competition problem; competition rules; and the competition registration form. Talk with your webmaster about the possibility of creating a "competitors only" section of the website, perhaps password protected, where you can house items that you want only competitors and their coaches to be able to access.

Ask your school's IT or events staff whether your school has a contract with a company that provides event-management software. Often, that software can help generate the event website, receive and process registrations and payments, develop email lists for sending information and reminders to participants, and more. Some event-management software pairs with conference apps that participants can download to their phones and receive event schedules and real-time information during the event. If your school does not already have a contract, depending on the size and complexity of your planned competition and your budget, you may want to research the cost of a contract to use event-management software and an app for your competition. Not only are apps useful in communicating information to participants before, during, and after the competition, many apps provide opportunities for banner and pop-up ads that may be attractive to sponsors.

As soon as you have set the dates and locations, you should design and create "save the date" postcards and mail them to the moot court director, legal writing director, moot court board president, or other appropriate individual at every law school in the country.[7] If your competition involves a specialty area of law, you also should target mailings to faculty who teach or run programs in those areas and student clubs focusing on those subjects. Again, you'll want to collaborate with your school's marketing staff in terms of design and branding. The postcard should include, at minimum, the dates of the competition, the location of the competition, any registration fees, the registration deadline, the web address for the competition website, and the contact information of the person on your team assigned to field inquiries about the competition. If you decide to cap the number of participants, you may want to add that information to your save-the-date postcard as well.

You also should market your competition using "free" resources like email. If you have an email list of moot court contacts or of faculty in a specialty field, you might start there. You should also publicize the competition on key listservs, including the online Legal Writing Institute Community (LWIC), the listservs for the Association of Legal Writing Directors and LWI Moot Court Advisors, and listservs that target professors who specialize in the legal subject matter of your competition.

C. Planning and logistics: Before the competition

In developing your own external moot court competition, you will need to do many of the same things you would do for an internal moot court competition, all of which are covered in detail in Chapter Three of this text:

- Create the competition format and rules;
- Create the competition problem and bench brief;
- Develop scoring rubrics for briefs and oral argument;
- Recruit and prepare judges;
- Distribute briefs for scoring and tabulate brief scores;
- Schedule oral argument rounds; and

---

7. This may be a project for your student moot court board. If you do not already have an up-to-date mailing list for the moot court contacts at each school, have the board research and create one. If you do already have such a list, a board member might be tasked each year with making sure the list is up to date.

- Determine oral argument pairings, which includes selecting a seeding or ranking scheme and how you want competitors to advance from round to round.

The nature of external competitions introduces additional considerations. As discussed above, if you are creating your own moot court competition, you will make many more of the decisions about the competition, and those decisions have broad-ranging ramifications that will impact your school's reputation in the broader academic and professional community. Although this presents opportunities and flexibility, it also puts the onus on you to plan early and in detail.

1. SETTING YOUR COMPETITION TIMELINE

Very early in the process, perhaps even before you pitch the competition to your school's administration, you need to develop a timeline for your competition. This timeline should include the following dates:

- Registration opens;
- Registration closes;
- Problem released;
- Deadline to request clarification;[8]
- Briefs due;
- Trainings for brief judges;
- Briefs distributed to judges;
- Brief scores collected from judges;
- Trainings for oral argument judges;
- Any times to send reminders for judges or competitors;
- Date(s) of oral argument rounds.

Most competition administrators determine dates by working backward from the dates of the oral argument rounds. Permit enough time between the time briefs are due and the dates of oral argument rounds

8. Some competitions permit teams to seek clarification regarding ambiguities in the problem materials. Teams send requests for clarification, generally by email, and then competition administrators review those requests and determine which requests require responses. Competition administrators then compose responses to the selected requests and publicize those responses to all competitors, usually by posting responses on the competition website. It's probably best, particularly in the early years of a new competition, to permit requests for clarification, but to be judicious in which ones you answer.

to score briefs, tabulate brief scores, and seed or rank teams as necessary to set oral argument rounds. Many competitions allow six to eight weeks for that process, although time spans range from over three months to just a few weeks.[9] You will also want to think about how long to give the student teams to draft their briefs. Generally, competitions allow between eight and twelve weeks for this endeavor, but competitions dealing with more complex or unfamiliar legal frameworks—such as the Jessup International Law Moot Court Competition—may have a longer span between when the problem is posted and when the briefs are due. Finally, think about whether you want to cut off registration before the problem is released, or whether you want teams to be able to see the problem before they decide whether to register.

2. COMPETITION RULES

Early in the process, you should devise the rules for your competition. Those rules should be posted on the competition website before registration closes and before the problem is posted. Chapter Three's advice regarding rules for internal competitions largely applies here, but you can also model your rules on those from other competitions. The online appendix includes some sample rules that you can use as a guide.

Competition rules generally cover, in detail, the logistics, practices, and procedures that govern your competition, including but not limited to:

- Who is eligible to compete;
- Participant cap and team composition;
- Key deadlines, including registration and brief submission;
- Rules governing brief format;
- Rules governing oral argument;
- On-site schedules and protocols during oral argument rounds;

9. For example, for the 2022–23 ABA National Appellate Advocacy Competition, briefs were due on January 9, 2023, and the first regional oral argument rounds began on February 16. The 2023 Pace Environmental Law Moot Court Competition had a longer span between the brief deadline and oral arguments: oral argument rounds began February 22, 2023, but briefs were to be postmarked no later than November 22, 2022. The Jessup timeline was shorter: briefs were due January 17, 2023, and qualifying oral argument rounds began as early as late January.

- How teams will be paired / seeded in oral argument;
- How overall team scores will be calculated;
- How the competition will determine which teams advance to additional rounds;
- Penalties for rule violations;
- How protests will be handled;
- Who can attend oral argument rounds;
- Assistance;
- Scouting; and
- Awards.

This section discusses some of these rule provisions that warrant particular consideration.

a. Participant cap and team composition

For your first year running a brand-new competition, you may want to cap the total participants at a relatively small number, so that you can better anticipate and manage your costs. A cap will also make your initial planning and budgeting much simpler. Depending on the popularity of the competition in its first year—and on the number of interested teams that you must turn away—you may wish to raise that cap in future years if your facilities can accommodate greater numbers.

As part of the competition rules, you also will determine how many students can be on each team and what role each student will be permitted to play. As discussed in Chapter Three, you always have the option of requiring students to compete as individuals. External moot court competitions rarely employ this structure, however, in large part because external moot court is more of a "team sport." As discussed in more detail in Chapter Four, one common team composition is the three-person team. In that situation, the competition problem poses two issues, and often one student on the team is responsible for each issue, with the third student serving as brief editor, bailiff, and alternate. Sometimes the third student also participates in oral arguments, perhaps arguing one side of one of the two issues. Other competitions, such as the Jessup International Law Moot Court Competition, have four- or five-person teams, with the teams briefing both sides of the issue. Keep in mind, however, that the more complex your team structure becomes, the more logistically challenging seeding, oral-argument scheduling, scoring, and awards become.

b. Assistance

As discussed in Chapter Four, most competitions have rules prescribing what type of assistance teams can receive from faculty or coaches. First and foremost, your rules should be clear. Beyond that, you need to balance how much you want teams to rely on their own existing skills and knowledge against how much you want to ensure that teams gain an accurate and complete understanding of a particular issue or area of law. Many competitions bar teams from receiving any assistance from anyone—including coaches, law faculty, attorneys, family, and friends—before the brief is due. If one of your goals is to enhance student knowledge of a particular area of law, however, you may decide to permit teams to discuss the general legal framework, or even legal arguments, with faculty or coaches during the brief-writing process, but still prohibit teams from receiving specific feedback on drafts.

Many competitions prohibit teams from engaging in oral argument practice with non-team-members as judges before the briefs are due. On the one hand, this limits the amount of guidance others can offer regarding the strengths, weaknesses, and nature of the arguments the teams offer; on the other, if the area of law is particularly dense or difficult, you may want students to receive a little more guidance, so long as that guidance stops short of providing feedback on drafts of the brief.

c. Schools sending multiple teams

You'll also want to consider how many teams an individual law school may send to your competition. If you are capping the total number of participants at a relatively low number, you'll want to limit each school to one team. If, on the other hand, you anticipate a larger number of participants, you may permit schools to send up to two teams. Allowing multiple teams from one school complicates administration, however, because you will need to schedule oral argument rounds so that you never have two teams from the same school arguing against one another, at least in the preliminary rounds.[10] This can force you to

---

10. Some competitions permit teams from the same school to compete against one another in the elimination rounds (but not in preliminary rounds). If you can avoid having teams from the same school compete against each other, though, it's probably best. Many times, teams from the same school have the same coach, have argued against one another repeatedly in practice rounds, and both feel and behave more like a single team than two separate teams. Moreover, having two teams from the same school argue against

disrupt seeding, and it becomes particularly cumbersome during elimination rounds. We do not recommend allowing any one school to send more than two teams.

Be sure to provide clear instructions to schools that send more than one team if there are special rules that apply to them. For example, many competitions require teams from the same school to brief different sides of an issue. Further, your competition's assistance and collaboration rules should clearly explain whether teams from the same school may read each other's briefs before they are submitted, practice oral arguments together before the briefs are submitted, and practice oral arguments together after the briefs are submitted.

d. Team anonymity

Be sure to include clear provisions in your competition rules to protect team anonymity. Most if not all external moot competitions protect against unconscious (or conscious) school-related bias in judging by preventing the judges from knowing which school any competitor attends. As discussed below in the section on "processing registrations," teams are usually assigned a number at registration. Teams put that number, instead of names or school affiliation, on their briefs. Although oral argument nametags generally bear the competitors' names, they also show only the team number and not the school name. Your competition rules should caution competitors not to identify their school affiliation to judges, whether affirmatively or passively. Students should not carry portfolios with their school's insignia on it, for example, or wear lapel pins with the school's logo, and if observers are permitted in the courtroom, they should not wear anything identifying the school. And, of course, students should not tell judges which school they represent. The rules should explicitly outline the penalties for violating this rule.

---

one another in any round but the final round means that at least one team from that school will be eliminated (although it also means that at least one team from that school will advance). That said, if two teams from the same school advance to elimination rounds, it makes your scheduling and seeding much simpler if you allow them to argue against one another, assuming that the competition's rules would ordinarily dictate that result.

e. Conflicts

To avoid potential conflicts or the appearance of impropriety when hosting an external moot court competition, many schools opt to bar students from the host school from participating. Since judges generally come from the local legal community, it is more difficult to ensure a school's anonymity if students from that school participate. If you and your moot court board administer the competition, the appearance of impropriety increases and may not only reduce faith in the fairness of the competition but also tarnish any victories your students earn. This potential conflict becomes more politically sensitive, however, when a school hosts a competition in a niche subject area in which the school has some expertise; it may seem unfair to many, including your school's administration, to deprive your students of the opportunity to participate. Regardless, unless you can delegate administrative responsibilities to someone outside your law school, it seems difficult to run a reputable competition while allowing students from your own school to participate.

Although this policy need not necessarily be in your published competition rules, it may be a good idea to include it to provide comfort to schools that may have specific concerns about conflicts of interest, perhaps because of past negative experiences. Make this decision early and be prepared to defend it to your school's administration, faculty, and student body. If you do decide to bar your school's students from participating, consider soliciting support from others in faculty and administration who can help you make the case that your decision is in the best interest of the competition and the school.

3. SPONSORS

Early in the process, you will also want to think about funding sources outside of registration fees. Local or national law firms, bar associations, professional organizations, and commercial legal vendors and publishers often are willing to sponsor all or part of a competition or to provide in-kind services to offset costs. Vendors and publishers such as Carolina Academic Press, Barbri, LexisNexis, Westlaw, Aspen, and others all have budgets for supporting interschool events, and they can provide materials, sponsor meals or receptions, and provide access to research resources. They need to be invited early, however, before their budgets are allocated to other events and initiatives. Reach out to potential sponsors in writing and by telephone (or in person, if possible) as early as you can. Different sponsors are on different budgeting cycles, and sponsorships and charitable donations are budgeted items that sometimes must go through several rounds of approval, particularly if you are dealing with a large company or national law firm. Make your ask as long before the competition as possible to increase your chances of being included in the budget for the next fiscal year. In exchange for this type of support, vendors and publishers often wish to have an information table at the event. The host school also should thank all sponsors publicly with signage and, if appropriate, notations in the competition materials or on the competition website.

When it comes to sponsors, you might also think a little bit outside the box and solicit in-kind donations from local businesses that might appreciate the opportunity to showcase their wares to your out-of-town guests. Again, coordinate closely with those inside your law school who might be reaching out to those businesses on a more regular basis to make sure that you do not undermine their efforts or inundate the same businesses with requests. But you may be able to provide continental breakfast items, local coffees or teas, afternoon snacks, gifts at an awards ceremony, pens and notepads, or other items at no or low cost, so long as you also acknowledge sponsors with signage.

Even if you cannot secure food donations, you most likely can negotiate discounts at nearby, locally owned restaurants for participants who present a coupon or other evidence that they are with your competition. You might task your moot court board with developing a list of local bars, restaurants, coffee shops, and other locations that visiting competitors and their coaches might find attractive and identify those that offer discounts associated with the competition. The more that your school can be a good "host" in every sense of the word, the better experience competitors will have, and the more likely they—and, perhaps most importantly, their coaches—will be to recommend your competition in the future.

4. HOTELS

Generally, the host school arranges for a hotel that will host the traveling teams, or, at the very least, recommends affordable lodging near the competition site. Again, your school or university may already have relationships with area hotels; many institutions have contracts with negotiated rates for anyone traveling on institutional business. If you negotiate with the hotels yourself, keep in mind that guaranteeing a minimum number of rooms often will garner a lower per-room rate. If you secure a room block, however, you must be sure that you will need people to book at least that many rooms, or the hotel may require you to make up the difference. To avoid being stuck paying for unsold rooms, you should negotiate a reservation cut-off date a couple of weeks before your competition, after which the hotel will release the block and no longer honor the lower rate. You can also secure a lower per-room rate by paying to use some of the hotel's facilities. For example, you may book a banquet room for your awards ceremony, or you may wish to hold some competitor meetings at the hotel.

As early as possible after the date and location are announced, the host school should post to the competition website and distribute to all participants the names, negotiated rates, and cut-off dates for the host hotels so that teams can calculate budgets and make travel arrangements. Some hotels will also help to arrange discounted airfare, car rentals, and taxi or shuttle transportation for competition attendees. Many teams may need to submit this information to an administrator or finance office to obtain approval before booking, so you should compile and communicate that information as soon as possible. Remember also that many schools require documentation that the team is staying at the "conference" hotel before they will reimburse expenses, so it is helpful to label this information clearly on the competition website.

5. PROCESSING REGISTRATIONS

Well before you open registration, you should have a process in place for handling it, including receiving registration fees and assigning team designations. Some of this you can do through your competition website; your school's webmaster can probably guide you through dealing with mechanisms to accept credit card payments and registration information online. You can also provide schools with the option of paying by check. Often the online registration and payment system can be designed to send a confirmation email once it processes the information and payment successfully. Ask whether your school has a contract with a company that provides event-management software designed to process registrations and payment.

Once you receive payment and registration information, you should assign each team an individual competition number. Most competitions do this to maintain anonymity. You can then either notify the team contact of the number by return email, or you can publish a chart of team numbers and school names on a "competitors only" section of your website.

6. RECRUITING VOLUNTEERS

Chapter Three goes into detail regarding how to recruit judges to score briefs and oral argument rounds. You will also need other volunteers, however, to run aspects of your competition on site. Volunteers run check-in tables and information desks, supervise the collection and tabulation of scoring sheets, troubleshoot issues, field protests and referee disputes, run information from courtrooms to a central administration office, and handle any food and beverage. You may decide to use your own moot court board for most of this, but you may need to recruit other faculty or staff to assist. Early in the process, determine how many volunteers you will need, and plan for back-up in case of illness or emergency.

7. RELEASING BRIEFS

Many competitions—whether internal or external—allow competitors access to all the competition briefs at some point before the oral argument rounds. This access often increases the quality of oral arguments and enhances the overall learning experience, as competitors see different ways of framing the arguments, learn of different authorities to cite or different arguments to make, and see the issues from the other side's perspective. This process can also help teams anticipate what arguments will be most difficult to counter and which teams will be the most formidable competition. Your webmaster can probably design a place on the "competitors only" section of your website where you can post, and competitors can download, the teams' briefs, or that may be something you can do through event-management software, if you chose that route. Post the briefs by team number. You probably want to remove those briefs or deactivate that page at some point after the competition has concluded.[11]

8. BRIEF SCORING

Chapter Three goes into significant detail regarding how to select and recruit judges for brief scoring, how to determine how many judges you need, how to craft a fair and effective brief-scoring rubric, and how to communicate with your brief judges. This section highlights a few quirks particular to external moot court competitions.

If you allow students from your own school to compete, you should not use your own faculty as brief judges. If students from your own school are barred from competing, though, your faculty can be your best judges, particularly those faculty with special expertise in the subject matter of the competition. You also probably want to recruit multiple judges to score each brief to ensure objectivity. Particularly if you anticipate a relatively small number of competitors, you may want to use this method, described in Chapter Three: Have each brief scored by five judges, then drop the high and low scores and average the three remaining scores to arrive at the final brief score. Remember to check and double-check your calculations and your judges' calculations. Errors in brief scores undermine competitors' faith in the fairness and accuracy of scoring overall.

You'll also need to determine when you will inform teams of their brief scores. Many competitions release brief scores in writing when teams arrive at the competition, at the initial competitors meeting, but inform teams in advance regarding any scoring penalties, such as subtractions for late filing, failing to comply with format requirements, or other deviations from the competition rules. The upside of informing teams of the brief score in advance is that you can resolve any computation errors or challenges before the oral argument rounds begin. The risk in informing teams of their brief scores before they arrive is that some teams may be discouraged by a low brief score and elect not to attend the competition, particularly if they are traveling from somewhere that does

11. Most competitions contain provisions in their rules that the competition owns the copyright to the record, the competition materials, and any briefs submitted in the competition.

not require them to purchase plane tickets. You also want to be sure you maintain confidentiality when it comes to brief scores, so take care in considering how to transmit them.

9. PREPARING ORAL ARGUMENT JUDGES

As soon as you have finalized the bench brief, send it to your judges. Most of your judges are busy professionals and giving them plenty of flexibility regarding when to review the materials will help ensure better-prepared judges at the oral argument rounds. If you plan to conduct an in-person training session for your judges before the competition—which is ideal but not always feasible—make sure to plan that date early and inform your judges when you are recruiting them. If you cannot train the judges before the competition, try to have at least a short session before they take the bench for the first time. Some competitions allegedly provide the bench brief to the judges for the first time on the day of oral argument rounds. Providing the bench brief shortly before judges enter oral argument seems like a recipe for inadequate judging, arbitrary scoring, and disappointing outcomes. You can strike a balance between respecting your judges' time and making sure they are thoroughly prepared by providing the bench brief by email a few weeks before the competition and then reviewing that material shortly before oral argument begins. Providing the option of online training or a pre-recorded training video also makes it easier for your judges and thus more likely that they will have time to prepare thoroughly.

The better prepared your judges are, the more satisfying your competition will be, and the more faith competitors and coaches will have about the fairness of the scoring. Chapter Three contains more information on how to conduct a training session to ensure that your judges understand the problem, the competition, the scoring process, and anything else you want them to know. In addition, Chapter Three includes information on how to prepare the bench brief and the role the bench brief plays in ensuring that your judges are well prepared.

10. SEEDING TEAMS

Once you have received the brief scores, you then will implement your competition rules to develop any seeding or ranking for the oral argument rounds. You can find more detailed information on how to seed teams in Chapter Three. Ideally, you will complete the seeding and round-scheduling process the week before the oral argument rounds. You may want to email competitors their pairings, at least for the initial rounds, before the competition begins (or push them through the event app, if you chose to use one). This approach has downsides, however, particularly if teams cancel at the last minute, or if you discover computation errors or other things that affect seeding. Although some competitors appreciate knowing pairings, heat assignments, and room assignments in advance, it is far more disruptive to have to change them at the last minute.

11. CONTINGENCY PLANNING

As we have all learned of late, the unexpected happens. A storm of the century prevents some or all teams from traveling to your location. A broken water pipe makes facilities unavailable at the last minute. A global pandemic prevents travel and gathering.

Expect the best but have a plan for the worst. Discuss what happens if you need to cancel or drastically modify the competition at the last minute. To the extent possible, be sure that any contracts with vendors include provisions that protect you in the case of circumstances outside your control. Plan back-up locations for arguments and events should planned facilities become unavailable or unworkable. And definitely know and train competition staff in your institution's emergency plans and procedures in case something should happen during the competition.

One option to explore if unexpected, last-minute circumstances make it impossible to proceed with the competition as planned is to conduct the competition virtually. Chapter Six of this text discusses in detail the logistics of a virtual moot court competition. Sometimes, however, simply cancelling the competition is the only reasonable course of action, and you should have a plan for that possibility.

D. Planning and logistics: Right before and during the competition

As the dates for the oral argument rounds approach, prepare to have most of your time consumed with final competition details. If possible, clear your schedule for the days of the oral argument rounds. If that's not possible, make sure you have a cadre of well-trained and informed help—whether student moot court board members, administrative staff, or other volunteers—to handle last-minute details.

1. PRE-COMPETITION COMMUNICATIONS

In the days leading up to the competition, you will want to send reminder emails to all your volunteers and judges. If you used event-management software for registration and payment, that same software often allows you to write reminder emails in advance that the software will then send to all registrants at designated times. As Chapter Three suggests, those emails are a good place to convey information about parking or transportation, meeting locations, attire, and any other last-minute information you need them to know. If you used an event app, you can use that app to communicate useful information like the schedule, team pairings, information about local attractions, hotel information, and more before the competition. Whether you use email, the event software, or an app, you will also want to send teams any last-minute scheduling information and to let them know where to go for initial check-in and the competitors' meeting. It's always thoughtful to provide maps to guide teams to key locations from the competition hotel, and this might be a nice time to transmit any restaurant or other recommendations. All this information should also be on your competition website.

2. COMPETITORS' MEETING

Schedule an orientation meeting for competitors and coaches before the first oral argument rounds begin. First, introduce all the key members of the on-site competition administration team and identify their roles. Then go over any rules pertaining to the facilities and review key provisions of the competition rules relating to oral argument rounds. You can also review the competition schedule, including the timing of different rounds and heats. If team members have obligations relating to scoring or interacting with the judges, discuss this as well. Introduce competitors and coaches to the process for lodging and resolving protests. Be sure to discuss the mechanism for seeking sanctions against other teams for violation of the competition rules.

It is also important to review any logistics with the bailiffs, competitors, and judges. You probably want to answer at least these questions:

- Do competitors enter the courtroom first, or do the judges?
- Do the bailiffs have any formal responsibilities to call the case, introduce the judges as they enter the courtroom, or escort judges from their meeting room to the courtrooms?
- Who times the arguments? How is that time calculated? How do the judges know when a competitor has used all their time? Do the judges have discretion to extend a competitor's allotted time?
- What happens at the end of the arguments? Do competitors leave the courtroom for some period to allow the judges to discuss and score the competitors' performances before the competitors return for in-person feedback?
- Who conveys scoring information to the central competition administration? Do bailiffs have any responsibility for calculating scores or determining their accuracy?
- How and when do competitors lodge and resolve complaints about things that happen during oral argument?

Often, uncertainty about these types of logistical details can cause competitors, coaches, and judges more stress than the oral arguments themselves, so the more detail and reminders you can provide regarding the procedural steps of your competition, both in the written competition rules and during the on-site training, the better.

Consider also talking to competitors about what any observers can and cannot do in the courtroom. Observers should comport themselves as in an actual courtroom, rising when the judges enter, remaining silent during arguments and feedback, and departing when instructed. All attendees should be reminded to keep phones and other noise-generating devices turned off.

Finally, often the competition administrator distributes brief scores and team pairings at this initial competitors' meeting. If you distribute this information, be sure to allow time for competitors to review their brief scores, check for any computation errors, and lodge and resolve any challenges to the brief scores, seeding, or pairings.

Although you will be discussing serious matters, like scoring, sanctions, rules, and regulations, try to keep the tone of the meeting upbeat and the energy positive. Think carefully about who will present and consider scripting key parts of your presentation. Competitors and coaches quickly form impressions regarding the competence and professionalism of competition administrators and staff, so put your best, most polished foot forward at the competitors' meeting.

3. JUDGE ORIENTATION

If you were unable to conduct an in-person or virtual training session for your judges in the weeks before the competition, gather your judges right before the oral argument rounds to review last-minute issues and logistics. To uncover any potential conflicts, make sure to inform the judges of the names of the students who will be competing before them so that judges can let you know if they know any of the students outside of the competition. This is also a good time to review the most important rules and priorities of your competition and any key points about the competition problem. As with the competitors' orientation, take time to walk the judges through some of the competition logistics, including the overall structure of the oral argument, to avoid any confusion or miscommunication. Do not rely on this meeting, however, to communicate everything you want the judges to know. That communication should take place in writing well before the competition date.

4. RUNNING ORAL ARGUMENT ROUNDS

Chapter Three provides detailed advice on arranging and running oral argument rounds in internal competitions, and most of that advice applies to external competitions as well. All the admonitions regarding logistics, properly arranging rooms, providing directional signs, and, most importantly, staying on schedule, are as—if not more—important in external competitions as they are in internal ones.

External competitions pose additional concerns. If you have two teams competing from one school, you may not wish to have those teams compete against one another in the preliminary rounds (or at all—we discuss this in greater detail in the "competition rules" section). Most competition rules for external competitions warn competitors against wearing or carrying anything that identifies their school and prohibit them from mentioning their school in front of oral argument judges.[12]

5. HANDLING SCORING DISPUTES/SANCTIONS

Chapter Three also thoroughly discusses handling protests and other complications. Responding to protests with diplomacy and fairness is particularly important in external competitions. The last thing you want is for your competition to be viewed as "rigged" or otherwise unfair. If you have written your competition rules well, you will be well prepared for most situations that arise, and competitors and coaches will be able to anticipate the procedures for seeking sanctions and the specific penalties for rule violations.

Try to avoid penalties for inadvertent rule violations. For example, as discussed earlier, the rules for many external competitions bar competitors or their spectators from wearing or carrying anything identifying their schools. If someone shows up to the all-competitor meeting carrying a briefcase with the school insignia on it, warn that student before the team heads to the courtrooms.

As Chapter Three emphasizes, you should strive for transparency, consistency, timeliness, and respect in handling rule violations, requests for sanctions, and other complaints. Hear and respond to issues immediately. Listen. Ask questions. Allow competitors or coaches to air their concerns and make it clear that their concerns are heard. Although you should respond promptly, do not be rash. As discussed earlier in this chapter, decide well in advance how you will handle different violations, and publish your rules early and on the website. Then be consistent.

12. Some competitions even identify competitors by letters (such as competitor A or competitor B from team 123) instead of by first and last name. Some people prefer this; names could invoke unconscious judging biases, particularly where a name reveals something of a student's personal background. On the other hand, a student cannot mask every trait that makes him or her an individual and that therefore might provoke bias.

6. FOOD AND BEVERAGE/OTHER AMENITIES

Most competitions provide at least continental breakfast items, coffee, and tea the mornings of competitions, and perhaps portable fruit (apples, bananas, and oranges) and cookies in the afternoon. Everyone appreciates bottled water (or iced water in a dispenser) at any time of day. In light of recent concerns about communicable diseases, it may be best to provide pre-packaged snacks. Provide hand sanitizer and wipes at any food stations and in all competition locations. Many companies sell branded hand-sanitizer containers and wipes; if you have money in your budget, such items are nice for competitor and judge swag bags.

Many competitions also provide some full meals. Most provide a lunch for competitors advancing to the semi-final or final round. Often this is a box lunch that competitors can take with them to practice locations. And most competitions have some sort of final banquet and awards ceremony. This event is usually a lunch or dinner, often buffet-style, and generally lasts about an hour. Again, depending on concerns about disease, it may be best to provide pre-packaged meals, like box lunches.

Generally, if you provide full meals, people expect vegetarian or vegan options to be provided alongside the more traditional meat selections. Asking competitors for information on dietary restrictions and allergies at registration, however, can open the floodgates. Generally, if someone has a significant allergy, that person will inform you or will avoid unlabeled food items at the competition. If you do provide a buffet at one meal, it doesn't hurt to try and at least have side items that are vegan, gluten free, and nut free. Salads without dressing, unbuttered rice, unbuttered mixed veggies, beans, and pasta with tomato sauce are all inexpensive options that meet most, if not all, dietary needs.

Many competitions also provide food and beverage for judges and other volunteers. As Chapter Three advises, stock your judges' area with light refreshments and plenty of water. If volunteers will be tied to the location during mealtimes, provide simple box lunches.

7. AWARDS

Be sure to include money in your competition budget for awards and an awards ceremony. Most of the awards can be simple—certificates for oral advocate and brief awards, for example—but you will want to provide at least one nice plaque or trophy for the team that wins overall, and perhaps for the top oral advocate and top brief.

Most competitions conduct an awards ceremony at a luncheon or dinner. If you base oral advocacy awards on performance in the preliminary rounds, you probably want to schedule the awards ceremony after the preliminary rounds but before any elimination rounds. This serves two purposes: It makes it more likely that teams that fail to advance to the elimination rounds will attend, making for a nicer ceremony overall, and it permits you to combine the awards ceremony with an announcement of the teams that will advance. If you prefer to have an overall awards ceremony after the final rounds, keep in mind that attendance will be spottier—some teams will head home as soon as they can after they are eliminated, and still others will opt to enjoy your city over attending a competition-related event after they are eliminated.

Depending on the number of teams and individual students that participate, you may want to have different awards. Most competitions give at least three oral advocate awards and three brief awards, in addition to the overall top team award. Some give commemorative items to any teams that advance to the elimination rounds or to a particular level of elimination (semifinals or finals). You can print certificates on site, and you can order plaques or other commemorative items from a local trophy shop; if you do not already have a relationship with one, check with your alumni relations office to see which vendor the law school usually uses.

If you have the facilities at your law school, you can certainly hold the awards ceremony there. Most hotels have banquet facilities, and you may garner a better per-room rate at the host hotel if you hold the awards ceremony and a meeting or two there. Restaurants tend to be more expensive and cumbersome to arrange, but many do have large private rooms that you can reserve.

Wherever and whenever you hold the awards ceremony, the key is to make competitors feel appreciated and recognized. Do not rush through the announcements. Have winners walk up to be recognized, particularly for the more significant awards. And select attractive, distinctive awards that competitors and schools will be proud to display. Many schools display team awards in a trophy case in the lobby or in the law library; often a distinctive award can encourage students to investigate a competition that they would not otherwise consider, and, for better or worse, the quality of the award can affect perceptions of the quality of the competition. Of course, you do not want to blow your budget on trinkets and trophies, but you should consider all potential audiences when designing and selecting the keepsake awards.

E. Planning and logistics: After the competition

As soon as possible after the competition, you need to write thank-you notes or letters to all your competition sponsors and volunteers. A form letter on your school's stationery (or competition stationery, if you have it) is more than adequate, but handwritten thank-you notes from you or from your moot court board can add a more personal touch.

While memories are still fresh, assemble your team to debrief. Ideally, make notes throughout the competition of what went well, what unanticipated issues arose, and what problems occurred. Once the competition is over, pull together everyone's notes and add them to your list for next year. Anyone involved in the competition should have a voice in the debriefing, including anyone from other departments who assisted (especially anyone involved with marketing or website matters). Of course, you should spend some time at the debriefing meeting thanking everyone and congratulating your team on a job well done.

Do not forget to send follow-up communications to your contacts at the schools that sent teams, and to the coaches if you have that information. A simple thank-you letter will suffice, but if you have information on the next year's competition (even if it's just competition dates), you should send that as well. Be sure to include a line inviting the school to send a team the following year. If competitors were unable to attend the awards ceremony but won awards, mail those as soon as possible to the school's dean with a nice cover letter containing your congratulations and thanks. Some competition administrators send letters to the dean of each school that sent a team, praising the team and its coach, and congratulating the school on its performance.

To improve the competition even more in future years, create an online survey for competitors and coaches to provide feedback on the competition—everything from administration, to the hotel, to logistics, to scoring and judging, to food and beverage. You can create the survey using any one of several online services (such as Survey Monkey). Check with your school's administration to see if your school has a subscription to any of these services. The website will usually give you a link that you can email to participants and that you can post on your competition website. Such a survey might not only give you perspective on what really went well or not-so-well but might also alert you to issues of which you would otherwise remain unaware.

You should also send out an email to all faculty, staff, and the communications team at your school, providing details on the competition—how many students attended and from how many law schools, how many outside lawyers and judges attended, and any other details that provide a picture of how the competition might help your law school. Do not forget to use this opportunity to publicly thank those within your own school who supported you and facilitated your competition's success, including but not limited to your dean.

III. Conclusion

Hosting or founding an external moot court competition can enhance your school's reputation, draw attention to areas of specialty, and provide positive publicity for your school's faculty, facilities, and location. Although founding an original competition involves a great deal of planning, money, and work, the rewards can be significant. Your school can provide an excellent learning experience for law students across the country while highlighting what you do best. The key is to make sure you have the resources, support, and planning to do it right.

CHAPTER 6

Virtual Moot Court Competitions

THIS CHAPTER WILL HELP YOU TO:

- **Evaluate whether and how to move your internal or external moot court competition or activity online;**
- **Plan and execute an effective virtual internal moot court competition;**
- **Plan and execute an effective virtual external moot court competition;**
- **Prepare your teams for success at virtual moot court competitions;**
- **Enhance the overall student experience in virtual moot court competitions; and**
- **Train more effective virtual advocates.**

In an era when state and federal appellate courts across the country have conducted oral argument over video-conference platforms—and when even the notoriously tech-shy United States Supreme Court has heard remote oral arguments and streamed them online[1]—it can come as no surprise that virtual moot-court competitions have become increasingly popular. Even absent public-health emergencies, lawyers continue to face the need to conduct oral advocacy and other aspects of law practice in a virtual environment. Some courts have permanently shifted

1. *See Press Release Regarding April Oral Argument Session*, Sup. Ct. of the U.S. (Mar. 19, 2021), https://www.supremecourt.gov/publicinfo/press/pressreleases/pr_03-19-21.

select hearings and other specific proceedings to videoconference.[2] Much alternative dispute resolution has moved to virtual formats,[3] and court rules permitting even party depositions to be conducted online appear likely to become permanent.[4] Not only will the effective lawyer of the twenty-first century require competence and confidence practicing oral advocacy in the virtual environment, but also virtual moot court competitions share with their real-world counterparts significant cost-saving benefits and the potential to increase access for a diverse array of participants.

In short, although in-person competitions have resumed and will persist, virtual moot court opportunities appear to be here to stay. This chapter sets forth some best practices in running virtual internal and external competitions and in preparing teams to participate in virtual competitions. With thoughtful planning and preparation, virtual moot court not only can help prepare students for the realities of twenty-first century legal advocacy but also can provide students with rich educational and extracurricular experiences.

I. Virtual Internal Competitions

In spring of 2020, many legal skills and moot court programs faced an unanticipated dilemma: cancel all internal oral argument activities and moot court competitions, or quickly pivot to a virtual format.[5] Fortunately, no future program need ever make that pivot without guidance.

---

2. *See, e.g.*, *Electronic Hearings*, Ariz. Jud. Branch, https://www.azcourts.gov/Electronic-Hearings (last visited Aug. 2, 2022).

3. *See* Meredith McBride, *ODR in the Era of COVID-19*, Am. Bar Ass'n (Oct. 27, 2020), https://www.americanbar.org/groups/family_law/committees/alternative-dispute-resolution/odr/.

4. *See* Nicole Black, *Conduct Depositions Remotely with These Virtual Technologies*, ABA J. (Mar. 25, 2022), https://www.abajournal.com/columns/article/conduct-depositions-remotely-with-these-virtual-deposition-technologies.

5. *Law Professor Takes 1L Zoom Oral Arguments Nationwide (and Here's How She Did It)*, Legal Skills Prof Blog (June 1, 2020), https://lawprofessors.typepad.com/legal_skills/2020/06/law-professor-takes-zoom-arguments-nationwide.html. Of the 76 legal-writing programs that responded to an informal poll in spring 2020, almost half had canceled all oral arguments in response to the pandemic. Of the half that conducted oral arguments that semester, 80% did so remotely using Zoom or another video-conference platform.

Through the experiences of the intrepid pioneers of 2020—and drawing on the advice of advocacy professors and real-world advocates, judges, and other experts—this text offers tried-and-true best practices for organizing and executing a virtual internal moot court competition that maximize educational benefit for the participants and minimize hassle for the administrator while replicating the best aspects of an in-person competition.

A. Should we go virtual?

In the absence of a public-health emergency or other exigent circumstances that compel you to move activities online, you may still wish to conduct an internal moot court competition in the virtual environment. Maybe you have a significant number of students for whom the commute to campus creates a barrier to participation. Perhaps your law school lacks adequate courtroom or classroom space to conduct multiple rounds of oral argument within the contemplated time frame. Or maybe you want to create a competition that simulates virtual law practice. In deciding whether to conduct your competition virtually rather than in person, you will wish to consider several factors:

- *Cost.* Virtual competitions can be less expensive than in-person ones. To the extent that a competition has invited out-of-town judges for semifinal or final rounds, the competition will not need to pay travel expenses for those judges. The competition need not provide food, beverages, or other amenities to judges or competitors. You need not incur any costs to rent space, and any extra security for after-hours use of the law school building, courtrooms, or classrooms will be unnecessary. On the other hand, depending on the existing resources at the law school, the competition may incur costs in paying for an adequate virtual platform on which to conduct the competition or for supplemental technology for students, such as webcams, microphones, headsets, or wireless internet hotspots.
- *Space.* Moving the competition online dramatically reduces the amount of physical space required. The virtual competition eliminates the need to reserve courtrooms or class-

rooms for arguments, judge robing and deliberation, and tabulation.

- *Accessibility.* Accessibility issues can cut both ways. On the one hand, some students find traveling to campus or an off-site competition location after hours challenging, whether because of family obligations or other issues. Such students may have an easier time participating in a virtual competition or may be more likely to participate if the competition is elective. Certainly, if you are running an online course or program or one in which some percentage of students are participating virtually from a distance, an online competition becomes a necessity. On the other hand, students who lack access to reliable, high-speed internet face material disadvantages that risk impairing oral-argument performance, including screen freezing, inconsistent audio, and even periodic disconnection.
- *Access to Judges.* Moving a competition online makes it possible to invite a wider and potentially more diverse group of judges. Alumni or friends of the law school who reside in other cities, states, and even time zones can participate in competition judging. For example, schools that moved their internal competitions to the online format have taken advantage of federal circuit court judges in other jurisdictions, sometimes even building full panels that mix judges from various circuits. Or a competition could target volunteer judges with practice backgrounds and expertise matching the topic of the competition problem, enabling those judges more easily to assess the substantive performances of the participants, score more accurately, and provide more helpful constructive feedback. Inviting them to participate as judges in a virtual competition can also be a great way to connect with distant alumni.
- *Logistics for administrators.* Although a virtual competition requires solid planning, execution, and pre-competition communication to succeed, in some ways running a virtual competition can be easier and more convenient for administrators than an in-person competition. Administrators can move from virtual courtroom to virtual courtroom from

the comfort of their own living rooms or offices and, with the proper equipment, can even monitor multiple competition rounds simultaneously.

B. Specific best practices for planning and executing virtual internal competitions

Although virtual moot court competitions are relatively new, a couple of years of conducting competitions online—with some thoughtful planning and some trial and error—have highlighted some key considerations and best practices that increase the likelihood of a relatively smooth competition and one that offers optimal educational value to its participants with minimal hassle or risk of unfairness. In addition, at the beginning of the COVID-19 pandemic in 2020, when it became apparent that many of the external moot court and trial advocacy competitions for the coming academic year would be conducted virtually, a group of almost 100 law-school advocacy educators convened over Zoom in connection with the nascent National Association of Legal Advocacy Educators (NALAE) to develop a best-practices document to help guide organizations hosting virtual competitions.[6] To the extent that any advice in this chapter is informed by that document, citations are provided in footnotes.

This section focuses specifically on internal competitions, but most of the best practices listed here also apply to external competitions. Any advice unique to external competitions will be provided in a later section.

1. BEFORE THE COMPETITION

This section sets forth decisions to make and actions to take before launching a partially or totally virtual internal competition at your law school.

a. Decisions

Planning a virtual competition first requires several key decisions about the mode of the competition, the platform, the schedule, and ways

---

6. *Guidance for Conducting Moot Court Competitions (2020–2021)*, Nat'l Ass'n of Legal Advoc. Educators.

to make the competition broadly accessible to all participants (students, judges, and competition staff).

i. Mode

First, the competition administrator should decide whether the competition will proceed entirely in virtual format, or whether some rounds might be held in person. For example, a competition might hold preliminary rounds online but semi-final and final (or just final) rounds in person. This system may make particular sense if the competition is moved online for space reasons, to minimize crowding, or better enable social distancing.

Having competitors argue in different modes in the same round, on the other hand, risks unfairness in scoring and should be avoided if possible. Certainly in "real world" lawyering, one attorney may appear telephonically or by videoconference while another is in the courtroom, but that circumstance is probably suboptimal for all concerned. In the moot court setting, it creates the perception (and perhaps the reality) of an uneven playing field. Competitors appearing virtually may experience actual disadvantages resulting from issues of audio or video quality or simply from not being physically in the room, and judges may unconsciously penalize those competitors for a perceived diminishment in their persuasive force or may actually overcorrect for what they see as unfairness. Either way, to preserve both the appearance and the reality of fairness, any individual round—and definitely any individual argument—should be conducted entirely in the same mode, whether that be virtually, telephonically, or in person.

ii. Platform selection and configuration

The vast majority of law schools opted for a single video-conferencing platform for conducting classes and other school activities during the abrupt shift to online learning in 2020.[7] Because competition administrators and students likely are familiar with the platform their law school already uses—and because law schools may not be willing to pay for appropriate access to a different platform just for moot-court activi-

---

7. For a personal perspective on video-conference teaching, see Kia H. Vernon, *Zooming Through Law School: Lessons Learned from Remote Learning During the Covid-19 Pandemic*, 65(3) Saint Louis Univ. L. J. (2021).

ties—most competition administrators will opt to use the school's existing platform. Whichever platform you choose, however, choose a single platform and conduct all competition activities on that platform. Competitions that did otherwise—by allowing judges or bailiff to choose their own platforms for their own rounds, for example—generally ran into more logistical difficulties and had more issues with competitors being unable to access the virtual courtroom in a timely fashion.

Competition administrators should also consider how they wish to configure the platform for the competition. That decision will depend in part on the platform selected and the options it presents. Institutional accounts with most of the major platforms offer the option of creating a giant complex of breakout rooms that can be accessed with a single meeting ID and password that can be given to all participants. Choosing this option requires someone with access to the account to create a meeting for each day of the competition, including breakout rooms that can serve as each virtual courtroom. Administrators may also wish to create waiting rooms where competitors can wait while judges are deliberating, a judge check-in room where judges go to receive last-minute training and courtroom assignments, and a tabulation room where competition administrators and bailiffs can discuss scoring questions.

Designing the virtual experience this way allows for some advantages and in many ways mimics the real-world experience as much as may be possible online. All participants enter through the same "courthouse lobby" and then can move to the assigned courtroom at the designated time. Participants can also congregate and chat or commiserate in designated breakout rooms before and after the arguments. Competition staff can move from room to room with a single mouse-click, eliminating the need to log in and out of various meetings. All participants are in a single meeting and names appear on a single participant list, enabling competition staff to verify at a glance that all necessary parties are present and to identify any missing individuals. In most platforms, the administrator can move individuals from one breakout room to another, and, perhaps more importantly, with a single click of the mouse remove a participant from a room in which they do not belong. Although many host errors or internet glitches at the host site will affect all participants, at least this circumstance is fairer than an error that only affects some competitors. Most platforms allow the administrator to broadcast messages that will reach all participants in all rooms.

A single competition staffer can open or close the entire complex of rooms simply by starting or ending the meeting. And, of course, having a single meeting ID and password means fewer meeting IDs and passwords to manage for participants and for administrators.

This format also has disadvantages, however. The sheer number and variety of rooms multiplies the potential for error in the creation. A single errant mouse-click by the meeting host—or a momentary internet glitch—can affect all participants and disrupt all competition rounds. Having a single log-in for the entire meeting that is sent to all participants makes it possible for participants to inadvertently or deliberately enter rooms in which they do not belong. With most platforms, a limited number of administrators can be designated as hosts or co-hosts and thus can move participants or broadcast messages. Although administrators do have the power to remove participants from rooms in which they do not belong, this requires administrators and staff to be vigilant in monitoring the participant list for each room.

To mitigate some of the risks of the single-meeting format, competition administrators can:

- Assign at least one co-host to the meeting;
- Launch the meeting from a site with strong, reliable internet access, like (presumably) a computer in an office on the law school campus rather than a private home;
- Have a competition staffer other than the meeting creator review each created meeting to ensure that all necessary courtrooms and auxiliary rooms have been created appropriately;
- Conduct multiple test runs before the competition to uncover any lurking issues;
- Arrange to have someone from the school's IT department monitoring the meeting and able to respond quickly to any technological glitches.

Another option that many smaller, internal competitions use is to create a separate meeting ID and password for each virtual courtroom, as if it were an individual real-world site. This strategy requires a meeting host for each courtroom, and that host must open and close the courtroom and will have the power to move individuals from room to room. Creating individual meetings for each courtroom enables the meeting host to create breakout rooms tied to each individual courtroom; some administrators use the main room for the judges and have the competitors wait in a breakout room before the argument and during judge deliberations. This format mitigates the consequences of a single user error or an internet outage affecting a single meeting host, but it also means that multiple hosts need to have access to highly reliable internet connections and to be accountable and responsible for their own individual meetings. This strategy also means that each courtroom will have its own meeting ID and password, which on the one hand mitigates the risk that any unauthorized person will join the wrong courtroom but on the other hand may create a more cumbersome process in communicating those meeting credentials to participants and puts the onus on participants to manage multiple meeting IDs and passwords. To mitigate some of these risks, each meeting should be assigned a co-host—perhaps the overall competition administrator—in case one of the individual hosts has a technical glitch or some other issue (or simply fails to meet their responsibilities for some other reason).

For the final round or any other round where you desire an audience for the arguments, a webinar format—where the host, advocates, judges, and bailiff can be visible and audible as panelists but all other meeting participants are view-only attendees—makes most sense. The webinar format prevents audience members from disrupting the argument with noise or video but usually permits them some ability to communicate with the host through a chat and Q&A function as necessary.

Regardless which option a competition chooses, administrators should keep in mind these key best practices:

- Have more than one person check and double-check the meeting set up and the accuracy of the text of any emails communicating meeting IDs and passwords;
- Have more than one co-host for any meeting;
- Use a waiting room function or similar mechanism (like pre-authentication mechanisms) to enable the meeting host to ensure that no unauthorized individuals join the meeting. Not only does such a procedure prevent participants or judges from joining the wrong meeting, it also guards against outside "Zoom bombers" or similar miscreants;

- Ensure that those hosting the meeting have the most reliable internet connection available. Those hosting individual courtrooms should do everything possible to avoid situations that might compromise internet reliability or speed, such as using a shared connection or simultaneously streaming other content while hosting the meeting;
- Strongly consider requiring each participant to attend a test session on the platform before the competition to ensure that they can access the platform and that cameras and microphones work properly. With student competitors, practice rounds before the official competition rounds may address these concerns. With judges, a pre-competition judge orientation—either right before the rounds or at an earlier time—provides an opportunity to address these issues.

iii. Accessibility

Competition administrators should consider how to address accessibility issues for competitors, judges, and competition staff with disabilities. Research and evaluate options for making the virtual competition accessible to individuals with sensory impairments and other disabilities. For example, the platform chosen should be compatible with assistive technologies some participants may be using, such as screen readers, magnification, and captioning. Some platforms themselves provide a form of closed captioning.

Competition administrators should also make sure that the meeting host for any competition round is familiar with the platform's accessibility features, how to use them, and how they might interact with assistive technologies participants may be using. For example, if a participant is using a screen reader, that screen reader likely reads aloud all chat messages, which would argue for limiting use of the chat function.[8] Before competition rounds, make sure to communicate to participants details regarding accessibility and provide opportunities for partici-

8. For a useful checklist on making online meetings more accessible, see American Bar Association Commission on Disability Rights, *Virtual Meetings: Accessibility Checklist & Best Practices*, Am. Bar Ass'n (July 1, 2021), https://www.americanbar.org/groups/diversity/disabilityrights/resources/covid-resources/virtual-meetings-checklist/.

pants to communicate any accommodations they may require. The virtual environment may provide opportunities to level the playing field in some ways for some participants, and the competition should do what it can to capitalize on those opportunities.

In addition, administrators should assess the risks that disparate socioeconomic circumstances and associated issues with access to a stable internet connection, an adequate webcam, and an adequate microphone will affect student accessibility. The competition should coordinate with the school's IT department to investigate the availability of loaner equipment for students in need. To the extent that program administrators anticipate conducting significant moot court activities online in the future, the program should strongly consider investing in things like hotspots, webcams, and microphones that it can loan to students who lack access to those resources.

iv. To record or not to record

Holding competitions online facilitates recording arguments. Most video-conference platforms enable the host to record a session simply by clicking a button or to select an automatic recording option when creating the meeting. The host then has access to the recording, which they can download as video or audio files to save or share with participants.

Recording sessions presents advantages. Although this text recommends having a competition staffer—whether that be a student bailiff, an administrator, or a professor—in each virtual courtroom during the argument, that may not always be practicable. And certainly the overall competition administrator cannot be in every courtroom at all times. Should a participant raise an objection to some aspect of a competition round, recording each round enables the competition administrator to review and assess the challenged conduct and evaluate what remedies or penalties might be appropriate.

To the extent that professors or administrators find it appropriate to provide individualized feedback beyond that provided by the competition judges, recording rounds enables professors or student mentors to review a student's performance with that student in detail. Some internal competitions serve as feeders for a school's external competition teams; recording internal competition rounds enables programs to use those recordings to evaluate skills, argument styles, and strengths and weaknesses of potential team members.

Recording also presents disadvantages, including the temptation to second-guess or attempt to relitigate round scoring, which can undermine finality, consistency, and the integrity of the competition, as well as create headaches for the competition administrator. Furthermore, some volunteer judges may be less inclined to judge if the rounds are recorded for later scrutiny. Some of these disadvantages may be addressed easily by adding provisions to the competition rules that limit the use of recordings to competition administrators and only under narrowly defined circumstances. Whatever the competition administrator decides regarding recording, it should be implemented uniformly and consistently for all competitors and all rounds. And of course, coaches and competitors should be notified of the recording policy in advance through the competition rules.

v. Schedule

Chapter Three of this text details various considerations and best practices relevant to constructing a competition schedule. In the virtual environment, competition administrators should weigh the following additional variables and considerations:

- As with in-person competitions, administrators should weigh course schedules for students and work schedules for both judges and students in setting the competition rounds. The virtual environment provides some flexibility in this regard, as it does not require judges or competitors to travel to the law school campus, but judges who wish to judge from their offices—for superior internet access, for example—may prefer earlier round times.
- In setting competition round times, coordinate with your IT department to ensure that someone is on call to troubleshoot and resolve emergency technical issues that may arise.
- If the competition involves multiple rounds occurring simultaneously in multiple courtrooms, you may consider staggering the start times slightly to enable the competition administrator to connect directly with each courtroom before each round begins and at the end of the judges'

scoring deliberations to make sure all is well and to address any questions or concerns.[9]

- Administrators may wish to build into the schedule a time slot or two for "do over" arguments to remedy situations where technology issues prevented an argument from occurring or continuing as scheduled.
- Although the virtual environment eliminates concerns related to finite physical space to conduct multiple simultaneous rounds, staffing and administrative issues as well as student schedules likely still limit the number of rounds you can realistically conduct at one time.

b. Logistics/Procedures

Chapter Three covers the logistics of moot-court competitions in exhaustive detail. This section flags logistical considerations and procedural issues particular to or heightened by the virtual environment.

i. The Role of the Bailiff

As Chapter Three discusses, although some competitions run successfully otherwise, having a bailiff in each courtroom helps a competition run more smoothly. Bailiffs—who can be faculty, law-school staff, student moot-court-board members, or other volunteers—serve as courtroom hosts, greeting the judges and answering any procedural questions, calling the case, timing the round, coordinating communication with the advocates, advising on competition rules, coordinating scoring of the round, and serving as an overall point person for the competition administration.

In a virtual competition, the bailiff's role is even more crucial, and best practices dictate having a bailiff in each courtroom.[10] If you choose the option of having an individual meeting for each virtual courtroom,

---

9. Professor Tessa Dysart, who runs University of Arizona Law's internal competition, recommends staggering start times by up to fifteen minutes. Tessa L. Dysart, *My Final Thoughts on Moot Court in the Age of Coronavirus*, App. Advoc. Blog (Apr. 27, 2020), https://lawprofessors.typepad.com/appellate_advocacy/2020/04/my-final-thoughts-on-moot-court-in-the-age-of-coronavirus.html.

10. *See Guidance for Conducting Moot Court Competitions (2020–2021)*, Nat'l Ass'n of Legal Advoc. Educators.

the bailiff can be the meeting host, communicate the meeting ID and login information to the participants and judges, and create breakout rooms and move people in and out of those rooms during the competition round.[11] Even if you choose the option of one giant meeting for each day, having a bailiff assigned to each courtroom makes it easier for competition administration to monitor proceedings in each courtroom and more promptly address technological and other issues. As meeting host, the bailiff can ensure that no unauthorized individuals enter the courtroom. The bailiff can answer procedural questions for the judges before or during the round, provide guidance on how to handle internet or other issues that affect a judge or an advocate's participation in the round, and serve as a contact point with IT support. The bailiff also can watch for potential rule violations, review scoring forms and resolve any questions, omissions, or errors with the judges before submitting the scores for tabulation, and generally serve as liaison with the competition administration. Finally, the bailiff can serve as a witness should a participant challenge anything about the conduct of a particular round.

ii. Timing

Competition administrators should consider whether they wish to have bailiffs time the arguments and display physical timecards onscreen to signal time increments or whether they wish to use one of the many online timer widgets or programs. Many competitions prefer to use the online timers, which count down the time onscreen. Using bailiffs may increase the risk of human error, but it may reduce the risk of technological glitches. Consider using the timer method but having bailiffs prepared to keep time as a backup option.

iii. Scoring

Both internal and external competitions have had success using collaborative online platforms like Google Forms or survey software to create virtual scoring forms for judges to complete and submit at the end of a competition round. Anyone who has administered a competition using paper forms and discovered errors or omissions only after judges have departed for the evening will appreciate the option of creating a

11. Some recommend having someone other than the bailiff be meeting host, assuming the competition has sufficient staffing to permit this approach.

form that can only be submitted when all fields are complete and when scores fall within a permitted range. Absent such a feature, choose a scoring mechanism that permits the bailiff or another representative of competition administration to review each judge's submission for completeness, accuracy, and scoring within permissible ranges before the judge leaves the virtual courtroom. Many such mechanisms automatically feed data from scoring forms into a spreadsheet that then calculates scores, making it possible for competition administrators to see and troubleshoot scoring results almost instantaneously.

c. Competition Rules

Competition administrators should augment their existing in-person competition rules[12] with supplemental guidelines for virtual competitions. Rules should specify not just required or prohibited behavior but also consequences—including possible scoring penalty ranges or disqualification—for violations. At minimum, the rules should address the following questions.

i. Who can be in the virtual "room"

Rules should specify who can (and should) be in each virtual courtroom and at what times. In general, a bailiff or other competition representative should be in each virtual courtroom at all key times, including during the entire competition round and during the scoring period. The rules should specify when competitors should join the courtroom and when they should leave. If the competition is using one meeting ID for the entire competition, the rules should specify in which breakout rooms competitors should wait during times when they are not required to be in the virtual courtroom.

For preliminary argument rounds, most internal school competitions provide that only judges, bailiffs, and the advocates competing in a given round should be in the virtual courtroom during the round.[13] This best practice reduces screen clutter and reduces the gatekeeping burden on the bailiff. Rules should specify whether any other observers are permitted and who those observers may be. For semifinal and particularly final

---

12. *See supra* Chapter Three.

13. External competitions should also permit coaches to be in the virtual courtrooms with their teams. *See infra* section II.B.7.

rounds, you likely wish to permit observers, but—as discussed earlier in this chapter—you may opt to use a webinar format to keep the audience invisible and muted while the advocates and judges take center stage.

Rules should also address who can be in the actual physical room with the competitors during their rounds. In general, rules should require or strongly encourage students to argue from a space where they can isolate themselves from distractions, including other people and pets. If students are competing in pairs, rules should address whether competitors must sign in individually or whether they may share a login and computer.[14] The rules should also specify whether team members can be in the same room while arguing.[15] The competition may consider reserving physical spaces at the law school for students who might not otherwise have a private space from which to argue (or access to adequate internet service). If so, competition rules should address use of that space.

ii. Who can be seen and heard (and when)

Audio: In general, rules should provide that any individual not speaking at a given moment should have their audio muted. As a general best practice, many competitions set up the videoconference so that all participants are muted upon entry, just as a default. The advocate currently arguing likely should remain unmuted throughout their argument—even when they are not speaking—but often it is a good idea to gently advise judges to mute their audio when they are not actively asking a question. First, muting eliminates the possibility of outside noise or interference that could make it difficult or impossible for judges to hear the advocate. Second, the act of unmuting the microphone alerts the advocate that a judge is about to ask a question, something that is always a little more

---

14. NALAE's Guidance for Conducting Moot Court Competitions 2020–2021 advises that "if teammates who are arguing are permitted to be in the same physical room, each should be required to sign on to the platform independently." *Guidance for Conducting Moot Court Competitions (2020–2021)*, Nat'l Ass'n of Legal Advoc. Educators, at Standard 1.2(A)(2).

15. Rules should specify that team members logging in individually and from separate devices should avoid being in the same room to minimize the risk of audio feedback or other interference. At minimum, such students should be encouraged to remain muted unless the teammate is muted.

difficult to anticipate in the virtual environment. Of course, frequently muting and unmuting creates the risk that a judge will forget to unmute before asking a question. Bailiffs should remain muted during the entire argument but may unmute as necessary before and after arguments.

Video: Rules should specify at which points individuals should have their cameras on or off during an argument. Many competitions request that judges keep their cameras on at all times during the arguments themselves, but that an advocate not currently arguing turn off their camera. This policy eliminates some visual clutter and opportunities for distraction, but it also prevents the bailiff or judges from observing the non-arguing advocate's expressions, demeanor, and conduct during the opposing advocate's argument. Competition administrators concerned about those matters—and about mitigating opportunities for cheating or other unauthorized advocate behavior—should require all advocates to keep their cameras on throughout the argument.

If bailiffs are acting as timekeepers during the argument, they will need to have their cameras on for at least a portion of the time. Some competition rules provide that bailiff cameras remain off during the arguments unless the bailiff is showing a timecard to an advocate; this policy has the advantage that the bailiff suddenly appearing onscreen makes it more likely that the advocate will see the time warning. The disadvantage of this approach is that, in many conference platforms, a participant suddenly turning on a camera rearranges the order of faces on the screen, which can be distracting and disruptive to both judges and competitors. As a result, some competitions instead use a countdown clock that remains visible on screen throughout the round.

Judge deliberations: Some competitions provide that judges deliberate in the courtroom but simply turn their cameras and microphones off during that time. This policy has some disadvantages. Competitors and others in the courtroom should be warned that the mere fact that judges cannot be seen or heard does not mean that the judges cannot see and hear. Further, having judge cameras off makes it harder for bailiffs to monitor the progress of deliberations. And, of course, having advocates remain in the room largely prevents judges from conversing with each other or with the bailiff. Where possible, it probably works better to move the advocates or the judges to a separate breakout room during the deliberation and scoring period to eliminate these issues.

iii. Competitor conduct

Competition rules should clearly dictate required and prohibited conduct by competitors, specify the penalties—if any—for violating each rule, and prescribe a procedure for raising and adjudicating rule violations and appealing penalties.

iv. Scheduling

Rules should set forth the general schedule of the competition, including any required meetings and the times when competitors and judges should arrive for a particular argument. Competitors and judges should be required to arrive anywhere from fifteen to thirty minutes before the start time of an argument to permit check-in, technological troubleshooting, and transmitting necessary competition information.

v. Naming conventions

Competitions should dictate how participants should name themselves when they enter the courtroom, largely to make it easier for judges to identify all the players and assign scores accurately. Most internal competitions do not require anonymity at oral argument, but it will be helpful to judges if advocates name themselves with their party affiliation and full name. If competitors are assigned numbers or other codes, those should be included as part of their screennames for ease in scoring. Judges should name themselves "Judge" and then their full name. The bailiff should use the name "Bailiff" and then their full name.

vi. Standing vs. sitting

Most competitions—and, indeed, most courts[16]—allow advocates to choose whether they prefer to sit or stand during oral argument.[17] The

---

16. Task Force on Remote Oral Argument, *Remote Video Argument: Suggestions for Arguing Counsel*, AM. ACAD. OF APP. LAWYERS 7–8, https://www.appellateacademy.org/publications/Counsel_AAAL_Remote_Task_Force_Recommendations_for_Counsel_Final.pdf; *Virtual Oral Advocacy* 2 (2020), http://www.adi-sandiego.com/practice/mcle/MCLE_Virtual_Oral_Argument_Presentation.pdf.

17. For example, the ABA National Appellate Advocacy Competition does not specify whether participants must stand or may sit. *2021 NAAC Competition Rules*, AM. BAR ASS'N (Nov. 15, 2021), https://abaforlawstudents.com/wp-content/uploads/2020/11/2020-2021-ABA-NAAC-Rules.pdf. Indeed, the final round of the 2021 NAAC included one team that had argued all rounds while standing and another team that had argued all rounds while sitting, suggesting that neither approach presented a disadvantage. The

competition rules should clearly specify whether advocates are required to sit or stand or whether they are given the option to do either. Permitting advocates the option of sitting or standing enhances accessibility and inclusion and better mirrors what students will experience in real-world virtual advocacy.[18]

vii. Access to technology (tablets, phones, computer screen)

Similarly, rules about advocates' use of technology and communication tools immediately before and during the argument somewhat mitigate the risk of cheating. Competition administrators should consider including provisions specifying whether and the extent to which competitors can use tablets, smartphones, and additional computers or computer screens during arguments. Competition rules should address when, how, and with whom competitors may communicate during rounds; if competitors are arguing in teams, for example, consider whether to permit teammates to communicate during the other side's argument or before rebuttal. Rules should also address the use of a plat-

---

seated team won that final round. Similarly, the rules for the Pace Environmental Law Moot Court Competition explicitly give advocates the option of sitting or standing during oral argument (although they encourage advocates to stand). *Jeffrey G. Miller National Environmental Law Moot Court Competition, 2021 Official Rules for Virtual Competition* Rule VII(F) (2020), https://law.pace.edu/sites/default/files/nelmcc/2020/2021/2021_Official_Rules_Sept_29.pdf. The rules for the National Online Moot Court Competition are silent on whether advocates must sit or stand. *See National Online Moot Court Competition, 2021 Rules*, https://drive.google.com/file/d/122MjQR0HgFzLm-WfbBWtgRhTEgrt873n/view. And it seems that courts permit advocates the option of sitting. *Virtual Oral Advocacy* 2 (2020), http://www.adi-sandiego.com/practice/mcle/MCLE_Virtual_Oral_Argument_Presentation.pdf. Anecdotally, it seems seated competitors may score higher than do standing competitors.

18. *See* Susie Salmon, Training Effective Virtual Oral Advocates in Law Teaching Strategies for a New Era: Beyond the Physical Classroom 403, 406 (Tessa L. Dysart & Tracy L.M. Norton, eds., 2021). Permitting advocates to argue from a seated position fosters inclusion for individuals with mobility and vision disabilities, among others. Furthermore, many students lack the resources or flexibility in their living situations to devise an effective mechanism to mount a camera and microphone at an effective height or distance to allow them to argue from a standing position while still being able to see faces on a screen and their notes. Finally, the insistence on standing during oral argument to manifest formality, deference, and authority is a relic of the Classical ideal of the male warrior as the paradigm of credible advocacy. *See* Susie Salmon, *Reconstructing the Voice of Authority*, 51 Akron L. Rev. 143, 154 (2017).

form's chat function during the argument, which may function similarly to handwritten notes during an in-person argument.

viii. Virtual backgrounds

Rules should address the use of virtual backgrounds during the arguments. On the one hand, prohibiting the use of virtual backgrounds altogether has some advantages. Because older computers do not support the use of virtual backgrounds without external green screens, requiring students to use a standard background creates unfairness. Ensuring that backgrounds are appropriate adds to the administrative burden, but it also provides an excellent opportunity to educate students in netiquette and professionalism in the online environment. Backgrounds can also complicate lighting and other decisions, and anyone who has attended enough online meetings know that sometimes people—or parts of people—inexplicably disappear into the background, creating distractions. On the other hand, prohibiting backgrounds altogether disadvantages students who otherwise may struggle to mitigate distractions in their real-world backgrounds.

If administrators do permit backgrounds, they should provide clear guidelines on the types of backgrounds that are permitted.[19] In any case, rules should strongly encourage students to do what they can to prevent anything distracting, inappropriate, or otherwise unprofessional from appearing on camera.

ix. Procedures for handling technical glitches

Competition rules should specifically address how any technical glitches—whether on the part of a competitor, a judge, a bailiff, or the competition administration—will be handled and set forth clear procedures for addressing glitches that disrupt an argument or prevent it from continuing. Such provisions should consider:

- How technical glitches or "freezing" will impact timing. At what point should the round clock be paused or stopped, if at all?

---

19. Competitions may consider creating and sharing a standard virtual background that all competitors, judges, and competition staff able to use backgrounds must use.

- What circumstances will compel the competition to stop an argument, and how and by whom is that decision made? Is the result different if the issues affect a competitor's audio or video than if they affect a judge?
- If a judge is disconnected from the argument or has persistent and unresolvable freezing or other audio or video issues, can the round continue without that judge?
- What happens if an argument must be stopped because of technical issues?
- Should competitors be required to take certain steps—texting or calling the bailiff, for example—when connectivity issues arise?
- If audio or video slowness can be remedied by moving to a "cameras off" round, should that be permitted, and, if so, how will that be handled?
- If a competitor or judge loses the ability to connect by computer during a round, should they rejoin by telephone or other mechanism, and, if so, how will that be handled?
- If an argument is affected by technical issues but is not stopped and rescheduled, what is the remedy?

Rules should specify that no student score should be affected by a technical glitch. As discussed in the "scheduling" portion of this section, ideally a competition would build time into the overall schedule in the event that re-arguments are required for any round.

x. Scoring

Competition rules should specifically address scoring criteria, how scores will be recorded, procedures for verifying scores before they are submitted, and the extent to which judges may confer with one another or with the bailiff or other competition staff during scoring.

If the competition is using a mechanism that permits rapid tabulation and verification of scores, consider when students should be able to see their scores and who won a given round. Many competition administrators prefer to wait until the end of preliminary rounds or even until the end of the entire competition before releasing scores of an individual argument to prevent scoring from affecting future student performance in or engagement with the competition.

Rules should provide specific guidelines for aspects of an advocate's performance that should not be addressed in scoring. In particular, aspects of the argument over which the advocate may have little control, whether because of disparate socioeconomic circumstances or simple bad luck, should be exempt from scoring penalties. Such aspects may include technical glitches, whether an advocate argues from a sitting or a standing position, background environment, lighting, and audio and video quality or speed. Because of communication lags, things like crosstalk and a student failing to stop talking promptly when a judge begins a question are unavoidable artifacts of the virtual environment that should not impact a student's score unless they appear unrelated to such technological delays.

Of course, scoring provisions should address penalties and challenges. Rules should detail the procedure for levying scoring penalties against competitors for violating rule provisions, the nature and extent of those penalties, and the process for appealing those penalties. Rules also should set forth the timing and procedure for asserting challenges arising from the conduct of a round.

d. Communications

Clear, detailed, and thorough communication is indispensable to the success of any moot court competition, but this is particularly true for virtual competitions.

i. General communications

Administrators should communicate rules and procedures to competition staff, students, and judges early, through multiple mechanisms, and repeatedly. Rules should be formatted in a way that enables users to navigate them quickly and find needed information quickly[20], and those rules should be readily accessible to all parties. Judges and students should have easy access to contact information for technical support and competition administration.

As a general best practice, competition rules should be available on a website where students, judges, and competition staff can access and consult them readily as questions arise. Competitions may also consider creating a "frequently asked questions" (FAQs) page highlighting those

---

20. A PDF with detailed table of contents that hyperlinks to rule sections works well.

rules, tips, or procedures that most often arise in the competition setting. Every communication with judges and students should include links to the full competition rules and schedule as well as to any other helpful information housed on the competition or program website. But competition administrators should also send multiple communications to those audiences before the competition, highlighting schedule details, what to expect during the competition, specific procedures and sequencing during an argument round, contact information for technical support and competition administrators, and frequently implicated competition rules.

Most law schools use some form of course management software. Even if the competition does not take place in the context of an official class, competition administrators should explore creating a course site for the competition. Even if you have a competition website with rules, procedures, and FAQs that remain more-or-less constant year after year, a course site with information specific to a particular year's competition—such as round schedules with competitor, bailiff, and judge information—with links to the competition website can be helpful.

Competitions also should be sure to send the competition link and password at least twice: once well before the competition, and once close to the argument time.

To ensure rounds are as seamless and successful as possible, competitions likely will also wish to communicate to both students and judges some key technology tips and other best practices of virtual interaction. Those include:

- *Eliminating distractions.* To the extent possible, encourage judges and students to connect from a location that enables them to control noise, visual background, and other potential distractions. If possible, they should position themselves in front of a solid, neutral-colored wall. Pets should be kept out of the room. Silence phones and other alerts and turn off any televisions or music. Judges and competitors should consider wearing a headset or earbuds to mitigate background noise and enhance audibility. And, of course, people should mute themselves when not speaking.
- *Maximizing internet stability.* Again, to the extent possible, students and judges should access the arguments from a

place that has the strongest possible connection. If they share internet access with others, they should try to minimize competing usage during the argument. People should close all applications on their computers other than the videoconference platform and any permitted notes.
- *Enhancing the visual experience.* Participants should practice with lighting and position to make sure they are as visible as possible. Discourage back lighting, which can transform a person into a mere shadow, obscuring facial expressions; if possible, people should position a soft light behind the camera, directed at their face, or sit before a window. As much as possible, cameras should be positioned at or above eye level.
- *Where to look.* In a video interaction, the natural inclination is to look at the people onscreen. To better simulate in-person direct eye contact, people should look at the camera as much as possible.

ii. With judges

As Chapter Three and other parts of this handbook repeatedly detail, well-trained judges are indispensable to a competition's success. This maxim holds particularly true for virtual competitions, where judges may be unfamiliar or uncomfortable with the technology or other quirks of the virtual competition environment or the ways in which their role in a virtual competition will differ from that to which they may have become accustomed in in-person competitions. Clear guidelines not only further the goals of consistency and fairness, they also give the judges the knowledge and comfort to confidently execute their crucial roles.

To further this goal, competitions should offer judges detailed information in as many forms as possible and make that information easy to navigate and access.

First, competitions should offer both live, interactive virtual training as well as a training video (which can simply be a recorded version of the live training) that judges can consult on their own time. Those materials should cover:

- A substantive overview of the problem, including facts and law;
- Key rule provisions and procedures relevant to the virtual competition;
- A primer on using the videoconferencing platform, including how best to format the screen during arguments to see competitors;
- Tips for best practices in videoconferencing;
- A step-by-step description of what to do and what to expect during an argument round;
- How to access and complete scoring forms; and
- A review of "what if" scenarios, such as what to do and whom to contact in the case of technological glitches or other emergencies.

The competition training and video should also alert judges to key differences between in-person and virtual argument, and in particular those differences that may impact scoring. For example, in a virtual argument, there may be a delay of one to several seconds between the time someone speaks a word and the time another person on that conference hears the word. Thus, some crosstalk may be inevitable, and students may unintentionally talk over judges, which of course would be perceived as a sign of disrespect in a live, in-person environment. You may also suggest that judges incorporate some "filler" signaling language into their questions to ensure that delays do not prevent students from hearing and understanding the substance of the question. For example, beginning a question with a hand gesture, a lean forward, and then "counsel, I have a question" may buy enough time to ensure that an advocate can stop talking and start listening before the actual question begins. If you have added other provisions to your rules on scoring to adjust for the virtual environment, you may wish to highlight those as well.

Because virtual competitions create a greater risk of miscommunication and confusion, you may wish to be more prescriptive in telling your judges how to run their virtual courtrooms. For example, you may wish to provide a script for how arguments might begin, including calling the case, asking advocates to state their appearances, and inviting advocates to begin their arguments. You can provide similar guidance for the end of the round, with judges taking the case under advisement and instructing the competitors either to move to breakout rooms or to remain in the room while the judges score the round. This approach, although more rigid, removes some unnecessary stressors from both judges and students—at least at the beginning and end of the argument, everyone will know when their turn to speak has arrived!

The day before a judge is set to hear an argument round, the competition—perhaps through the individual who will serve as bailiff for that argument round—should send the judge an email with the following key information:

- The date and time of the argument;
- The time judges are asked to log on to the meeting platform (no later than fifteen minutes before the argument is set to begin);
- The link and password to the meeting room where the argument will be held;
- Instructions to log on to the meeting platform;
- Contact information—including mobile phone number—for the courtroom bailiff and the competition administration contact;
- Contact information for IT support during the competition;
- A link to the competition rules and a sample scoring sheet;
- Any other materials that might be useful to the judge during the argument, such as a copy of the bench brief, any script you wish to provide, and some sample questions.

iii. With students

The successful virtual competition will also communicate clearly and consistently with the student participants. In fact, the competition should strongly consider providing students access to competition rules, procedures, and FAQs before students enroll or elect to participate.

Ideally, all students would attend a training session that covers key competition rules and procedures and enables students to test technology and experiment with things like lighting, backgrounds, and assistive technology. Of course, if the competition occurs in the context of a class or workshop, these issues can be covered there. Practice argument rounds present an excellent opportunity to troubleshoot issues and for students to receive feedback on presentation and technology issues.

As it does with judges, the competition should send a written communication to student participants shortly before the competition rounds begin. That communication should include at least the following information:

- The date and time of any preliminary rounds in which the student is expected to argue;
- The time students are asked to log on to the meeting platform (no later than fifteen minutes before the argument is set to begin);
- The link and password to the meeting room where the argument will be held;
- Instructions to log on to the meeting platform;
- Contact information—including mobile phone number—for the courtroom bailiff and the competition administration contact;
- Contact information for IT support during the competition;
- A short reminder of how the competition round will proceed, including any details about breakout rooms and when students should and should not be in the courtroom;
- Reminders of any key rules or guidelines, such as required backgrounds, tips to maximize internet strength, and restrictions on communications before and during the arguments;
- Information on any accessibility features of the meeting platform.

iv. With bailiffs

As the liaison between the judges and competitors in a particular argument round and the competition administration, bailiffs play a crucial role in ensuring that the competition runs smoothly and in avoiding issues that may result in scoring complications or challenges to the conduct of a round. Thus, even more so than with in-person competitions, bailiffs for virtual competitions should receive thorough training and communication in competition rules and round procedures.

In providing instruction to the bailiffs, competition administrators should consider the following:

- If bailiffs will take the lead in communicating with judges and competitors before the competition, clearly communicate and document the nature and scope of their responsibilities. Prepare sample email language and timelines or checklists for bailiffs to use and follow to ensure clear, uniform communication and administration.
- Confirm that bailiffs have a strong fundamental understanding of the competition platform. Conducting a "dry run" where bailiffs must launch meetings, move people between virtual rooms, share scoring forms or spreadsheets with judges, and troubleshoot technical issues can help ensure a smoother experience for everyone during the actual competition. In particular, if you are aware that a participant will be using assistive technology, be sure that bailiffs know how to troubleshoot any issues stemming from how that technology interacts with the meeting platform.
- Prepare troubleshooting guides with recommended courses of action for different exigencies. For example, bailiffs should receive information on (1) a sequence of steps to take if a judge does not check in on time, (2) a sequence of steps to take if a competitor does not check in on time, (3) how to handle technical issues with a scoring form or spreadsheet, (4) how to guide a judge or competitor through basic technological issues, and (5) whom to contact for additional technical assistance.
- Provide bailiffs with a script or checklist of items to cover with judges and competitors at the beginning of a round, such as (1) reminders regarding timelines and basic procedures of a competition round, (2) reminders regarding technical issues, such as when cameras should be on or off, how cameras should be placed, and muting and unmuting microphones, and (3) any reminders of significant rules impacting competitors, such as what and whom they can have with them during a round.

- Provide bailiffs with a script or checklist of items to say during the round, such as (1) any calling of the case at the beginning, (2) instructions to judges and competitors when arguments conclude and judges begin scoring, (3) items to verify with judges after they have completed scoring, (4) instructions before judges provide feedback to competitors, and (5) instructions to provide judges and competitors once feedback is complete, including conveying appreciation to judges and encouraging competitors to do so, sharing information about where to find round scores (if applicable), and any details about next steps on the competition.
- Each bailiff should receive mobile phone numbers and email addresses for the judges and competitors for whom they are responsible, as well as for any backup judges.
- Although in general bailiffs should be able to handle issues that arise during their rounds with minimal assistance—and of course most rounds will proceed without incident—nonetheless a wise administrator will provide bailiffs with clear guidance on what issues must be escalated to someone else within the competition administration, how to contact those individuals, and what information to document and provide to those individuals.

2. DURING THE COMPETITION

Chapter Three provides detailed guidance on how to structure and run competition rounds, but the virtual environment requires a few additional steps and best practices. The potential for technical glitches amplifies the need for contingency plans and for all participants to arrive and check in with competition administration early.

a. Timeline of a competition round

The sequence of events in a competition round will vary slightly depending on whether all simultaneous rounds take place in breakout rooms under one global meeting ID or whether each virtual courtroom has its own meeting ID. In general, however, rounds will consist of these basic steps: (1) competitor and judge check-in, (2) argument rounds,

(3) score tabulation and verification, (4) judge feedback, and (5) communication of round results to competitors.

i. Check-in

All competitors and judges should log into the competition site no later than fifteen minutes before the argument is set to start. If the competition is using one large meeting for simultaneous courtrooms, all participants will arrive in the main room. Judges can be sent to their courtrooms, and participants can either remain in the main room or be sent to a waiting room associated with the courtroom. If each individual argument session has its own meeting ID, the bailiff associated with each courtroom should launch the meeting no later than thirty minutes before the argument is set to start. Judges can be placed in the main room, and participants can be held in a breakout room until it is time for the round to begin.

Bailiffs should verify that all judges and competitors are present and communicate that information to the competition administration. Should a competitor or judge be missing, the bailiff will follow a prescribed protocol to address that issue, whether that involves tracking down the missing person or contacting a substitute.

Once all required persons are present, the bailiff can provide any pre-round instructions.

ii. Argument rounds

If competitors and judges are in separate virtual rooms before the competition, the bailiff or competition administrator can move them or direct them to move to the appropriate courtroom a few minutes before the scheduled argument start time. If multiple competition rounds are being held within the same large "virtual courthouse," the competition administrator can broadcast a message to all rooms with a five-minute warning to alert everyone to move to the appropriate courtroom, followed by a second message directing participants to begin arguments.

The argument rounds themselves should proceed much as they would in an in-person competition. If you are conducting two or more arguments sequentially in the same virtual space—just as if you were conducting sequential arguments in a physical space—bailiffs will need to ensure that arguments run on schedule. Participants in the next round can be held in a waiting room or can wait in the main room or a designated breakout room until it is their turn to enter the virtual courtroom.

iii. Score tabulation, feedback, and communication of results

Once arguments conclude, the judges should either move to a breakout room or turn off their microphones and cameras so that they may complete scoring forms out of view of the competitors. If the judges simply turn off their cameras and microphones while remaining in the same room with the competitors, bailiffs should remind competitors that judges can still see and hear them if they speak. Although it may add time when bailiffs need to bring judges and competitors back together for post-round feedback, it is probably a best practice to move either competitors or judges to a separate virtual room for scoring.

Judges should notify bailiffs when they have completed scoring so that competitors can receive their feedback. Even if you choose a scoring mechanism that allows competitors to see their scores immediately after a round, competitors should be prevented from seeing those scores until the judges have provided their feedback; otherwise, competitors may be distracted and not benefit as much from any useful feedback.

3. AFTER THE COMPETITION

Make it a priority to celebrate achievements in the virtual competition just as much as you would those in an in-person competition. If you have an in-person overall awards celebration for your advocacy program, of course you will want to include those students who participated exclusively in virtual competitions.

No one has cracked the code to successful virtual celebrations. No online interface permits the kind of casual, self-directed, unstructured social interactions one can enjoy in person; even small-group activities in breakout rooms retain an element of stiltedness and artificiality. And, of course, providing food and beverages to enhance the celebratory mood simply does not work the same way online as it does in person. That said, if an online awards ceremony is your only viable option, having one still provides a valuable opportunity to recognize accomplishments and build community. Invite speakers to keep remarks brief, but do not deprive students of their moments in the sun to have their hard work and accomplishments acknowledged and celebrated before their peers and any friends or loved ones they wish to invite.

II. Virtual External Competitions

Virtual external competitions involve many of the same best practices and considerations as do virtual internal ones. This section addresses some additional matters relevant specifically to external competitions.

A. Should we go virtual?

In evaluating whether to launch a virtual external competition or to take an existing external competition virtual, of course the reduced cost and reduced need for space may make such an option attractive. Moreover, planning a virtual competition eliminates the need to undergo much of the work detailed in Chapter Five! If circumstances make in-person competitions impossible or impracticable—as they did during the height of the Covid-19 pandemic—advocacy programs may have few alternatives and may opt to send students to virtual competitions rather than forego competitions altogether. In that situation, an existing competition likely will draw a significant percentage of the participants it would have drawn if it were in person. Thus, as long as you have the staffing and interest within your institution, it likely makes sense to continue with that competition in the virtual mode.

Under ordinary circumstances, where government and institutional policies permit programs to send student teams to external competitions, programs may still find virtual competitions attractive for various reasons, many of which this text addresses in the next section. In determining whether to pursue a virtual external competition in that situation, you need to consider whether enough teams will find your particular competition compelling in order to make it worth your while. Perhaps your virtual competition addresses a subject-matter area that other competitions do not. Perhaps the virtual format allows you to draw noteworthy judges who might not be available individually or in combination for an in-person competition. Or maybe you offer a unique format, more oral-argument rounds per advocate, or compelling prizes.

You will want to think carefully about what value you add to the crowded competition landscape and the likelihood that you would be able to convince enough programs to send teams to make the effort of marketing and running a virtual competition worthwhile.

A competition might draw participation by marketing itself as a relatively inexpensive, less time-consuming opportunity for students to develop and practice oral-advocacy skills as a supplement to any in-person competitions teams may attend.

B. Specific best practices for planning and executing virtual external competitions

Once you have decided to run a virtual external competition, you will want to consider all of the same issues raised in the section on internal competitions, as well as some additional matters specific to external competitions, including how many teams to permit, what fee to charge, timing of rounds, how to handle all-teams meetings, and any swag or awards.

1. HOW MANY TEAMS?

Without the constraints of physical courtroom space to consider, it becomes tempting to set a high cap for the number of teams who can compete in a virtual competition. Resist that temptation, and instead think realistically about the number of teams you can handle while still ensuring adequate staffing and well-prepared judges for every round. When in doubt, start small. A modest competition that provides knowledgeable judges, seamless coordination, and prompt technical support one year may draw—and be able to accommodate—more teams in later years by building a reputation for delivering a quality educational experience and fair competition.

2. REGISTRATION FEES

In general, registration for virtual competitions should be less expensive than for in-person competitions—in most instances, significantly less expensive. As discussed in more detail in the section on internal competitions, virtual competitions incur fewer costs to administer; your registration fees should reflect that magnitude of that difference. Your competition is unlikely to draw significant participation if it does not provide good value for the dollar.[21]

3. TIMING OF ROUNDS

With a virtual competition potentially drawing teams and judges from many different time zones, competition administrators will need to think carefully about when to begin and end rounds and other competition activities like team meetings and awards presentations. As much as is practicable considering your participant population, you probably want to schedule rounds to begin no earlier than 8 or 9am and no later than 7 or 8pm in any time zone in which you have participants.[22] If you hold any competition rounds or activities Monday through Thursday or Friday, you also will want to consider work and school schedules; you will draw more judges if you schedule rounds to begin between 5 and 8pm in their time zones, and your competition may be more attractive to teams if they do not need to miss class to attend.[23] Timing becomes more difficult, of course, if you draw teams and judges from around the world.

4. TEAM MEETINGS

Many external competitions commence with an all-teams meeting, where advocates, coaches, and other team participants are all required to attend. Administrators use these meetings to disseminate key information, share seeding and scheduling information and brief scores, highlight key competition rules and procedures, review competition logistics, and introduce key competition personnel and their roles, among other things.

---

21. The NALAE guidance document suggests registration fees of $300–500 or less for virtual competitions, and it strongly recommends that the fee "bear some relation to the cost of running the competition." *Guidance for Conducting Moot Court Competitions (2020–2021)*, Nat'l Ass'n of Legal Advoc. Educators.

22. The NALAE guidance document, based on a consensus of the advocacy educators weighing in, suggests beginning rounds no earlier than 8am and no later than 8pm in any time zone in which you have participants. *Id.* at § 2.1(c)(1).

23. *See id.* at § 2.1(c)(2).

In a virtual competition, such a meeting also presents opportunities for competitors and coaches to explore the competition interface, navigate to key locations in that interface before they need to do so in a competition round, test their own equipment, troubleshoot possible technical issues, and ask any questions about competition rules or procedures specific to the virtual environment. Administrators may consider creating a checklist or other activity—maybe even a scavenger hunt—that encourages participants to systematically explore the interface and test their equipment.

5. ANONYMITY, SCREENNAMES, AND VIRTUAL BACKGROUNDS

The issues discussed in section I.B.1.c. of this chapter regarding screennames and virtual backgrounds can be even more significant in external competitions where competitor anonymity is often a key component. Most external competitions have rules requiring that judges not be able to identify the school with which a team or competitor is affiliated. If your virtual competition has that rule, be sure to emphasize it with teams and judges and to highlight scenarios that may compromise anonymity in the virtual environment. Teams should be sure that nothing visible onscreen reveals their school affiliation; teams arguing from school facilities should make sure no school logos or other identifying features are visible.

To further eliminate the risk that a student's surroundings might inadvertently reveal something that creates a conflict or reveals the student's school affiliation, competition administrators may consider requiring competitors to use a standardized virtual background designed and provided by the competition. One downside of requiring the standardized background, however, is that it also requires the student to have a computer that supports using backgrounds without an external green screen, which may put additional burden on students and schools with fewer resources.

Competitors and coaches should be instructed on how to change their screennames on the competition interface to comport with competition procedures; be clear and consistent with judges, team members, and coaches in instructing precisely what screennames should include. Where possible, people affiliated with competition teams, such as coaches, advocates, and observers, should change their screennames immediately upon entering the competition space, preferably where no judge can see them doing so.

In general, any coach, competitor, and observer names should prominently feature the team number for the team with which they are affiliated; this requirement makes it materially easier for competition administration to see at a glance whether any individuals who should not be in a particular courtroom or breakout room are present. Some competitions ask competitors to identify themselves using team number, side, a number indicating the order in which the competitor will argue for their team, and a last name.[24] So, for example, Janie Jones, the first student to argue on the petitioner side for team 234 would have a screenname of 234 Petitioner 1 Jones. Judges generally label themselves with "Judge" and last name or first and last name, making it easier for competitors to address and refer to them during argument.

As in an in-person competition, judges should be instructed to do nothing that would lead them to learn with which school a competitor is affiliated. If a judge even suspects they know a particular student, they should notify the competition administrator of the conflict. Administrators may even consider detailing what a judge should not do, including Googling competitor names.

6. COMPETITION APP

Administrators may consider investigating the cost and feasibility of having a competition app that competitors, coaches, and observers can download onto their phones and that will provide up-to-the-minute schedule information, round results, key rule provisions, and other useful information. An app would enable competition administrators to push notifications to those using the app to alert them to changes in schedule, delays, technological issues, or other timely information.[25]

Many event management software platforms include an app option. If your virtual competition is sufficiently large and complex—or if your

24. Some competition rules omit the last name and instruct competitors to label themselves solely with team number, side, and number, but two years of experience suggest that judges find it useful to be able to address advocates by their last name during the argument.

25. Instant-messaging and private-server apps like Slack and WhatsApp also have some of this functionality.

institution runs enough events that it already has a subscription to such a platform and personnel on staff familiar with how the app operates—it may be worth using the app rather than relying on communicating timely information through phone calls, text messages, or the event platform itself.

7. WHO CAN BE IN THE COURTROOM

As with an internal competition, an external competition should have clear rules regarding who can be in a competition courtroom and at what times. Rules should explicitly address whether team coaches, non-competing team members, or observers affiliated with the team may be present during the round. If observers are permitted, the rules should address how many such observers may attend.

Because moot court should be, above all, an educational experience, competition administrators should permit—and actually encourage—team coaches to observe competition rounds and listen to judge feedback. Barring coaches from attending prevents them from providing helpful, personalized feedback to their students on their round performance and from helping their students sort through sometimes contradictory, confusing, or imprecise feedback provided by judges. Coaches should remain muted with their cameras off at all times while in the virtual courtroom, which prevents them from adding to the risk that the judge will have a conflict of interest. Any concerns about improper communication between students and coaches during rounds can be addressed through rule provisions with strict penalties for violations. Further, any downside associated with permitting coaches to observe argument is significantly outweighed by the substantial—indeed, indispensable—educational benefits.

8. CREATING A SENSE OF PLACE AND COMMUNITY

For many students, part of the value of participating in moot court is traveling to a new place and mixing with students from other law schools. In general, even the best-run virtual competitions to date have not been able to provide these benefits in any meaningful way.

Competitions can do a few things, however, to make it easier for competitors from different schools to socialize with one another. First, immediately after a round, while the judges are deliberating, is a natural time for competitors to chat informally. Keeping the judges and competitors in the same virtual room while the judges score inhibits or completely prevents this unstructured, informal socializing and decompressing. Implementing a system where the judges move to a deliberation room to complete scoring forms enables at least this small amount of networking and connection among competitors.

Second, often students from other schools are able to meet and chat during all-team meetings, either at the beginning of the competition or during re-seeding or elimination discussions. One way to encourage some conversation and connection might be to have students from different schools navigate a "scavenger hunt" together to learn the nuances of moving around within the competition platform.

The most successful virtual social activities are usually structured around a game or activity. The competition could host an off-hours trivia competition about the simulated virtual location, allowing interested students to meet and work with one another.

Finally, as with internal virtual competitions, being thoughtful about how to recognize students for outstanding achievement in the competition can make the experience more memorable and rewarding. Perhaps instead of simply announcing the names and school affiliations of students who won brief or oral advocacy awards, the emcee might read some judiciously selected comments from judges about the student's performance.

III. Coaching Teams in Virtual External Competitions

In recent years, moot court programs faced a stark decision: send teams to virtual competitions or resign themselves to a year of no external moot court options for students. We all hope those decisions remain in the past, but schools may nonetheless have good reasons for requiring some of their teams to attend virtual competitions, adding some virtual competitions to their roster, or offering students the option of attending virtual competitions. This section outlines matters you should consider in evaluating whether to send a team to a virtual competition—and which competition to select—and sets forth some best practices in preparing teams to succeed in virtual competitions.

A. Should we attend a virtual competition?

Although for many, virtual competitions were a distant second-best option to in-person competitions, they do provide significant advantages. First, and most obviously, virtual competitions require no travel and thus sending students and coaches to a virtual competition imposes significantly less expense. Because virtual competitions cost less money to run, registration fees also are generally lower. A school could send two three-person teams to a virtual competition for as little as $500, whereas sending two three-person teams and a coach to an in-person competition in another city could cost well over ten times that much.

Second, virtual competitions may in some instances be more accessible for some students—students with child-care or other responsibilities that make travel difficult or costly, students with mobility impairments or other disabilities that make travel challenging or uncomfortable, or students who prefer not to miss days or a full week of classes in the middle of a semester. Attending virtual competitions also imposes less burden on coaches, who similarly will not have to miss work or class time or incur collateral costs of travel.

Additionally, schools may consider sending students to both a virtual and an in-person competition in the same year, seeing the virtual competition as a relatively inexpensive practice round for the in-person one. Or schools may send second-year students to virtual competitions and third-year students to in-person ones.

As with other competitions, however, schools should avoid sending students to a competition unless they will have adequate support to prepare to succeed in that competition. Resist investing less effort in virtual competitions; students who attend virtual competitions should receive just as much preparation and encouragement as those who attend in-person competitions.

In determining whether a particular virtual competition is worth attending, pay careful attention to (1) whether the competition has been run online in the past, (2) whether the competition rules demonstrate a thoughtfulness about how to run a virtual competition effectively, and (3) any information you can obtain from past participants about the quality of the competition experience. The meeting platform may influence your decision, both based on accessibility features and existing familiarity with that platform. Accessibility may be an issue for some of your students; competitions should provide information about any accommodations enabled or provided. Additionally, investigate whether the rules permit coaches to watch arguments; competitions that bar coaches from attending arguments deprive students of the opportunity to receive feedback from someone who has watched their progress and who can help evaluate and interpret feedback from the competition judges.

B. Preparing teams for virtual competition

In preparing teams for the virtual competition, you will want to keep in mind many of the same principles as you do in preparing teams for an in-person competition; in particular, you will want to simulate competition conditions in your practices as much as possible. Simulating competition conditions in the virtual setting means doing all the same things Chapter Four recommends in terms of timing and presentation, and also:

- Conducting almost all practices virtually. When possible, competitors should log onto the virtual platform from the location where they intend to be when they deliver their competition arguments, whether that be from a quiet location at home, an office, or a room on campus. Similarly, competitors should use the same computer, webcam, microphone, lighting, and other equipment they plan to use during the competition. Practicing this way not only builds comfort with competition conditions and allows fine-tuning of lighting, sound, and other aspects of presentation, but also provides opportunities to identify potential technical glitches and troubleshoot them.
- Conducting almost all practices on the virtual platform the competition will use. In general, competitions should communicate that information well in advance.

In preparing teams, take advantage of the opportunities the virtual environment provides. Cast your net widely in recruiting judges; virtual practices allow you to use judges in different geographic locations and even different time zones, enabling you to bring back past team members who may have moved out of town after graduation and to tap into your network of alumni with expertise in particular subject-matter areas. Virtual practices often make volunteering as a guest judge more attractive and accessible even for attorneys, judges, and faculty who live nearby; people can simply sign on to the virtual platform from their offices or even homes, making it less burdensome to volunteer and possibly enabling them to spend more time interacting with the students instead of traveling to and from the practice location. Evening and weekend practices become less burdensome for everyone involved; coaches and students can log in from home rather than traveling to campus and struggling with parking or other issues.

Virtual practices also make it more convenient to record and rewatch practices, which can provide invaluable learning experiences for the students. Instead of grappling with unwieldy recording equipment that you may have to take time to borrow from and return to your IT department, you can record with a simple click of a button, or you can even preset all your practices to record automatically. Just make sure you obtain permission from everyone involved; generally, judges are happy to consent to being recorded with the idea that it will help the students obtain more value from the experience. Often, coaches find it helpful to watch the recordings with students individually to highlight certain aspects of a student's argument but enabling the students to watch their own arguments alone has its own advantages.

Before the first practice, you will want to devote some thought and discussion to where you want the students to be when they argue. Some competitions allow students to be in the same room with their teammates during the argument, just as they would be in an in-person competition. This arrangement has some advantages: it more closely simulates an in-person experience, to the extent that the competition permits teammates to communicate during the argument, it makes that somewhat easier, and it enables students to provide moral support for one another with their simple presence. Some coaches believe strongly that if students are permitted to be in the same room during arguments, they should do so.

That said, arguing from the same room has some disadvantages. First, you will want to consider whether the two students should argue using the same computer, microphone, and webcam. Having the students sit near one another on different devices can create issues with feedback, even if the non-speaking student mutes their microphone; the student will also need to silence the speaker on their computer, which makes it more difficult for that student to follow the proceedings. But some competitions require all competitors to be visible onscreen during the entirety of the argument, or at least the entirety of their side's argument, which can be difficult if two students share one webcam.

Moreover, arguing from the same room likely means students will argue from a room at the law school. At many schools, reserving the same room for weeks at a time may be difficult or impossible. Events at the law school may create noise or distractions that create issues during the competition.

Either approach has its advantages and disadvantages, and likely neither approach uniformly suits all teams. Thus, discuss the pros and cons of each approach with your teams, get their thoughts, and proceed accordingly and consistently from there.

C. During the competition

Virtual competitions require more effort for a coach to connect with and support the team. The fact that the coach and team will not travel together to a different city also eliminates many opportunities for in-the-moment mentoring and bonding. Extra effort to schedule time to meet with team members at crucial moments during the competition can pay educational dividends:

- As with an in-person competition, coaches should exchange mobile phone numbers and other contact information with team members to enable them to contact one another;
- If possible, coaches should consider being in the law school building during competition rounds, which will enable students participating from rooms at the law school to meet with the coach before and between rounds;
- If the coach cannot meet with some or all team members in person, the coach should take advantage of any team

breakout rooms provided on the competition interface to meet with teams during the competition. Team members and coaches should arrive in that breakout room fifteen to thirty minutes before the scheduled round time. Not only does this habit enable coaches to call or text team members who are running late and eliminate last-minute stress wondering if a competitor will miss a round, it also allows time for coaches to provide support and last-minute pep talks before teams argue;

- If coaches are allowed to be in the virtual courtroom during rounds, they absolutely should take advantage of that opportunity. In some ways, requirements that coaches keep cameras and microphones off provide advantages. Coaches need not worry about keeping poker faces during arguments and feedback and can take notes on opportunities for improvement and consider how to discuss critical feedback during a post-round debriefing;
- Competitors and coaches should connect after the round to debrief and evaluate what, if any, feedback to implement and how to do so;
- Just as coaches might offer students opportunities for additional practice during off-hours at an in-person competition, competitors and coaches can connect for targeted virtual practice sessions or in-person brainstorming during a virtual competition;
- To the extent that schedules and budgets permit, coaches should explore ways for team members and the coach to share one or more meals together during the competition, just as they would during an in-person competition in another city. During the height of the Covid-19 pandemic restrictions, some coaches sent team members gift codes for online food delivery services for a celebratory meal after the competition;
- Just as they would in an in-person competition, coaches should foster professionalism and grace; teams should attend any awards ceremonies or other gatherings, regardless of whether they anticipate winning anything.

D. After the competition

Win or lose, coaches should reconnect with their teams after the competition to debrief and discuss lessons learned. And students who participate in virtual competitions should be included equally in any moot-court celebrations or awards ceremonies.

IV. Conclusion

Although virtual moot court competitions differ in meaningful ways from in-person ones, they can still provide valuable—and increasingly relevant—advocacy experience for law students. Rules and procedures for virtual competitions should anticipate and address the challenges and limitations of the virtual environment and do everything possible to ensure equitable access. As in coordinating any large event, planning and communication are key. Competition administrators and coaches need to be particularly thoughtful about how to create a collegial atmosphere and opportunities for students to connect with one another, with judges, and with their coaches to maximize the educational experience and make the virtual experience as fun as it can be.

Index

Note: Page numbers followed by '*n*' indicate a note.